UPRISING!

The police, the people and the riots in Britain's cities

Martin Kettle
and Lucy Hodges

UPRISING!

**The police, the people
and the riots in Britain's cities**

Pan Books London and Sydney

First published 1982 by Pan Books Ltd,
Cavaye Place, London SW10 9PG
ISBN 0 330 26845 7
Photoset by Parker Typesetting Service, Leicester
Printed and bound in Great Britain by Collins, Glasgow

Contents

This is a work of collaboration but the chapters were the work of one co-author or another. Martin Kettle drafted the Introduction and wrote Chapters 3 , 5, 7, 8 and 9. Lucy Hodges was responsible for Chapters 1, 2, 4 and 6.

Acknowledgements

We should like to record our gratitude to Paul Gordon and Michael Ignatieff for their assistance in the preparation of this book.

Abbreviations

ACPO:	Association of Chief Police Officers
CARD:	Campaign Against Racial Discrimination
CCRL:	Council for Community Relations in Lambeth
CRC:	Community Relations Commission
CRE:	Commission for Racial Equality
DPP:	Director of Public Prosecutions
IRR:	Institute of Race Relations
JCAR:	Joint Committee Against Racialism
JCWI:	Joint Council for the Welfare of Immigrants
LAG:	Legal Action Group
PEP:	Political and Economic Planning
PSI:	Policy Studies Institute
RRB:	Race Relations Board

Introduction:
A riotous history

The riots that blazed through Britain's cities in the summer of 1981 shocked the nation and the world. Unprecedented images of police in familiar helmets crouching behind unfamiliar riot shields, illuminated by the glare of burning buildings, were beamed daily into homes around the globe. Hitherto obscure inner-city districts – Brixton, Toxteth and Moss Side – became familiar overnight to millions who would never visit them.

There had been warning voices. Some had said that when unemployment rose to its highest level in half a century social strife would surely follow. Others looked at the decade of conflict in Northern Ireland and feared that what had become a way of life in Belfast and Derry might one day happen in Britain too. Within black communities all over the country, men and women argued that unless white society and white institutions changed their ways, what had happened one April night in Bristol in 1980 might be repeated elsewhere.

But it is doubtful whether many were prepared for the scale and rapidity of events in 1981. What happened broke the seismograph, and left the British people groping for explanations of events whose anger seemed all the more extraordinary when set against the summer's other dominant collective experience – the wedding of the Prince of Wales and Lady Diana Spencer.

This book is both an account of these events and an attempt to understand them. We have tried to put the riots into a broad historical and social framework. But the emphasis throughout is on the immediate importance of relations between communities – especially black communities – and the police. There is no doubt that broad social and economic explanations are relevant in some degree, and we have not ignored their importance. Indeed, in Chapter 5 they are looked at in detail. But our underlying argument concerns the way that Britain is and should be policed.

A brief word about terminology: there has been some dispute, both legalistic and political, over the question of whether what happened in Britain in 1981 can properly be described as 'riots'. It is ultimately a sterile argument. Existing English law, for instance, defines a riot in a very specific way. It requires three or more people with a common purpose to be prepared to help one another, by force if necessary, against anyone opposing them. If they then carry out that purpose and force or violence takes place that would 'alarm at least one person of reasonable firmness and courage', then, says the law, that is a riot.[1]

The common usage of the word is, however, much broader. Most people would probably agree that when a large group of people use violence in public against people or property and the authorities cannot immediately control them, then that is a riot. Even so, this leaves scope for disagreement and different interpretations. Some will object on principle to the use of the word riot at all. In a special 140-page issue of its journal, *Race and Class*, published in November 1981, the Institute of Race Relations consistently talks of the 'riots' of 1981 in inverted commas.[2] They were anxious not to appear to collude in describing the summer's events in the same way as the police and government.

The use of the word riot is therefore a problem. But none of the other words that have been used causes any less difficulty. Hooliganism, public disorder, protest, rebellion, uprising – all present their own problems. In the circumstances, 'riot' will have to do.

Britain, like every other society in human history, has

never been wholly free from riot. It is an error and a denial of history to suppose otherwise. Indeed, there is a nice irony in the fact that almost six hundred years to the very day before events in Toxteth set in motion the most widespread phase of the 1981 riots, England was witnessing the massive outbreak of popular anger that is known in every school textbook as the Peasants' Revolt.

Throughout British history, powerless people, feeling themselves oppressed and seeing no effective response to their grievances, have despaired of any improvement, formed themselves into crowds and physically challenged the world that seemed to deny them what they wanted. This is not to say that there is a historical continuum of rioting. The history of riot is heterogeneous and complex. Riots, like other forms of violence, do not just 'erupt'. Riots have reasons and need to be understood as a specific popular activity.

In the 1370s reduced demand for labour and attempts to force down wages provoked the revolt of 1381. The preamble to a statute of 1377 already reflected the fears of feudal lords at the growing protests. The peasants, it said,

do menace the ministers of their lords in life and member and, which is more, gather themselves in great routs and agree by such confederacy that one should aid the other to resist their lords with strong hand: and much other harm they do in sundry manner to the great damage of their said lords and evil example to others.

In June 1381 a concerted revolt throughout the south and east of England marched on London where supporters opened the city gates to them before the rioting was eventually quenched by a series of promises made by the king, which were never kept.

The list of riots and risings that followed down the centuries is long and varied. Some are celebrated and familiar, while others are obscure and forgotten: Cade's revolt of 1450 and the Norfolk rebellion of 1549 threatened the state itself and were put down only with great violence and difficulty – as many as 3000 rebels were killed in the suppression of the 1549 rising, for example; other instances were more local and short-lived. Yet it has been calculated that between 1450 and 1640 there were more 'internal disturbances' in England than anywhere else in Europe.

In the eighteenth century, when the cities of Britain began to grow and the map of the country took on a more recognizably modern form, riot was frequent, even endemic. Most common was the food riot at times of bad harvest or shortage. In the countryside, riot was also likely to be provoked by the enclosure of common land. In both cases, rioting had a deeply legitimating quality, aimed at setting right a profoundly felt grievance. This sort of action can be seen from the fourteenth century right through to the 1840s. A common factor to both urban and rural cases was violence to property – destruction of buildings, smashing of machinery, burning of houses, barns and hayricks. Violence to people was much less common, though rarely altogether absent. Nevertheless, the risk to life was much greater for the rioter than for his opponent. The historian George Rudé has calculated that between 1736 and 1848 rioting crowds killed twelve people at most, while troops shot dead 630 rioters and the courts hanged a further 118.

In this riotous century, the most sustained violence came in the Gordon riots of 1780, vividly depicted in Charles Dickens' novel *Barnaby Rudge*. The writer Horace Walpole was amazed by the Gordon riots: 'I remember the Excise and Gin Act and the rebels at Derby and Wilkes's interlude and the French at Plymouth, or I should have a very bad memory; but I never till last night saw London and Southwark in flames!'

Beginning at Westminster with the presentation to Parliament of an anti-Catholic petition, the riots spread into the City of London and the West End. During the next week, the riots surged all over the capital city, still anti-Catholic (and anti-foreign) in mood but also directed against the houses and the symbols of the wealthy and the powerful. By the time that the army regained control of the city, 450 people had been arrested, of whom 25 were later hanged. The troops shot 285 rioters dead and wounded another 173. The damage to property was assessed at just under £100,000, two thirds of it to private buildings.[3]

There has been no concentration of civil disorder in Britain to rival this since 1780. But while some historians have seen the Gordon riots as marking the climax and conclusion of a characteristically eighteenth-century form of crowd violence – in which there was a tacitly accepted role for the crowd in the unreformed political process – they certainly did not mark the end of rioting in English cities. The forms of rioting changed in various ways as society changed, but riots never disappeared.

On the land, there were peaks and troughs in rioting in the first half of the nineteenth century. There were times when by sheer numbers rural anger forced its way into the national newspapers and the history books. One such was the East Anglia rising of 1816. Another, more famous now, was the Captain Swing riots of 1830 and 1831, as a result of which 1976 people were brought to court, 252 sentenced to death, 19 executed and 505 transported. But, as A. J. Peacock puts it:

they were only exceptional years in the *amount* of violence that took place. No year in the first half of the nineteenth century was a quiet year in the east. Every year was violent and the amount of violence that took place was very great indeed.

Or, as the MP for Cambridgeshire put it in 1846;

If gentlemen think there is nothing to be dreaded from our rural labourers, I fear they are greatly mistaken. I do not believe there is a village in my neighbourhood that would not be ready to assert by brute force their right (as they say) to eat fully the fruit arising from their own labour.[4]

Urban industrial society produced new forms of social protest and new forms of law and force to combat them. During the French Revolutionary and Napoleonic wars, a tough clamp-down on labour organizations and radical ideas and protest was attempted. But food riots, machine riots and agitation for political reform persisted in spite of and because of the repression. As E. P. Thompson wrote:

The hundreds of men and women executed or transported for oath-taking, Jacobin conspiracy, Luddism, the Pentridge and Grange Moor risings, food and enclosure and turnpike riots, the Ely riots and the Labourers' Revolt of 1830, and a score of minor affrays, have been forgotten by all but a few specialists, or, if they are to be remembered, they are thought to be simpletons or men tainted with criminal folly.[5]

Direct action is a recurrent theme of this era and the one which followed.

Sometimes it had an explicitly political character, as in the Bristol riots of 1831 or the Birmingham Bull Ring riot of 1839. Sometimes it had a more industrial or economic character, as in the Merthyr Tydfil rising of 1831 (where at least twenty-four people were shot dead by the army and one man hanged) or in the 'Plug Plot' riots that swept the North and Midlands in 1842. Even in the Chartist period of the 1840s and early 1850s strikes, marches, sabotage and even near-insurrection formed integral parts of a wide movement which had a more modern party political character and which was 'led' by men dedicated to achieving their aims more by what they called 'moral force'.

The middle decades of the nineteenth century saw the gradual incorporation of working-class organizations into the framework of the emerging modern state. Governments chose reform rather than resistance. But thousands of people never signed any treaty with the parliamentary or judicial systems of the time and angry disorder could and did spring up when least expected. Strikes were one focus of such incidents. The campaigns of the unemployed were another. In 1886 and 1887, years at the heart of a recession, the mass protests of the jobless led to rioting in central London and fierce attacks by the police. Political militancy too could produce a riot. In 1866, crowds demanding an extension of the right to vote broke into Hyde Park to meet.

The twentieth century is not riot free either, although the intensity and danger to life and limb have undoubtedly grown less. In the decade before the First World War, industrial disputes continued to lead to occasional serious disturbances. The miners' strike of 1910 and the rail strike of 1911 were particularly ferocious. In Liverpool and in Llanelli in 1911, troops fired at crowds of angry strikers, killing two people in each case.

Even during the war itself outbreaks were not unknown, notably on Clydeside. The return of peace even led to an upsurge. There were mutinies at Calais and Folkestone among soldiers anxious for demobilization, and in January 1919 3000 discontented soldiers occupied Horse Guards Parade demanding an early return to civilian life. A mutiny among Canadian soldiers at Rhyl was put down only after five soldiers had been killed. In Glasgow, supporters of a demand for a forty-hour week fought the 'battle of George Square' with police. In Liverpool, it was police on strike who themselves rioted, smashing town centre windows; order was restored by the army.

Violence flared too in the interwar years. During the General Strike of 1926, there were outbreaks of violence in Glasgow, several west Yorkshire towns, east London, Preston, Hull, Liverpool and Edinburgh. As a result of the strike, there were 3149 prosecutions for incitement to sedition and for violence. One historian concludes: 'It is, of course, a fable that there was no violence during the general strike.'[6]

Nor were the unemployed of the 1930s mere passive protesters. Modern generations have seen that newsreel film of the Jarrow march so often, with its image of peaceful, disciplined, fife-playing workers, that a misleading image of protest in the Depression has emerged. In reality, the early 1930s were marked by repeated battles between the unemployed and the police in cities all over Britain: London, Bristol, Glasgow, Manchester, Stoke, North Shields, Belfast and Birkenhead, to name but a few. In the Birkenhead violence of 1932, for instance, the police were attacked with iron railings, one officer was thrown through a plate glass window, another shoved down a manhole, while women pelted police with missiles from upstairs windows. Indeed, it was the degree of violence that had occurred when previous marches arrived in London that led to the setting up of the National Council for Civil Liberties, in order to observe police treatment of the 1934 hunger marchers.

Racial street violence is no child of the postwar era either. In 1919 there were outbreaks of black militancy in several ports. In Liverpool, a black seaman, Charles Wootton, drowned while trying to escape a white mob. There were similar clashes in the early years after the Second World War, often local and short-lived, but culminating in the riots of August 1958 in Nottingham and London's Notting Hill. The two decades which separate Notting Hill and the Bristol riot which is the subject of the first chapter of this book were themselves marked by occasional riots in cities such as Leeds, Liverpool and London.

Race is not, of course, the sole feature of the riots that have from time to time erupted in postwar Britain. There have been violent clashes over international issues such as the bomb, South Africa and, perhaps most notably, Vietnam. Industrial disputes have also produced uncontrolled fighting and destruction, such as the clashes at Saltley during the 1972–3 miners' strike and the Grunwick dispute of 1977. Demonstrators were killed, for the first time for decades, at Red Lion Square in 1974 and at Southall in 1979 – not to mention Northern Ireland.

This is no more than a thumbnail historical sketch. But it should have established that riots were not invented in the 1970s. Such incidents form a persistent thread in British history, even if it is one that is often tangled and sometimes broken. This implies no particular moral view of rioting, that rioting is either right or wrong, good or bad, successful or unsuccessful, glorious or wicked. It is simply to stress that the 1981 riots were not something wholly unprecedented in British experience. When, for example, Richard Clutterbuck – a former soldier and an expert on terrorism frequently consulted by the media, the army and the police – tells us that the 1970s were 'exceptionally violent years' he is correct only in terms of very recent comparisons.[7] Looking back over centuries rather than decades, it is more accurate to say that the post-1945 era has been exceptionally peaceful.

Equally, though, it would be wrong and confusing to stereotype all these outbreaks. They obviously have important differences. In different eras and in different societies, different sorts of crowd have gathered for different reasons and have acted in different ways, with different degrees of organization.

The intensity and the particular characteristics of the 1981 riots dispelled an illusion which has affected British society very widely. It is the view embodied in Richard Clutterbuck's important book, *Britain in Agony*. It is the view implicit in the now famous remark of the Secretary of State for Employment, Norman Tebbit, in his speech at the 1981 Conservative Party conference when he said that when his father was out of work he didn't riot but got on his bike and looked for work. It is the view that our democratic system, with its universal suffrage, representative institutions, relative prosperity and welfare state – however essential and desirable these things are – represents some kind of historical plateau on which crowd militancy or riot can have no place.

The 1981 riots exposed the loose ends of other assumptions too. Writing in 1969, the Marxist historian George Rudé tried to impose some intellectual order on the evolution of crowds. He argued that popular movements have had distinctive and particular characteristics according to the sort of society in which they spring up. He tried to show that the 'pre-industrial' crowd in western Europe of the eighteenth and early nineteenth centuries was different from the crowds of other eras. He suggested that the special features of the behaviour of the pre-industrial crowd were its association with food riots, the resort to direct action against property, its spontaneity, the fact that the crowd had no leaders within it, its mixed social composition and its concern for the restoration of 'lost' rights. The industrial crowd – that is, the crowd in our own society – didn't share these characteristics.

Rudé recognized that this sort of analysis could easily become simplistic. Although he was distinguishing between the pre-industrial and the industrial crowd, he was honest enough to admit that he saw many recent examples of pre-industrial features in what should, according to his model, have been mature, modern industrial crowds. The final example of this modern pre-industrial behaviour that Rudé chose is now especially relevant. 'And what of the Negro rebellion that has been erupting in the Northern cities of the United States since 1964?' he asked. 'Hasn't this, in certain of its aspects at least, a distinct flavour of the "pre-industrial" riot? I think the answer is yes.'[8]

The American riots of the 1960s showed up the weakness of attempts to cram historical events into neat categories. They didn't fit the traditional Marxist mould because the organized labour movement did not play a decisive role (except in a negative sense). By rights, the labour movement was supposed to act as the engine and negotiator of workers' economic and political grievances. In America, as in France in 1968 and in Britain in 1981, it stood by. But the American riots showed another thing; they reiterated the lesson that there are important aspects of crowd behaviour which transcend and defy the moulds. In no sense were the British riots a slavish copy of what happened in America, but they pose the same challenges of interpretation.

In the last decade, historians and social scientists have begun to respond to these challenges. In the early 1970s, books like Richard Cobb's *The Police and the People*, a study of French popular protest between 1789 and 1820, and

Gareth Stedman Jones's *Outcast London*, which deals with the Victorian period, moved the focus away from politically organized collectivities. A continuing impetus has been given by the work of the History Workshop, originally based at Ruskin College, Oxford. All this work has been directed towards a mass of detailed local studies, emphasizing the great diversity of popular militancy and violence from one time and place to another.

E. P. Thompson, writing in 1971, developed the point in a way which is especially relevant. He satirized what he called the 'spasmodic' school of historians who explained rioting in terms of response to quantifiable measures of social tension. According to the spasmodists, Thompson said, rioting followed a simple causal sequence. Labourers clapped their hands to their stomachs, registered that they were suffering from hunger, and set off to liberate the nearest bakery or burn the nearest farmer's house. Instead, he emphasized the 'legitimizing' behaviour and the restraints operated by the eighteenth-century crowd.[9]

The result, in Tony Hayter's judgement, is that 'we are a long way from the idea of mob as a vain and crazy rabble whose aim is destruction and anarchy'.[10] The historians are producing a much more dappled picture of riot than could be allowed within the liberal democratic or the old Marxist analysis – or, indeed, within any analysis which is based on race. Paradoxically, this is helping to open up fresh lines of historical and behavioural continuity which should form an important part of any analysis of today's riots. These enable us to see things in common betwen, say, the Notting Hill carnival riots of the 1970s and the events of 1579–80 in Romans, described by Emmanuel Le Roy Ladurie in his book *Carnival in Romans*.

Take, for example, the very obvious but unexplored point that most of the rioting in 1981 took place at night or at weekends, not during the so-called working day. A similar tendency was noted in the Kerner Commission's report on the American riots of 1967. Richard Cobb's work on revolutionary France makes a similar point: 'Nights were of course more dangerous than days . . . The night favoured violence as well as love.'[11] The advantages of the blanket of the dark may well be self-evident, but doesn't this say something relevant about the self-imposed restraints on what some see as open rebellion?

Or take another, more explicit, continuity, the language of authority in response to riot. Some newspapers and authorities were obsessed in 1981 with the desire to find a conspiracy behind the riots. 'Search for the Masked Men', said the *Daily Mail* banner headline on 9 July: 'The hunt is on for the hidden men who directed the riots in Toxteth, Liverpool, on Saturday night.' Three days later, the *Mail* was back with 'Extremists' Master Plan for Chaos', while the London *New Standard* followed up that evening with 'Riots: Four Men Hunted: Special Branch work on link theory'. Beneath a front page photograph of an overturned car, the caption read: 'Last night in Woolwich . . . another planned disturbance?'

The conspiracy theory is just about the oldest card in authority's pack. In 1780, during the Gordon riots, it was French and American agents slipping across the Channel, pockets bulging with gold, who were said to be behind things. Witnesses at the subsequent trials of the rioters spoke of conspiratorial lists of houses 'that had to come down'. An informer told the government that the mob consisted of 200 housebreakers, 550 pickpockets, 6000 'all-sorts' and 50 men that 'gives them orders what to be done; they only come at night'. In the event, no French agents, no secret plans, no ringleaders were ever found.[12]

For every mass event, it seems, there is a police conspiracy theory. During the Captain Swing riots of 1830 and 1831, for example, scores of official reports attributed the arson campaign to 'Jew-looking fellows' or 'distant and foreign incendiaries'. Subsequent inquiries never found them.[13]

In 1979 in Southall, 342 people were arrested after a

day of fierce fighting with police. The Metropolitan police commissioner, Sir David McNee, attributed the confrontation to outsiders 'hell-bent on violence'. The *Daily Telegraph* reported that the demonstrators were known to have been gathering for three days beforehand. The charge was taken up by the Home Secretary. Later, it became clear that the overwhelming majority of the people protesting against the National Front's meeting in Southall were local and that the bulk of those arrested were Asians living in the area.

The language used to describe the events follows well-established historical grooves of its own. In March 1981, thousands of black people marched to central London from the south-eastern suburb of New Cross, to protest at white apathy over the unsolved deaths of thirteen young West Indians in the Deptford fire two months earlier. The march was militant, uncooperative with police and, at times, violent. Windows in Fleet Street were smashed, a newspaper stall overturned and a jeweller's shop looted.

'Rampage of a Mob', said next morning's *Daily Express* headline. 'For seven hours a frenzied mob took part in an orgy of looting and destruction in the West End', said the *Sun*. Unconsciously, these headlines were reviving, almost word for word, the coverage given by the press a hundred years previously to the unemployed's protest in Trafalgar Square in February 1886. Then, said *The Times*, 'The West End was for a couple of hours in the hands of the mob.' The next day, it reported 'roughs in 1000s trooping to West'. This was echoed in the *Daily Express* of February 1981 with its warning about 'gangs of rowdies'. But the most uncanny parallel with 1981 was the report in *The Times* of 1886 that '10,000 men were on the march from Deptford to London, destroying as they came the property of small traders'.

Not only the language but the events themselves provide useful parallels. The New Cross marchers' first confrontation with the police came just south of Blackfriars Bridge. A brief skirmish developed. Bricks were thrown at the police, who brought out their protective riot shields. Whether they knew it or not, the police who chose that point in the route to attempt to funnel the march into an orderly shape had chosen to act where their predecessors down the years have chosen to act. The crossing of London's river is a challenge to authority, an invasion of the City and all it represents. Here, more than five hundred years before, Kentish rebels under Jack Cade fought to gain control of London Bridge, while in 1848 the army and a vast force of special constables manned the bridges to stop a huge Chartist rally on Kennington Common from spilling across the river to challenge Parliament with its demands. In its rhetoric, the British state fights on the beaches. In practice, it fights on the bridges across the Thames.

Finally, in trying to place the riots in context, some note must be taken of the characteristics of crowd behaviour. What is it that draws people into crowds? What changes come over people in a crowd? What sorts of satisfaction do crowds seek? What turns a static crowd into a moving crowd? What is the psychological explanation of the pleasures to be gained from destruction, noise and fire?

It is easier to ask such questions than to answer them. But it is well established that all societies have had to negotiate some sort of tolerance of such behaviour.

Christopher Hill points out that medieval society recognized certain days of the year when social hierarchies and decencies could be turned upside down: 'It was a safety valve: social tensions were released by the occasional *bouleversement*; the social order seemed that much more tolerable.'[14] And Cobb observes that the French police had to be 'well acquainted with the calendar of violence and riot, almost as fixed as that of the saints'.[15]

Perhaps Britain's police should study history more closely. For all their diligence, dedication to intelligence gathering, and planning, they obviously possessed no calendar to forewarn them about the summer of 1981.

1 The forerunner: Bristol 1980

Bristol was a turbulent port, containing all the ingredients for a riot.

Michael Brock: *The Great Reform Act* (1973)

When the leader of Bristol city council, Claude Draper, was telephoned on the night of 2 April, 1980 and told there was a riot taking place in the St Paul's district of Bristol, he thought it was a joke. 'Quite frankly I would never have expected a riot in St Paul's,' he said.[1]

Though many forecasts of riots had been made in the 1970s, no one had expected that it would really start in Bristol. Riots were forecast for dramatically deprived inner-city areas such as Brixton or Handsworth, Birmingham, publicly well known for their concentrations of blacks; few people had even heard of St Paul's. While it is run-down by Bristol standards, and has a thriving black youth culture, the area has not been totally neglected.

Over recent years money has been put into redeveloping and rehabilitating its rows of small houses. The result is that it has lost a sense of cohesion, that new estates have destroyed the old patterns of streets, and that there is an odd mix of newly done-up homes, decaying shops and some bleak council housing. The blight has been made worse by the building of the M32 motorway right through the centre of St Paul's, dividing the community and carving up the landscape. There have been complaints that it has no library, no public lavatory and few social centres for young blacks. All these are true. At the same time St Paul's is not the twilight zone it once was, though it is still the red-light district of Bristol and has made a name for itself in other ways.

Decades ago, long before it became multi-racial, the area acquired notoriety for servicing this West Country port with brothels. Black and white prostitutes can still be seen at all hours of the day soliciting openly on the streets. Since the bulk of the West Indian community arrived in the 1950s (mainly from Jamaica) the district has become known, to blacks rather than whites, as 'shanty town' or 'the jungle'.

A year before the Bristol riot, a West Indian sociologist, Ken Pryce, published a book on St Paul's;[2] it paints a lurid picture of the place: 'St Paul's is regarded as a place of "vice and shame", with a high potential for trouble.' In 1979 a total of 246 prostitutes were arrested, and police statistics show offences such as robbery, drugs and selling alcohol on unlicensed premises are rife in the subdivision which covers St Paul's.[3] Pryce's book later became known as the book that forecast the Bristol riot.

St Paul's is an area to which black people from all over the city come for parties, shebeens (illegal drinking clubs) and to play ludo, dominoes and pinball machines at the Black and White Café, the premises where the spark for the riot was lit. They come because there is nowhere else to go. Much of the activity is perfectly lawful and, even where it is not, it involves behaviour such as illicit drinking and cannabis-smoking which does other people no harm.

If the district is the focus for black social life in the city, the Black and White Café in Grosvenor Road, the 'front-line', is its nerve centre. When the riot broke out, it was the only black café (it is in fact run by a black and white husband-and-wife team) which had not been forced out of business for contravening local authority health regulations or for similar reasons. But it had had its licence to sell alcohol removed. A seedy joint created out of the ground floor of a terraced house, the café was of great importance to the black community. It was the only bit of territory they had left and they were prepared to fight for the right to do what they liked there.

The raunchiness of St Paul's should not be exaggerated. It contains the kind of black social life which exists in other multi-racial urban areas. To the outsider the part of St Paul's in which the rioting took place is cosier than, say, Handsworth in Birmingham or Brixton in London. Accurate statistics are hard to come by but it is safe to say that between thirty and fifty per cent of the area's population is black. According to the Home Office, they are better off for basic amenities than ethnic groups in the rest of the country, and are on a par with Bristol whites in this respect.[4] (Many local people would dispute that.) Two housing action areas have been designated in St Paul's and one in an adjacent area: it is well endowed with qualified social workers and day nursery places; and police–community relations were not at crisis point.

At the same time the black people, and particularly the young blacks who were born here, share the same kind of experience as blacks in most British cities. They cannot find work (unemployment among blacks doubled in Bristol during 1977–80, whereas it declined for whites) or at least the kind of work they would like, they feel discriminated against and they complain constantly about police harassment. They deal with this by rejecting the society which has rejected them, making them failures. They also reject their parents for accepting this state of affairs and end up drifting towards Rastafarianism or revolt. Ken Pryce explains:

For those who will eventually drop out, the syndrome is always the same: relationships with parents enter a period of strain – over matters of late hours, choice of friends and entertainments, involvement with the law and repeated work failure. The parents, for their part, find these deviations intolerable and view them as a betrayal, an undermining of the original purpose of their migration to Britain. They regard the emerging disreputable orientation of their children as utterly irrational and quite definitely a disgrace which makes it

25

impossible for them to 'hold their head up high' in the community. They react by rejecting them completely. Thus begins the drift and alienation of the would-be teenybopper into a life of homelessness and adventure which sooner or later brings him in conflict with the law.[5]

What brought hundreds of black – and eventually white – Bristolians up against the law on 2 April, 1980, a day when the schools closed at midday, was a police raid on the Black and White Café. This had happened many times before but serious violence had never broken out – though it had in London in connexion with the Mangrove and Carib clubs (see Chapter 3). On the Second, as the occasion become known, thirty-nine policemen armed with search warrants for drugs and illegal consumption of alcohol moved in; the majority were to go into the café and the rest were to be held in reserve. The operation had been planned nine days earlier and members of the West Indian community, including a well-known Rastafarian, Francis Salandy, had been consulted in a temperature-taking exercise. According to Vincent Arkell, the police superintendent in charge of the raid who was transferred from the area soon after, the community leaders had said that police–black relations could not have been better. What they could not have known was that tension was high in the Black and White that day. There was much talk about a St Paul's youth who had been arrested on 'sus' in London and was appearing in court the following day. Young blacks were angry about the 'police harassment' and talked of going to London to protest.[6]

At about 3.3 p.m. the officers, the drugs squad in plain clothes and the rest in uniform, raided the café. They searched the place and questioned the twenty customers, searching some of them as well. Bertram Wilks, the café's owner, was arrested and taken away in handcuffs, protesting loudly, to be charged with possessing cannabis and allowing it to be smoked on his premises. The police found large quantities of alcohol, including brandy, vodka and 132 crates of beer which they proceeded to load into a van in front of a growing crowd outside. The loading took a long time because there was so much liquor. As each crate was humped into the van, the crowd grew more restless, and when the van left a bottle was thrown, but there was no real violence as yet.

A man complained that his trousers had been torn by a police officer in the café, an allegation which was later canvassed as the reason for the riot, and drugs squad officers made a run for it clutching their booty. This was what really seemed to annoy the crowd. 'Let's get the dope, let's get the drugs squad,' they are reported to have shouted.[7] Missiles were thrown in earnest at a police car and at officers, and the riot had begun. The violence spread quickly: officers outside the café took refuge inside under a steady hail of bricks, bottles and stones from the crowd of black and white youths which had grown to about 150 (others were looking on) on the grassy area opposite.

The police radioed for help and at about 5.30 p.m., two hours after the raid began, reinforcements arrived, assembling down one end of Grosvenor Road and marching down the road to rescue their besieged colleagues. This was a hazardous operation, with officers coming under a terrific barrage and being forced to take cover under crates and behind dustbins. It was the start of the really serious violence. As a black prostitute told the *Sunday Times*: 'They came down the road, left right, left right, like they were on parade. They had dogs with them. When they came in front of the café, we let them have it.' The mistake the police may have made was to try to impose control with too few men. The marching column contained only 100 police and, on this interpretation, was a positive incitement to the angry crowd. Defence counsel at the riot trial months later suggested that the police had provoked the crowd by their military-style tactics. The police said, in turn, that they hoped this show of strength would disperse the crowd. It did no such thing.

Another possible provocation was the presence of dog handlers and about six to eight dogs which, according to Superintendent Arkell, were there to clear the grassy area in front of the café for the rescue operation. They had originally been on stand-by in case they were needed for sniffing out drugs and were brought in later because of the disorder. Afterwards the chief constable of Avon and Somerset, Brian Weigh, admitted that the use of drug dogs in a multi-racial area required 'very careful consideration' and that this was one of the lessons to be learnt from the riot.

Once the trapped officers had been rescued there was a lull in the violence. During that hour police reinforcements arrived from all directions. An officer who drew up in Grosvenor Road to ask another the way found himself and his companion assailed with flying objects. They had to abandon their vehicles and watch them being turned over on their sides by a group of twelve black youths. One was set on fire, the other was swiftly removed by officers arriving on the scene, and thirty men then stood guard on the burnt-out car to wait for a breakdown van. It took a long time to arrive and when it began to remove the wreck at about 6.30 p.m. it and the officers came under heavy attack. Serious violence began again. With hindsight, said Brian Weigh, it would probably have been better to have abandoned the vehicle altogether.

By this time riot shields had been rushed to the scene and distributed to the fifty to sixty policemen involved. The action shifted as a result of the towing away of the wrecked car. A cordon of police was formed across City Road and, under the command of the superintendent, began to move towards a group of about two hundred missile throwers. But the bombardment was so great that the cordon had to fall back. Officers were injured, police cars overturned and set on fire and the crowd started to loot. Lloyds Bank was attacked, broken into and set on fire. Firemen trying to quench the flames were also attacked. The police cordon split into two to try to protect the bank but failed and had to withdraw under extremely ferocious assault.

Of the 50 to 60 officers on the scene, 22 had been injured and had to be taken to hospital (27 more had minor injuries), 21 police cars were severely damaged and six were destroyed beyond repair. Eleven members of the public had to be treated in hospital. At the height of the violence it is estimated that the police faced a crowd of 2000 of whom many were under seventeen years old. Brian Weigh arrived on the scene, saw that his men were clearly overwhelmed and feared someone might be killed.

At 7.26 p.m. he decided to withdraw to collect reinforcements from neighbouring police forces, hoping the crowd would quieten down. This was perhaps the most controversial decision of all – to bring forth scathing criticism from MPs and other police forces and to be remembered the following year when violence broke out elsewhere. It meant that the police were conceding defeat, at least for a while, and that the large crowd was free to loot to its heart's content for the next few hours. This was when most of the looting took place, much of it by whites and much of it very selective; goods and property worth an estimated £150,000 were taken from stores. At 11 p.m. the police began to return in large numbers and by midnight were in control of the area; a total of 609 men had been called out in those four hours.

After the fire

As the ashes settled on the smoking buildings, local residents and businessmen counted the cost. At least £500,000 of damage was done to twenty-one buildings which were set on fire and/or looted. The police authority was liable for compensation under the Riot Damages Act of 1886 and was faced with forty-seven claims: some such as Lloyds Bank were very large, others quite small. Traders were given no help with the complicated procedure and some were unable to claim anything because they were late with their submission. In other cases the authority said the claims were ridiculously high so the parties entered into lengthy haggling. Eighteen months after the riot six claims had still not been settled and many of those that had were settled at around thirty per cent of what had been claimed. In autumn 1981 a firm of printers and stationers which had been burnt down opened again and work began on rebuilding the burnt-out shell of Lloyds Bank.

Once the fires had been put out the action shifted to the smoke-filled rooms of Westminster. Politicians began to shake their heads in wonder, the newspapers were full of the drama, spicing it with their own brand of reporting. ('A riot-torn immigrant part of Bristol was virtually a no-go area to police for five hours last night,' said the *Daily Express*. 'Mobs of black youths roamed the streets.') The analysis came thick and fast with observers falling over one another to point out that it was not a race riot, in the sense of black people fighting whites.

They missed the important point that, while not inter-racial, the riot was racial in that it began as a clash between black people and white policemen on a piece of black territory. It was a clash of cultures: a West Indian lifestyle of cannabis smoking and illicit drinking versus a white British view which condemns such behaviour. Persistent police attention to drugs and drink had led to trouble before and was to do so again. White youths did join in the rioting but were outnumbered by blacks. The reluctance to face up to the racial element, which occurred again in the more serious and prolonged rioting of 1981, was seen by blacks as a typically British response. To deny the racial aspect is to deny that blacks face special problems of disadvantage and discrimination. In 1981, the Home Affairs Select Committee pointed out that St Paul's suffered all those problems. Not to recognize the racial nature of them is to bury one's head in the sand, to lump black people's problems in the same bracket as poor housing and unemployment and to treat outbreaks of violence as aberrations.

Although Britain had witnessed violent street clashes between blacks and police, the Bristol riot shattered the cosy assumption that civil disorder USA-style could not happen here. David Lane, chairman of the Commission for Racial Equality, said somewhat desperately: 'Bristol should shock and shake us out of any complacency. What happened here could happen in other towns and cities.' But the lessons of Bristol were never learned. No official inquiry was held, nothing was said or done nationally about the complaints of black people, while police forces seemed willing only to learn technical lessons about dealing with disorder.

The following day, the Home Secretary, William Whitelaw, called for a report on the riot from Brian Weigh and dispatched his junior minister, Timothy Raison, to Bristol for an on-the-spot assessment. Like Raison, numbers of other politicians, journalists and black radicals (the police said Tariq Ali had been spotted) descended on St Paul's to find out what all the trouble had been about. David Lane and his deputy, Clifton Robinson, joined them as MPs of all parties and Bristol city council began to press for a public inquiry. William Nicks, chairman of the Bristol Council for Racial Equality, which also wanted an inquiry, said with some prescience: 'An outbrust of this ferocity is not going to be a one-off incident and unless there is a Government and a public response there will be further incidents of this kind.'

Whitelaw at first refused to commit himself on the question of an inquiry. Later, though, he turned it down, while Raison said that it would only cause recriminations and rancour. In the absence of any government initiative, widely differing reasons for the riot were offered. Derek Lane, community relations officer for Avon and Somerset police, blamed high unemployment and discrimination against blacks in the job market; others blamed a heavy-handed police operation. Rodney Usher, head of Pimlico School in London, wrote a letter to *The Times* reminding readers that black people were being constantly harrassed by the police.

All went quiet on the political front until the Home Secretary made Weigh's report public.[8] At the same time he got himself off the hook of having to announce an inquiry by referring to the Home Affairs select committee's decision to look at St Paul's as part of its racial disadvantage inquiry, and to Avon county council's and Bristol city's decision to investigate how they could improve community relations in the area. (Bristol and Avon, both responsible for different services in the city and representing opposite poles politically, had not been cooperating before.) The Home Secretary said these two investigations would meet what he called the 'community relations' aspect of the disturbances. He did not take the opportunity to comment on the position of black people here, to reassure them or to propose reform. The policing aspect of the riot was met by Mr Whitelaw's announcement that he was setting up an inquiry of police chiefs into the arrangements for handling spontaneous public disorder. This was in fact the only official government inquiry into Bristol – a revealing priority.

Chief Constable Weigh's report contained some reasonably frank admissions of where the police had gone wrong on 2 April. But it did not in any sense concede that the police had been wrong to withdraw from the area at the height of the violence, a step which had led to demands from one Tory MP that the chief constable be removed. Whitelaw said he understood why the police had withdrawn but that he did not approve of 'no-go areas', thus managing to have it both ways. One of the lessons the chief constable learnt was that, in future, decisions such as that taken to raid the Black and White Café should be made at the rank of assistant chief constable and above. He acknowledged that the day and time chosen were not the best because the schools had broken up at lunchtime, and that the police community relations officer should have been consulted. He also announced that the area would be policed henceforth mainly by officers on foot and not by panda cars. The community relations department would be strengthened and inquiries would be made into whether the police should be taught about the background and culture of black people. At the time of writing these reforms had taken place or were about to be implemented. In view of the force's inability to assemble reinforcements quickly, Weigh said the procedures for calling out men were being revised.

The question of gathering reinforcements was top of the agenda for the Home Office working party set up nationally after the riot.[9] It said that, while it would not be sensible to lay down a single comprehensive national scheme for emergency reinforcements, each force should examine its arrangements by setting up a planning team to work out a command structure and an operation plan. (Mutual aid of this kind has a long history and several forces had already done this). Chief officers agreed to set a minimum target for the number of officers on whom they needed to call in an emergency. Communications and equipment, as well as protective gear for officers, would be examined, as would police training in the use of shields. The report added that it was important for police forces to establish links with local community leaders and to involve local officers in the handling of disorders. On every single one of these points the police were found wanting when widespread rioting broke out in 1981. Reinforcements could not be assembled quickly or in sufficient numbers, communications were hopeless, protective gear inadequate and the police quite unable to handle their shields (which were in any case of defective design). Relations with the local political establishment were hostile and local beat officers were never called in.

The government's decision to reject a national inquiry made the job of the Commons select committee rather difficult. A subcommittee of five MPs visited Bristol to be told that it was 'a complete and utter waste of time'. No black youth were present at its session. This led to speculation that they were frightened to come forward because of the television cameras but an equally strong reason was a widespread cynicism about the willingness of government to do anything about their grievances. For some, this had evolved into a philosophy which made a virtue out of separateness. Francis Salandy, a St Paul's Rastafarian and organizer of the local advice centre, spoke on behalf of many black youths during the summer when he said he did not want a public inquiry and that the issue of black unemployment was simply a diversion. What had to be faced up to was that Britain was deeply racialist, he said.

In the end a group of the city's trade unionists and Labour Party activists set up their own local inquiry into the riot, chaired by Ian Mikardo MP.[10] It was boycotted by the police and the Conservative-controlled Avon county council. At the same time a working party of the National Union of Teachers in Bristol was preparing a report which concentrated on education and produced some detailed and hard-hitting recommendations.[11]

The riot trial

While the politicians and pundits sucked on their pens, the rioters themselves were being rounded up by the police. A total of 134 arrests (88 black and 46 white) were made. Community leaders objected that the police were picking up young people indiscriminately and detaining them when they were innocent. The chief constable denied it and offered to show critics round the cells. Eventually ninety-one people faced charges of criminal damage, assault, theft, burglary, handling stolen goods, public order offences or riotous assembly. Apart from the few charged with the last offence, they were dealt with fairly quickly in the magistrates' courts, and were in the main convicted. Some of the looters received hefty fines: from £125 for stealing two jars of coffee from a shop which had been sacked by rioters, to £500 for handling stolen electrical goods.

A small core of sixteen cases were isolated by the Director of Public Prosecutions as meriting more serious treatment. These people were all charged with riotous assembly, a serious and rarely used charge which carries a maximum sentence of life imprisonment. Lawyers acting for the prosecution admitted that these defendants were chosen to some extent arbitrarily but said the line had to be drawn somewhere. When they were first picked up, the sixteen had all been charged with lesser offences, which would not have warranted trial by jury, and the riot charge was only added at a later date. The way in which this charge was preferred brought strong objections from defence lawyers who said people should not be made scapegoats of and should be dealt with only for offences they had committed. In the end it was probably the controversial use of riot charges more than anything which led to the collapse of the trial.

The committal proceedings in the magistrates' court lasted six weeks and were tense, with fighting breaking out in the court room between youths and the police. Some of the accused leapt from the dock to join in and there were clashes later outside the court between about a hundred demonstrators and the police. The trouble was over the removal of the riot's alleged ringleader, Franklin Rapier, from the court for interrupting proceedings. There was more trouble when people were refused entry to the public gallery on the grounds that it was full. The magistrates found that twelve of the sixteen had a case to answer and committed them to the crown court for trial. After this the Director of Public Prosecutions decided to drop the lesser charges against eleven of the twelve defendants so they appeared at the crown court charged with one very serious offence – riot. This meant they were not simply accused of having been violent but of having been violent towards a common end. The only woman of the twelve, Doretta Maye, a prostitute with four children, was also charged with maliciously wounding a policeman. All were black except one white youth and all pleaded not guilty. Five were aged seventeen.

The trial did not take place until ten months after the riot and was perhaps most unusual for the composition of the jury: five of the twelve were non-white and eight were women. The black representation was therefore better than it is in Bristol generally (four per cent are black) and contrasted with the juries in the city the week before. A small survey carried out by the Bristol Council for Racial Equality at the same court the week before the trial revealed all the juries to be white, with more men than women. Lord Denning, Master of the Rolls, commented later that it was the composition of the jury which led to the collapse of the trial. He had a point but the defendants had a perfect right to reject the jurors they did not want so there was no abuse of the right of challenge, as Denning suggested. What must have shocked him was that the colour of a person's skin had become a criterion for selection of a juror. This had not come to his attention before.

The composition of the jury resulted from the determination of the judge and the barristers that the trial should be fair and seen to be fair. It had not escaped anyone that this case was important for race relations throughout the country. On the first day of the trial, 3 February 1981, the judge, Mr Justice Stocker, agreed that the whole of the jury panel, which amounted to scores of people, should be brought into court for inspection. He seemed to agree with defence lawyers' arguments that if there were no black people on the panel, from which the jury is chosen, he would have to think about discharging the whole panel and picking another, thus delaying the trial further.

More than one hundred bewildered-looking Bristolians packed into the court room among whom, to the court's relief, were a handful of blacks. There then began the lengthy but fascinating process of challenging the jury. A court official read out the name of members of the panel, they fought through the crush and processed solemnly past the barristers towards the jurors' bench. If a barrister (there was one for each defendant) objected to a potential juror, he or she was rejected and had to leave the court. Each defendant had three challenges and the defence used up thirty-five of their thirty-six challenges in order to get the jury they wanted. They did not have to give reasons but it was clear that anyone who was white and aged over fifty did not meet with favour. Crucially, the prosecution counsel agreed not to oppose any of the non-white jurors chosen.

The trial was better tempered than the committal. Mr Justice Stocker allowed the Rastafarian defendants to wear their brightly coloured woolly tams in the dock, a break with custom, and did not seem to mind when they fell asleep in court. At times proceedings were very informal, as when defendants joined in challenging members of the jury. In the fifth week of the trial, the judge directed the jury to return not-guilty verdicts against three of the accused for lack of evidence, and at the end of the seventh week, after hearing evidence from more than one hundred witnesses, the jurors retired to decide on the remaining nine.

They spent hours closeted up in hotel rooms and after the first day began to acquit. It was hard work. After deliberating for fifty hours over two and a half days, they acquitted five men. They were deadlocked on most of the remainder so the judge discharged them and the trial collapsed, having cost around £500,000 (the same as the cost of the riot damage). The result was seen as a resounding victory for black people and the rioters, and led the Director of Public Prosecutions, Sir Thomas Hetherington, to comment that it may have been a mistake to have brought riot charges at all. He decided not to press charges against the remaining four defendants, as he would normally have done, because it was not in the public interest. He said an important factor in reaching this decision was advice he had received from Chief Constable Weigh about the promotion of racial harmony in Bristol.

There were cheers, applause and clenched fist salutes when the trial broke up on 20 March 1981. Champagne flowed and impromptu celebrations took place in the pub opposite and later in the Black and White Café. Three of the non-white jurors, all men, joined in the festivity. What made it so difficult to convict in the end was that the jury was split on whether or not there had been a riot. In order for a riot charge to stick it has to be agreed that more than three people gathered, that they had a common purpose and that they carried out that common purpose.

Prosecution counsel said the common purpose in this case was a show of strength against the police, and the judge agreed that, if there was this show of strength, that could be considered common purpose. Some of the jurors thought otherwise. They may have agreed with the defence lawyers that the common purpose in the case was not obvious or even that the police themselves had started the riot by their drugs and alcohol raid.

Five days after the Director of Public Prosecutions announced he was not going to proceed against the remaining four, the inner London area of Brixton went up in flames. Some commentators saw a connection between the two events. They were most unhappy about charges having been dropped in the interest of 'good race relations' ('Was there one law for whites and another for blacks?' they asked) and thought this gave rioters elsewhere the green light to throw bricks and loot shops without fear of the law. But the DPP's decision can equally well be seen as a recognition that the first trial was a major blunder that he was anxious not to repeat.

Black youths in Bristol, celebrating the anniversary of the riot on 2 April 1981, saw it and the trial as an achievement which had put Bristol on the map and shown that black people could fight back. 'What happened here is something people should be proud of,' said Sibghat Kadri, one of the defence barristers. St Paul's had become a symbol of resistance and black youths were to be heard chanting: 'Bristol, Bristol' at police in Lewisham later that month.[12] Many felt it was only a matter of time before Brixton exploded, and a paint-sprayer in south London echoed that: 'Bristol yesterday, Brixton today', said the graffiti. But when the real riots came riot charges were nowhere to be seen.

2 Immigration and racism: Blacks in Britain

As long as the black man has a strong white Government and a numerous white population to control him he is capable of living as a respectable member of society.

The Times, 13 November 1865

Tolerance does not require that every Englishman should have a black man for his neighbour.

The Times, 10 July 1981

It's the totally racist nature of English society that leads up to the riots.

Jessica Mitford

Blacks have been in Britain for centuries, and so has the idea of getting rid of them. Queen Elizabeth I pronounced herself 'highly discontented' about 'the great number of blackamoors which are crept into this realm'. They were disturbing her liege people and did not understand Christ or His gospel. She decided that they should be expelled, and a Lubeck merchant was put in charge of the operation.[1] Two centuries later, in 1794, it was estimated that there were 20,000 black people in London.[2] Many were former slaves. They were mainly servants (like Dr Johnson's Frank).

Calls for blacks to be repatriated were heard at the beginning of the twentieth century too. Immediately after the First World War, there was rioting in Liverpool against black seamen and black residents. Four people were killed. *The Times* reported:

The police have issued a warning that severe measures will be taken against anyone attempting to attack members of the

39

coloured community, many of whom are inoffensive and have given distinguished service after the war. Scores of coloured men and women, some of them with their families, have gone to the local police headquarters asking for protection, and last evening over 60 of them were taken into the care of the police.[3]

The reasons that were given for the unprovoked attacks on black people were resentment that blacks had jobs when returning white soldiers had not, and that blacks had married local white women. The government offered a passage 'home' and some ninety-five were taken up.[4] There were other riots, in Canning Town in east London, Cardiff, Newport and Hull – all of them dockland areas.

Black immigration started on a large scale after the Second World War when West Indians began to cross the Atlantic. They came for jobs, and to improve themselves financially and socially. The first boat to make the journey was the famous SS *Empire Windrush* in June 1948 carrying 492 Jamaicans who were put up in an empty air-raid shelter in Clapham.[5] They were found jobs by the nearest labour exchange, which happened to be in Brixton, and thus put down roots in a part of London which was beginning to decay.

By 1950, the non-white population of Britain was estimated at 30,000, of whom 5000 had arrived in the postwar influx, and white political fears at the highest level were already growing. In June 1950, the Labour prime minister, Clement Attlee, set up a secret Cabinet committee to review 'means which might be adopted to check the immigration into this country of coloured people from the British colonial territories'.[6] The committee reported to the Cabinet in February 1951 saying that restrictions were unnecessary for the time being but might become 'essential' in the future.

A further boost to immigration was the passing of the McCarran-Walter Act four years later in the USA. This effectively stopped West Indians from migrating to America and forced them to look for a new destination.

Although the distance was great, Britain was still the 'mother country'. The early arrivals were skilled or semi-skilled workers and many had jobs lined up before they came. This was partly as a result of direct recruitment by British enterprises, such as London Transport, in the West Indies. This process was continued by the National Health Service, ironically then under the ministerial control of Enoch Powell. In the later phases of black immigration, by contrast, immigrants tended to be less well qualified, often totally without skills, and to come from rural areas.

The vast bulk of immigration from both the West Indies and Asia took place between 1956 and 1974 with a high point being reached in the eighteen months before the passing of the Commonwealth Immigrants Act 1962. People flocked to Britain then to try to beat the ban. Until 1962 there were no controls whatsoever on the movement of Commonwealth immigrants to and from the British Isles. In fact the two major political parties still thought it wrong to keep them out. They were, after all, 'our' citizens. The 1948 Nationality Act had made clear that all subjects of the Crown throughout the Empire and all citizens of independent Commonwealth countries remained British. An element of idealism still held sway through the 1950s though, as the Cabinet discussions of 1950–1 had shown, its days were numbered. Asians came to Britain later than the West Indians mainly because the Indian government refused to give passports to its nationals until it was forced to do so in 1960. Then the restrictions on emigration were lifted and the numbers began to grow, fuelled partly by rumours about impending immigration control in Britain. In 1960 there were 7500 immigrants from India and Pakistan; the following year the figure had risen to 48,000.

The influx of blacks to Britain was not some apparently arbitrary nomadic process. It was an influx of *labour*, paralleled in the economies of other Western European countries such as France and West Germany. Migrant workers came to these countries to do jobs which native

41

workers were reluctant to take – low paid and low status – but which were nevertheless so indispensable to the maintenance of the economy and social services that they had to be done. But they also came to better themselves economically. They came from poor countries – often single-commodity-producing economies. In the words of Robert Moore, an expert on race in Britain, 'Migrants are here because our rulers created the conditions in their homelands which made migration necessary, as well as a situation in Europe into which migration was possible.'[7]

Large scale migrant labour in Britain was no new phenomenon in the 1950s. The Irish had formed a subst-antial part of the workforce in trades such as construction from the middle of the nineteenth century onwards. What was new was that the migrants were black. They faced hostility and prejudice for that reason above all others.

The early West Indian settlers put up with the indig-nities of the 'colour bar', as it was then called, in ways which would not now be tolerated by their black British children. Dilip Hiro, an Asian writer, has collected numerous examples of this. A skilled West Indian welder explained what happened to him:

It didn't take me long to realise that I couldn't get a job in that trade . . . When I start riding the buses looking for job, I would jump off wherever I saw a chimney . . . At last I went to Lyons, and got a job there as a porter.[8]

At least he found work, even if he was over-qualified for it.

Finding somewhere to live was much more difficult. Signs reading 'No coloureds' and 'Europeans only' were common, but did not mean that houses without these signs were prepared to let rooms to black people. Surveys undertaken in the 1950s and 1960s revealed massive discrimination in the private rented sector. This meant that black people were forced into terribly crowded accommodation. Whole families would live in one room, saving up for the day when they too could put down a deposit for a home of their own, perhaps together with other West Indians in a 'pardner' group. David Smith, who has written definitive studies on racial disadvantage, concluded:

When they did escape to owner-occupation, they were very likely to buy properties in the same deprived areas where they already lived, first because they had jobs nearby, secondly because they knew little about opportunities in other areas where house prices were low. In these ways, discrimination in the rented sector has probably had long-term and far-reaching effects.[9]

Racial violence against black people and black counter-attacks began to be common occurrences. They climaxed in the major rioting of Nottingham and Notting Hill in 1958. In Nottingham, where black people had settled after West Indian servicemen had been posted there during the war, six whites were stabbed on 23 August 1958. A crowd of about 1500 white people then retaliated and eight people were injured and had to be taken to hospital. This was soon followed by an explosion in Notting Hill where, within hours of the news about Nottingham, a gang of teddy boys were searching for black people to attack with iron bars and knives.

The riots in Notting Hill were mostly whites assaulting blacks and continued for days, growing in scale and nastiness. A house was set alight and others were attacked, and there were also reports of petrol bomb attacks. Nine teddy boys were given gaol sentences by Lord Justice Salmon who commented, in a famous judgement, that they had filled the nation with horror, disgust and indignation. 'Everyone, irrespective of the colour of their skin, is entitled to walk through our streets with heads erect and free from fear,' he said – fine words which helped to calm the immediate situation but did little to dispel the growing bitterness of the black community or the fear of many white people that the influx of blacks was a threat which they were powerless to prevent.

Sir Oswald Mosley and his British Union of Fascists cashed in on these fears. Mosley decided to fight the North Kensington parliamentary seat in the 1959 general election on a platform of repatriation coupled with the fair treatment of blacks here. At the time repatriation was considered extreme; later it was to become a much more mainstream philosophy. Initially, the Conservative government resisted a move to restrict immigration from the colonies on the grounds that Britain was the mother country, but the racial unrest had left its mark.

In the years from 1958 to 1963 Britain became a country with net inward migration. The pressure to abandon the laissez-faire policy on *black* immigration, became irresistible. A motion demanding control was passed by a huge majority at the Tory Party conference in 1961 and the stage was set for the Commonwealth Immigrants Act of 1962.

Under the Act, Commonwealth citizens and United Kingdom citizens whose passports were not issued in Britain or through a British high commission abroad had to obtain an employment voucher to come to Britain. There were three categories of voucher according to whether someone was coming to a specific job, whether they had a recognized skill or whether they had served in the forces in the Second World War. While the Act did not actually say that its intention was to keep black people out of the country, that was its effect and that was why it was introduced. It made, and still makes, black people bitter on the grounds that it legitimized discrimination by writing it into law. It began what many choose to call the process of institutionalized racism. 'Racialism was no longer a matter of free enterprise,' said A. Sivanandan, of the Institute of Race Relations. 'It was nationalized.'[10]

The four years between the Nottingham/Notting Hill riots and the Commonwealth Immigrants Act marked a turning-point in the history of blacks in Britain. They made non-white poeple more politically conscious and aware of their common grievances and the Act ushered in a decade and more of British politics in which the race question was dominated by immigration. Politicians of the two major parties vied with one another as to who could introduce the most stringent control. In the process a consensus emerged that this island could only absorb a small and finite number of blacks. If it took too many, it was asking for racial trouble, the argument went. The indigenous white population would simply not stand for it. In other words, the victims of racism were blamed for being the cause of it.

While opinion polls conducted in the 1960s provide evidence that this view was widely held among whites, the damage to blacks in general was immense. The obsession with immigration inflicted untold damage not just on those who were subject to control but on those who were not. It also confirmed whites in their own feeling of superiority. In her powerful book on racism, published in 1973, Ann Dummett says she remembers an employer at a conference asking the very pertinent question: 'Why is it wrong for me to refuse to have any of these people in my firm when the Government is refusing to have them come into the country. If the Government doesn't want them, why should I want them?'[11] It was hard to introduce legislation to outlaw racial discrimination and make the law stick when new racial curbs on immigration were being introduced every few years.

A 'bipartisan' immigration policy emerged between Conservative and Labour, though it took some time to solidify. The 1962 Act was passionately opposed by the Labour opposition, led by Hugh Gaitskell, and Denis Healey initially pledged the party to repeal the law. What finally took the steam out of the opposition was the general election result in 1964 in the west midlands constituency of Smethwick. The Conservative candidate, Peter Griffiths, turned a national swing towards Labour of 3.5 per cent into a 7.2 per cent swing to the right. He had run a rabidly racialist campaign, endorsing the slogan 'if you want a nigger neighbour, vote Liberal or Labour' with the result that Patrick Gordon-Walker, the

Labour candidate and one of the new Labour government's leaders, was defeated. (Gordon-Walker had made a speech opposing immigration control three years before.)

This result (along with the defeat of Fenner Brockway in Eton and Slough) sent shock waves through the Labour Party leadership. Race had suddenly become a political issue and was so hot that it could cause the defeat of a respected Labour figure. Harold Wilson, the new Labour prime minister, called Griffiths a 'parliamentary leper', while recognizing his electoral success. The result was that the party did not fight what it saw as the clear message of the voters. Being soft on immigration might mean electoral defeat. In 1965, a private opinion poll confirmed the mood of the constituencies: 95 per cent of voters favoured stringent control of coloured immigration.

In his diaries, Richard Crossman, a Cabinet minister and west Midlands MP who was no great liberal on immigration, made clear how well he had taken the point.

Ever since the Smethwick election it has been quite clear that immigration can be the greatest potential vote-loser for the Labour Party if we are seen to be permitting a flood of immigrants to come and blight the central areas in all our cities.[12]

At the same time he emphasized that immigration control had to go hand in hand with measures to promote racial justice and to reduce racial disadvantage. He appreciated the importance of a balancing act, even if he did not see how difficult the tightrope trick might be.

Labour had come to power in 1964 committed to positive measures to prohibit racial discrimination at home but 'balanced' with more immigration control. Its majority in the House of Commons was wafer-thin and the Conservative opposition made clear it would agree to anti-discrimination legislation only if the offence of discriminating on racial grounds was not a criminal one and if conciliation machinery was set up to deal with it.

Labour agreed and its Race Relations Bill was changed by Sir Frank Soskice, the Home Secretary, between second reading and its committee stage. The Bill, which became law in 1965 with full Conservative support, was very narrow in its coverage because it applied only to discrimination in public places and left out the important areas of housing and employment. For Soskice, who sounded almost apologetic at promoting the Bill at all, it was obviously a relief to get it through, particularly with Tory support. To black critics and other lobbyists it was a feeble Act with feeble conciliation machinery – even if it was a beginning.

The years 1964–5 saw the forging (the word is not inappropriate) of a seamless unity between the two main parties on race relations and immigration. The precondition for good race relations was seen as the control of numbers; integration, an ill-defined concept, was seen as the ideal to be aimed for. Labour, egged on by the opposition, produced a White Paper suggesting lowering the number of work vouchers for Commonwealth immigrants at a time when there was an acute shortage of labour. It proposed that no more unskilled workers could come in unless they had jobs to come to, that 'strict tests of eligibility' should apply to the entry of dependants, that the dependants should have medical tests and that deportation powers should be extended. (This was carried through despite strong protest.) Richard Crossman mourned the fact that the government had become illiberal in the following words:

Nevertheless, I am convinced that if we hadn't done all this we would have been faced with certain electoral defeat in the West Midlands and the South-East. Politically, fear of immigration is the most powerful undertow today. Moreover, we had already abandoned the Gaitskell position when we renewed the Immigration Act [of 1962], and any attempt now to resist demands for reduced quotas would have been fatal. We felt we had to out-trump the Tories by doing what they would have done and so transforming their policy into a bipartisan policy. I fear we were right; and partly I think so because I am an old-fashioned Zionist who believes that anti-Semitism and racialism are endemic, that one has to deal with them by controlling immigration when it gets beyond a certain level.[13]

Crossman represented mainstream Labour opinion, the world of *realpolitik*. So did Roy Hattersley, another west Midlands Labour MP. In 1965 Hattersley explained that he regretted the Labour Party had not voted for the 1962 Act:

I now believe that there are social as well as economic arguments [for limiting Commonwealth immigration], and I believe that unrestricted immigration can only produce additional problems, additional suffering and additional hardship unless some kind of limitation is imposed and continued.

Hattersley is now on record as having regretted voting for the even more restrictive 1968 Immigration Act, an acknowledgement that perhaps reflects a change in *realpolitik* as much as one of consciousness.

During the 1960s, Asians and West Indians began to organize: the Indian Workers' Association was formed; so was the West Indian Standing Conference. Black people united to fight the 1962 Act and were soon borrowing tactics from across the Atlantic, where Martin Luther King's civil rights movement had begun to make dramatic impact. In April 1963 in Bristol, the city which was to experience serious rioting seventeen years later, they used the weapon of passive resistance in an almost exact copycat of Luther King's style. The Bristol Omnibus Company refused to employ blacks, so Paul Stephenson, a Bristol-born West Indian who had visited the USA, called for a boycott of the buses. This blew up into a full-scale dispute which lasted four months, produced demonstrations and brought forth comments from national politicians. The Transport and General Workers' Union refused to become involved but eventually the management capitulated and some blacks were hired immediately. The tactic had worked well; it made a local incident into a national *cause célèbre*.

Many of the attitudes of the mid to late 1960s were influenced by what was going on the other side of the Atlantic. A reawakening of black consciousness and pride was leading American blacks to search out their own history and culture. In 1964 Martin Luther King visited London on his way to receive the Nobel prize in Oslo and left behind him the idea for a British civil rights organization. This became CARD – the Campaign Against Racial Discrimination – which brought together Asian and Afro-Caribbean organizations and some white Labour Party radicals. It received a great deal of publicity because a need for such a pressure group was widely understood and CARD achieved significant success in pressing for new race relations law. But as a liberal, multi-racial organization with a fairly narrow brief and operating as a conventional pressure group, it had few roots in the rapidly changing black community. By 1967, CARD had fallen apart under the pressure of prolonged disagreements between the old guard and a more radical group who mistrusted it for its links with increasingly discredited parties and institutions. A similar fate befell the Institute of Race Relations, an academically oriented research organization, in the early 1970s. The institute, unlike CARD, survived, albeit in a completely altered state.

These developments reflected the growth of a more radical, autonomist movement in British black politics, frequently dubbed a 'black power' movement. It is important to see why it emerged. It did so because, in closing the immigration doors, white British institutions were seen to have closed the doors on blacks in more general terms. This weak move to the left was the natural consequence of a much stronger move to the right in Britain on race during the 1960s. The growth of a radical black politics had many strengths, but it arose from a position of weakness imposed by, more than any other factor, immigration control.

This was not, however, the whole story. The doors were closing, but where was the compensating equal treatment? In 1967, a report by Political and Economic Planning (PEP) proved what all black people had known for a long time, that there was still massive racial discrimination in Britain. This added weight to calls for a strengthening of the race relations law. But, first, the government, with unerring instinct, seemed to make that respectable by playing its immigration control card again. During 1967 growing numbers of Kenyan Asians had been entering Britain as a result of President Kenyatta's 'Africanization' policy. There seemed to be some confusion about their status in immigration law until the Court of Appeal ruled that they were not covered by the 1962 Act because they were citizens of the United Kingdom and colonies with passports issued by the British government. They therefore had every right to come into the country. There was nothing accidental about this. When Kenya was granted independence in 1963, the British government pledged to both European and Asian settlers that they could retain their British citizenship and have British passports if they chose to do so rather than become Kenya citizens. This was to prevent the possibility of them becoming stateless one day. Many accepted the offer.

But when, four years later, it looked as though this pledge was to be acted upon, it was met by an outcry from, among others, Enoch Powell and Duncan Sandys. (The latter had been Commonwealth and Colonial Secretary in 1963.) Powell said: 'Hundreds of thousands of people in Kenya, who never dreamt they belonged to this country, started to belong to it like you and me.' The government, with a new Home Secretary, James Callaghan, bent before the storm, and the Commonwealth Immigrants Act of 1968 was rushed through Parliament in three days of emergency debates. It became law immediately and meant that United Kingdom and colonies citizens who were not resident in Britain would not have the right to come here unless they had one parent or grandparent who was born here. The law was used to keep Kenyan Asians out while Kenya's white settlers could come and go at will. Despite the speed with which it was introduced, the Act did not escape bitter condemnation and was later found, in a report which remains unpublished, to have contravened the European Convention of Human Rights. It was, after all, preventing United Kingdom citizens from entering Britain when they faced expulsion from the country in which they lived and yet had no rights to enter any other country.

Like his predecessors, Callaghan balanced this particularly unsavoury piece of legislation with a new Race Relations Bill bequeathed him by his more liberal predecessor, Roy Jenkins. It significantly extended the scope of the 1965 Act by making it unlawful to discriminate on racial grounds in employment, housing and in the provision of commercial and other services. The powers of the Race Relations Board were strengthened to enable it to take a discriminator to the county court once conciliation had failed and to obtain damages from the discriminator if he was found guilty. (In fact this was rarely used.) The Bill established the Community Relations Commission to promote 'harmonious community relations', a job which had previously been done by the voluntary National Committee for Commonwealth Immigrants. Thirteen years on, this Act may not look very impressive, especially as it has been replaced, but at the time it was seen as an important victory, won at a time when immigration control had again reared its ugly head.

Three days before the second reading debate Enoch Powell made his notorious 'River Tiber foaming with much blood' speech in Birmingham. In it he advocated re-emigration, a word he has recently resuscitated, and suggested that the people who suffered discrimination and deprivation were not the immigrants but the indigenous white population. He gave a lurid example, that of an old-age pensioner, the only white left in a street now filled with blacks:

She is becoming afraid to go out. Windows are broken. She finds excreta pushed through her letter box. When she goes to the shops, she is followed by children, charming, wide-grinning piccaninnies. They cannot speak English, but one word they know. 'Racialist', they chant.

Mr Powell concluded: 'As I look ahead I am filled with foreboding. Like the Roman I seem to see "the River Tiber foaming with much blood".'

The speech caused a sensation. Powell was sacked from the Shadow Cabinet by Edward Heath but received phenomenal backing from the public: 110,000 letters poured in, mostly in support; and thousands of workers backed him with demonstrations. Thirty-nine immigration officers at London Airport publicly announced their support. On the day the Race Relations Bill was to be debated, 1500 dockers marched on Parliament; the following day the Smithfield meat-porters joined in. National opinion polls showed the extent to which the public was behind him. One poll showed that 82 per cent thought him right to make the speech, another that 74 per cent agreed with him in general. The same year Birmingham city council passed a motion saying it did not want any more immigrants allowed into Birmingham.

What Enoch Powell did was to take the concern with immigration control to its logical conclusion – there are too many black people here but controls on their entry are not enough so let us send them back whence they came. The politicians responded with a re-run, on a larger scale, of 1964. While Powell was denounced, the support which he received pushed politicians in his own Conservative Party as well as in the Labour Party to take up less liberal positions on race relations and immigration. New restrictions on immigration were introduced in 1968; after Powell's speech Callaghan introduced further controls: male Commonwealth citizens were barred from entering Britain to join their British wives and fiancées. A liberal measure which had been in the pipeline did, however, go though, introducing a complicated appeals machinery for immigrants who were prevented from entering Britain. But within this new law was a very important change: in future immigrants from the Commonwealth and colonies had to obtain an entry certificate before coming to Britain. This severely curtailed the inflow of dependants. Eventually the complex legislation on immigration was codified and tightened even further in the Immigration Act of 1971 which repealed previous Acts and is now the basis of our immigration law. It put Commonwealth citizens on much the same footing as aliens in relation to entering Britain. The effect of this was almost totally to close the doors to black immigration. The only people allowed in were the immediate relations of those already here and the East African Asians to whom we had promised our citizenship. The latter were allowed in only in a tiny and tightly controlled dribble after queuing for years.

There is no doubt that the support which Powell was able to ignite was an underlying political reason why no political party has attempted to liberalize the immigration laws in any very significant way since 1968. The tendency has been to tighten control still further, by law in 1971 and again in 1979, as well as by practice. In spite of some well-publicized cases of individual hardship, mainly involving Asians, the remorselessly humiliating and discriminating reality of everyday immigration control practice remains little known. But the response to the Ugandan and Malawian Asian expulsions in the 1970s is vivid proof that widespread white hostility to black immigration lies scarcely dormant. This explains why politicians today retain the priorities which Richard Crossman documented in the 1960s. The extraordinary tenacity of a degree of public support for Powell – who last held ministerial office in October 1963 – is a constant sanction for inactivity.

It also provides a backcloth of respectability for hostility to blacks. In the early 1970s this was marked by a revival of extreme right racist politics and by violence to individuals and communities. These developments are examined in relation to the police response in a later chapter. But it was a significant sign of the growth of racism that 'Paki-bashing' should break out in the early part of that decade. Tausir Ali, a Pakistani immigrant who lived in the East End of London, was murdered by two white eighteen-year-olds. His death highlighted what many Asians had been saying for a long time and are still saying today – that they are plagued with abuse ranging from verbal attacks to persistent stone-throwing to killings and arson, and that the police do not take it seriously enough.

This was only one area of complaint. A community under immigration control was also, it seemed, a community under special police control. A case from the same period in Brixton is indicative and still remembered. It concerned a Nigerian diplomat with an equally distinguished Nigerian name – Gomwalk. In 1969 Clement Gomwalk was the First Secretary at the Nigerian High Commission and lived in Chester Square, Belgravia. He had just bought a brand new white Mercedes-Benz and driven it over from West Germany himself. The car therefore had foreign number plates together with a British road tax licence that had just arrived. Mr Gomwalk was committing a minor technical offence for the few days the car was registered in this way but he hoped to escape attention with the CD signs he attached to the car, announcing his diplomatic status.

In fact he attracted attention. On 15 November he went shopping with his family in Brixton, parking on double yellow lines in Atlantic Road and thus committing another offence. Diplomats are frequent parking offenders because they have diplomatic immunity from prosecution, though this is no excuse for it. The inevitable happened: the police arrived, asked who he was and accused him of stealing the car. Gomwalk denied it twice but the police persisted, and in the end he said something to the effect that if they wanted him to say he had stolen the car he would. 'OK, I stole the car,' he said. This was silly and Gomwalk was to live to regret it.

Gomwalk was promptly dragged off by a number of officers, according to a signed statement he made later.

Protesting his innocence loudly, he was punched, hit in the groin and handcuffed. The officers also talked about killing him, he claimed. He was then made to sit in Brixton police station for an hour, still in handcuffs. Whenever he opened his mouth to speak he was told to shut up. Finally the handcuffs were removed and Gomwalk was able to prove what he had been saying all along — that he was a diplomat. The police accepted it but by that time a crowd of about two hundred people had gathered in Atlantic Road shouting for him to be released. Officers decided to try to disperse the crowd. Violence broke out, and five people were arrested who later claimed to have been beaten up by the police. Gomwalk got nowhere in the formal complaint he made about the incident in the same way as the vast majority of people who complain about police behaviour never receive the redress they seek. Moreover James Callaghan made a singularly unsympathetic statement in the House of Commons in which he reproduced a police version of events which did not correspond to Clement Gomwalk's. He had not spoken to Gomwalk first.

The incident illustrates a number of faces of the British police with which black people are only too familiar. The police clearly found it difficult to believe that a black man would own such an expensive car; they did not listen to what he said; according to his statement they hurled racial abuse at him; and when a group of people gathered to protest they waded in with truncheons instead of leaving them to disperse. But they got away with everything: they won the physical fight in Brixton and the verbal battle in the Commons.[14]

In the following years things got worse and there were clashes between blacks and the police in a number of big cities. Liverpool, with its long-established black community, was especially tense during the summer of 1971. That year, a whole decade before the riots which are the subject of this book, Margaret Simey, who now chairs the Merseyside police authority, said:

55

The coloured community is fed up with being hounded. No one is safe on the streets after 10 p.m. One gang we know has given the police an ultimatum to lay off within two weeks or they fight back. It could lead to civil war in the city.

The surprising thing is that it took ten years before anything happened. In 1974, Labour was returned to government and the liberal Roy Jenkins returned to the Home Office. Following a White Paper in 1975, Jenkins charted a new Race Relations Act through Parliament. The 1968 Act outlawing discrimination had not been a complete failure. There had been a sharp decrease in the overt discrimination which had appalled people in the early 1960s but the law had by no means eradicated many of the problems. This was partly because of weak enforcement mechanisms which rested on a process of conciliating the two parties. But it was largely based on the fact that the Race Relations Board could only act on complaints it received. It could not act on its own initiative; even where it was able to get organizations which had discriminated to pursue new policies, it could not ensure that this happened.

The 1976 Act set up a new race relations body – the Commission for Racial Equality (an amalgam of the old board and the Community Relations Commission) – with greatly increased powers. It is able to carry out its own investigations of organizations to find out whether they are discriminating; it can subpoena documents and witnesses and, where discrimination is proved, it can serve a non-discrimination notice telling them to stop their past practices. It can insist that certain steps are taken to remedy things and can check that these are being carried out. The new Act was not based on complaints received. It gave complainants direct access to the courts and industrial tribunals and enabled the commission to provide them with support. Moreover it extended the area of discrimination covered to include 'indirect discrimination'. This meant that a practice which was discriminating in its effect, even though it was a practice applied to everyone, would be unlawful. This was designed to catch a rule, say, which outlawed the wearing of a headress by employees. The effect of this rule, applied to all, would be that turbanned Sikhs would not be hired.

Despite the strength of the Act and the unprecedented powers given to the commission, it is clear that discrimination still flourishes throughout the country. (The household regiment, for example, which employs the soldiers who guard The Queen, refuses to recruit blacks. It is exempt from the Race Relations Act.) Some of the responsibility for this state of affairs must lie with the CRE; the rest undoubtedly lies with government and society generally, which has still barely learnt to accept that Britain is multi-racial. Industrial tribunals have been extremely cautious in interpreting the new Act and it has proved difficult to win individual cases in law. The commission, set up to enforce the law, is an easy target for critics. It comes in for constant abuse from sections of the black community, who blame it for failing to eradicate the discrimination and disadvantage from which they suffer. Right-wing Conservatives, resent many aspects of the race relations laws and regard the CRE as an unacceptable state intervention. In December 1981, the Home Affairs select committee published a violent critique uniting Labour and Conservative antagonists of the CRE. Much of the criticism of the commission is justified. It has undertaken too many investigations (forty-five in the space of five years) and finished too few of them. It has got involved in too wide a range of activities, without the resources (and sometimes the expertise) to follow them through.

To some extent this is the fault of the legislation; the commission was given the jobs of two former institutions and now has the unenviable task of enforcing the law, punishing people and holding them up to opprobrium, as well as trying to promote good race relations. It is not an easy task and many of the critics are increasingly coming round to the view that it would be better off enforcing the law in a really determined and effective way and leaving the social work to voluntary effort. This might ensure that the commission was less of a universal flak-catcher. As it is, the black community blames it for almost everything: for being mealy-mouthed and weak and at the same time taking the heat out of black unrest by giving the community funds and mediating its demands. The commission is also a bitterly divided and unhappy place.

From the other end of the political spectrum – from Tory MPs, the odd judge and a lot of employers – there is criticism that the new legislation is Draconian and somehow un-British and that the commission is a monster with monstrous powers. The CRE therefore has to walk the tightrope of meeting the expectations of blacks without antagonizing the white majority. It has found increasing resistance to the powers it has geen given in law and has ended up in court having to justify its decisions to investigate organizations. The ultimate challenge to its authority came in 1980 when the Home Office, the government department which set up the commission and drafted the 1976 Act, took it to court over its decision to investigate the immigration service for possible discrimination. The CRE won – but only just.

The problems that the CRE has faced are, in part, a reflection of the political contradiction that tight immigration control is indispensable for good race relations. The Home Office refusal to accept the immigration investigation was a classic illustration of the problem. Immigration remains the area into which 'good race relations' may not trespass. In 1979, just before she was elected to office, Margaret Thatcher said that some white people felt 'swamped' by immigrants. Quite apart from the fact that most black people here feel insulted to be called 'immigrants' (more than forty percent were born here), the message of rejection was clear:

They [the whites] have seen the whole character of their neighbourhood change. They feel their whole way of life has been changed. Small minorities can be absorbed, they can be assets to the majority community. But once a minority in a neighbourhood gets very large, people do feel swamped.

A subsequent Gallup poll showed that two thirds of the population agreed with Thatcher's words and that 46 per cent wanted an immediate halt to all coloured immigration, while 30 per cent said blacks not born in Britain should be 'sent back home'.

These replies showed serious ignorance. In reality, immigration has dried up, except for a small number of wives and children joining their husbands. Nonetheless, the new government felt that it was politically necessary and advantageous to stand on a platform of further immigration restriction. It has pursued a policy of tightening up further on the settlement here of dependants and began to apply immigration law in new and tougher ways. The immigration rules were changed to prevent black British women living in Britain from bringing husbands or fiancés into the country. (This almost certainly contravenes the European Convention of Human Rights.) And Home Office ministers began to exercise the discretion which they have in deportation cases in much more rigid ways. Whole groups of people, for example the Filipinos, were sent home as part of a widening of the definition of illegal entry. The removal of significant numbers, combined with new drives to check the passports of foreign-sounding or -looking people, created resentment. The passport checking was conducted either by immigration officials hunting for illegal immigrants or by officials in health, education and social services to make sure that someone not 'entitled' to free treatment was not getting it. The final straw for many blacks was the government's Nationality Bill, which became law at the end of 1981. It changed the basis of Britain's citizenship to bring it into line with its tight immigration law. In the view of many people (not only in the black community) these developments further institutionalized racism in British society. And yet, all the while, the government was supposed to be committed to good race relations.

The serious resurgence of racism against black people during the 1970s included the emergence of the National

Front as a powerful electoral force. In 1973 its candidate, Martin Webster, polled sixteen per cent of the votes in the West Bromwich by-election, and the success was repeated in local elections later that year. The party ran ninety candidates at the October 1974 general election, though its share of the poll was in single figure percentages. In 1977, the *Guardian* journalist Martin Walker could conclude his book on the NF with the observation:

Perhaps the best measure of the change that has come and the change that may yet be is that a bare four years ago, the prospect of a tiny band of former Nazis, Empire Loyalists, crackpots and cranks becoming the fourth party in the country was wholly unthinkable.

Events have proved that fear wrong for the moment, but Walker's comment was true of its time. It did seem as if the very future of the black people in Britain was at risk, a future of murder and attack. In 1976 Gurdip Singh Chaggar was stabbed to death by white youths in Southall. Afterwards, Kingsley Read of the National Party (a breakaway from the NF) made a speech in which he commented 'One down, a million to go.' Read was acquitted of incitement to racial hatred. The judge told him 'By all means propagate the view you hold. I wish you well.'

The death of Chaggar had other effects. It led to the setting up of the Southall Youth Movement, which is now 600 strong and is a powerful focus of local Asian militancy. The movement was paralleled by a rising tide of militant opposition to the National Front in many parts of the country through the Anti-Nazi League. These developments signalled a growing mood of frequently violent resistance to racism, which led to major confrontations with police, which we describe elsewhere. These were political movements of the streets. They were not, however, matched by the emergence of a black political culture with any purchase on the mainstream political process. There were no black MPs, for instance, and only a tiny handful of black councillors. The trade unions recruited blacks in large numbers but few blacks were elected shop stewards, still less as members of union executives or as full-time officials.

The racist threats to black people continued, in the form of attacks. On the political stage, the National Front waned but it was replaced by new groups, notably the British Movement, which were every bit as virulent, indeed more so. Meanwhile the visibility of racism increased. Racist graffiti continued to be daubed in the cities while the resurgence of the skinhead subculture was indissolubly linked with white aggression – whatever its deluded adherents on the left may claim.

The decline of the National Front's electoral support and the exclusion, to some extent, of Enoch Powell from respectable democratic debate on race are points worthy of note. But in no sense do they mean that racism and insensitive language have been purged from mainstream discourse. Far from it.

To take but one recent example, how were blacks in Britain supposed to draw security from the coverage of the closing months of white rule in Rhodesia? When Margaret Thatcher travelled to the Commonwealth conference in Lusaka, Zambia, in August 1979, the *Daily Mail* reported that she was greeted with the 'diplomatic courtesy a gang of muggers might reserve for a solitary woman travelling on the late night Tube'. The *Daily Express* headlined a picture showing Joshua Nkomo sitting behind Thatcher as 'The Killer Behind Maggie'. The press was only reflecting a racially patronizing tone adopted by the foreign secretary, Lord Carrington, when he told a BBC reporter: 'I find that if you tell the truth and say things clearly, Africans are just as capable of understanding them as Europeans.' Blacks in Britain, though, identified/strongly with the uncompromising policies of Robert Mugabe. (While Mugabe was in gaol in Rhodesia, his wife Sally lived in Britain, where she was involved in long and familiar wrangles with the Home Office over her immigration status and had great difficulties trying to obtain housing and work.) When Mugabe's ZANU-PF party won its landslide independence election victory, installing Mugabe as unchallenged leader of Zimbabwe's blacks, the *Daily Mail* was distressed. 'We of the white tribe,' said its editorial, 'cannot but be moved by an undertow of melancholy.'[16]

It was against this background that a major organizational development among London's West Indian population took place in the most tragic circumstances. On 18 January 1981, thirteen young blacks were burned to death after a fire in a family home in New Cross Road, Deptford. A party was being celebrated and in a ferocious blaze the house was quickly gutted. The national press reported the story and then forgot it.

The New Cross tragedy – or 'massacre', as it became known – roused the black community to enormous suspicion. The community had a history of arson attacks against it, including one close by at the Moonshot Club, which was burnt down in what was widely believed to be a racialist attack. Within days Darcus Howe, editor of *Race Today*, had moved in to set up the 'Massacre Action Committee'. He did what very few West Indians have been able to do – to provide leadership to angry and troubled people. Blacks accused the police of neglecting to investigate the question of an arson attack, the press of neglecting to investigate a potential scandal and the government of failing to show compassion for a community tragedy. They compared this with Prime Minister Margaret Thatcher's immediate transmission of condolences to Irish families bereaved after a discotheque fire in Dublin a few weeks later. For them it added up to one thing – they were ignored because they did not matter to anybody.

The Massacre Action Committee set out to put this right. It organized a day of action for 2 March when black people would march from Lewisham, across the Thames, along Fleet Street and into central London. To the amazement of many, 10,000 people, mainly black, turned out. It was a weekday; children skipped school to take part and others had the day off work. The march made maximum impact because of the turnout and because of the violence which accompanied it. As the march snaked up Fleet Street windows were smashed and shops looted. The popular press had a field day (as we noted earlier), but black people had been noticed, and other newspapers woke up to their grievances over the fire. The pressure was maintained right through the inquest into the death of the thirteen, during which the police suggested that there had been a fight in the house which had in some way led to the fire. One black youth after another came into the witness box and claimed that the story he had told the police about a fight was untrue. They said there had been no fight and that the police had forced them to tell lies. Counsel for the families thought the incendiary device found outside the house after the fire was much more significant. An open verdict was returned and the truth was never discovered.

The Deptford fire aftermath served to confirm what had become apparent throughout the previous decade – that blacks were rising up to protest and that their relationship with the police was in crisis. If they continued to be neglected they would fight back with organized protest and considerable violence. This and the Bristol riot of 1980 were clear signs that new levels of black resistance had at long last emerged.

3 'People don't like being lined up against a wall': Black people and the police

At two in the morning on 15 July 1981, London police officers burst into eleven black people's houses in Railton Road, Brixton. They smashed their way in through doors and windows, armed with sledgehammers and crowbars. Inside the houses, further damage was done to floors, doors, banisters, panelling and to occupants' property. The police raid followed a tip-off that petrol bombs had been stored on the premises. No petrol bombs were found, but seven arrests were made and five people were later charged with possession of cannabis. The police officer in overall charge of the raid was later quoted as saying, 'We were bound to do what we did.' Three months later, the Home Office published an internal Scotland Yard report which concluded that the raid was fully justified.

Early on the morning of 29 October, the same day that William Whitelaw released the report on the Brixton raid, a 52-year-old white car factory supervisor was sitting down to breakfast with his wife and pregnant daughter in their Birmingham home. Peter Moss heard someone at the door and went to answer. On the step were two men, one wielding a sledgehammer. As Mr Moss quickly pushed the door shut the hammer came through the glass front. 'I shouted at them not to come near. From their dress I took them to be thugs.' The men were police officers. They burst into the Moss home, and searched the house, looking for firearms. Eventually, Peter Moss was able to persuade them that they were mistaken. A man was later arrested in another house in the same street.[1]

The difference between the two cases is that afterwards,

when it was accepted that the police had damaged property in a fruitless search, the Brixton raid was strenuously defended and no immediate apology was made. But the residents in Railton Road were black. In the Birmingham case one of the officers on the raid came back to the house the same day with a bunch of chrysanthemums and an apology. But then Mr Moss and his family were white.

Policing without consent

British policing, as any police officer will tell you, is based on the principle of consent. The police can only police the community with the community's consent. That is the theory. In practice that consent has not always been self-evident or stable. When the modern police force was created in London in 1829, it was met with hostility. Radical crowds surged around central London to cries of 'No new police! No standing armies!' The first constables who patrolled through the West End were accompanied by abusive crowds of Londoners. The new police force had no immediate community consent. Nor did the resistance die away quickly. In 1833, police dispersed a reform meeting in Coldbath Fields with a sabre charge, but not before three officers had been stabbed, one of whom, Constable Culley, died. A coroner's jury returned a remarkable verdict of justifiable homicide on Culley, on the grounds that the police action had been 'ferocious, brutal and unprovoked'. The extension of the police force into the counties and towns of England and Scotland over the following two decades was also marked by resentment and hostility.

The police gradually evolved a less overtly antagonistic relationship with the people. The history of that negotiation is complex and it is often overlooked, in the official histories, just how pragmatic, uneven and unstable these relationships actually were. 'In each neighbourhood and sometimes street by street, the police negotiated a complex, shifting, largely unspoken "contract" . . . sometimes oiled by corruption, but more often sealed by favours and friendships. This was the microscopic basis of police legitimacy and it was a fragile basis at best.'[2]

The arrival of democratic government altered but did not erase the essential truth of this analysis. The police and the community have never made an absolute pact. On their side, the police have never enforced all laws with equal vigour no matter what the circumstances. For its own part, the community has never wholly rejected the notion that there must be police and that they have a legitimate job to perform. Neither the police nor the community is monolithic.

In many ways the development of the democratic system of government has made very little direct impact on Britain's police. Compared with other state agencies and services, the police are probably under fewer direct democratic constraints than any, save the courts of law. Parliament has traditionally exercised little control over policing, even in London where (as we shall see later) it has more constitutional sanction for doing so. Local authorities have rather more duties – but they are indirect, exercised at one remove, rather than as a direct local authority function. Both Parliament and the local authorities have long been content to take a back seat, on the grounds that policing, unlike welfare, education, planning, the economy and so on, is somehow 'above politics'. This is part of the reason why the people who have made the decisions affecting the development of policing have largely been the police themselves.

Two general observations about modern police practice need to be borne in mind when analysing the relationship of black people and the police. The first is the development in the past two decades of policing methods which are necessarily more antagonistic to black people than to others. The precondition of this was the rupturing by the police of those microscopic local contracts when they began to withdraw officers from the beat. In a series of largely self-determined reforms, police officers in the 1960s were transferred from local beats to mobile car patrols. The police force as a whole was reorganized with the prime aim of providing the quickest possible response to reported crime incidents. This sort of policing has gained the nickname 'fire-brigade policing'. It is dependent upon clear lines of control, lack of individual discretion, high quality communications and transport technology, and wide police powers. Special reserve squads are an integral part of the system. Although it is wrong to claim that fire brigade policing is *wholly* unconstrained by local sanctions, it is very much less constrained and tends to become less so as police officers are promoted to senior ranks without the experience of a community base to their job. As the communities which are being policed change – specifically as they become more multi-racial – so this form of policing is even more distanced from black people than from whites.

The second feature is the related decline of accountability and the growth of police autonomy. This is a wider set of phenomena than is sometimes acknowledged. It is not only that as democracy has advanced, institutional control of policing has remained unchanged (or in some cases has declined) thus creating less control in real terms and in relation to expectations. It is also affected by the growth of a more politically assertive generation of police leaders at command level and representing police rank and file. The autonomy of police is further strengthened by the overall reluctance of courts to control police action, the failure of complaints procedures to give effective redress to the public and by the absence of traditions of political criticism and language which can rein the police in at corporate and individual level while still supporting legitimate police functions. Both of these issues will be examined in detail later. However both create a form of racial disadvantage in the working of social control which strike deep into the heart of widely accepted notions of justice. The policing methods and the system of police accountability are both less sensitive to the policing needs of black people, for example protection from racist violence, and more likely to encourage an aggressive approach to blacks.

Racial attacks

Nowhere has the lack of police responsiveness and lack of police sensitivity been more emotively exposed than over the question of attacks on black people and their property. Racial attacks are not new. Minorities in this country have faced violence from the white English over many years, perhaps even centuries. Attacks on Jews, their homes, their businesses and their places of worship have a long history. Although anti-semitic violence reached its highest levels in the 1930s, when the Mosleyite movement was strong, it still occurs in Britain. Nazi insignia were daubed on synagogues, Jewish cemeteries were desecrated and a London synagogue was burned down in 1980. An upsurge of anti-semitic violence in several Western European countries in 1980 and 1981 culminated in the bombing of a Paris synagogue in October 1980 in which four people died. This led to calls in the Jewish community for special vigilante groups to protect buildings and people. Jewish leaders supported calls for greater police protection against racial attacks and participated in the campaign which led, in February 1981, to the setting up of a special Home Office inquiry.

In the 1930s, Jews faced particular racist violence in the East End of London. In the 1970s and 1980s, Asians have been repeatedly subjected to the same horror in this same district, which has a reputation for white working class racism second to none. Skinhead 'Paki-bashing' incidents first hit the headlines in 1971. There was a further upsurge of violence when Malawi Asians arrived in Britain, expelled by the Malawian government. Two black students were killed in Mile End in 1976. In 1978, more murders took place. Altab Ali, a 25-year-old machinist from Wapping, was stabbed to death in Whitechapel in May. The following month, fifty-year-old Ishaque Ali was attacked and killed in Hackney. These cases received prominent news coverage. But behind these most dramatic incidents were dozens, probably hundreds of others. An inquiry published by the Bethnal

Green and Stepney Trades Council in September 1978, *Blood on the Streets*, spoke of 'an almost continuous and unrelenting battery of Asian people and their property in the East End.' The report documented more than a hundred cases of physical assault in the home, the workplace and on the streets. Harassment, robbery, destruction of property, intimidation, abuse, vandalism and arson against Asians were repeatedly proved.

Racial attacks were not confined to the East End, nor to Asians, nor did they abate after the summer of 1976. Official figures admit the increase, but they fail to give the full picture because of under-reporting and because the police are frequently reluctant to classify an attack as racial unless proof of a racial motive can be established. Local attempts to keep track of the attacks give some sense of the true scale. In Newham, a dossier compiled by the local monitoring project was presented to the Greater London Council in October 1981. It showed more than eighty recent attacks. Details such as these are typical:

Mr A; E15. Attacked in house by local youths and also in street. Windows smashed, door kicked in. Threats to Mrs A. Youths known to Mr A; no police action.

Mr B; E15. Windows smashed, abuse in street. Threatened in telephone box by person with bread knife. Youth known to Mr B and the police; no police action.

Mr C and family; E15. Bricks through window. Fireworks through door. Windows smashed several times.[3]

In the London borough of Camden, fifty-nine cases of racial harassment were recorded on local council estates in the six months up to November 1981. The local community relations council dealt with 102 such cases between 1979 and 1981. Taken in isolation, the incidents may seem trivial – dumping of rubbish on doorsteps, verbal abuse or painting of graffiti – though they are no less disturbing for that. But when the incidents become cumulative, families are forced into a stage of siege. Moreover, the number of incidents seemed to increase

during 1981 and to become more serious, including stab-
bings and arson. Many local monitoring exercises in
other parts of London – notably in the boroughs of
Lambeth and Hounslow – point to the same pattern. A
report compiled for the Union of Pakistani Organizations showed that racist attacks had risen from an average
of 20 to 25 a week in 1980 to 50 to 60 a week in 1981.[4]

An important dimension of the racial attacks issue is
press treatment. Three inter-racial murders in 1981
showed how this could vary according to the race of the
victim. On 10 April, a seventeen-year-old black youth,
Marbland Chambers, was murdered in Swindon in what
local papers dubbed a race riot; national papers ignored
the killing altogether. At the end of May, Mian Azum
from Pakistan was murdered in Wandsworth, south
London. There were five lines of coverage in a *Daily Mail*
inside page and equivalent space elsewhere. A day later, a
nineteen-year-old white youth, Terence May, was murdered in Thornton Heath, south London, by a group of
blacks. This time the killing got detailed coverage under
headlines such as 'Race Murder in Suburbia' (*Daily Mail*),
'Innocent Victim of Race Hate' (*Daily Express*) and 'Ram-
paging Blacks Kill Youth After Wrecking Pub' (*Daily
Telegraph*). The killing was a particularly horrible affair,
but no killing of a black victim has ever received equivalent coverage.

Many attacks have been monitored by the anti-racist
journal *Searchlight*. A disabled Sikh woman burned to
death and her house gutted by fire in Chapeltown, Leeds;
a gang of skinheads threw a petrol bomb at an Asian shop
in Ilford; two arson attacks on Asian-owned shops in
Bolton; petrol bombing of a black family in Reading; a
white teenager seen hurling a bottle of blazing liquid
through the window of an Asian house in Middles-
brough; a fire attack on an Asian women's centre in
London; arson of Liverpool's largest radical bookshop;
vandalizing of a flat in Dunstable owned by a Nigerian
who had been stabbed earlier in the year; the windows of
Southampton Community Relations Council smashed;

attacks on Indian waiters in a Manchester restaurant; three Asians assaulted in a Reigate street; two Asians attacked by a hail of missiles in Walsall; a Bangladeshi doctor's house attacked in St Albans; two Arab storekeepers beaten up and their property firebombed in Liverpool.[5] This last example is a reminder that racist violence was not confined to attacks on Asians and blacks. Jewish people, as noted earlier, were still at risk and in July 1981 four petrol bombers attacked the home of a Chinese family in Norwich.

In addition to these cases, 1981 saw two particularly vicious attacks which became the focus of large local campaigns. In July, the Khan family of Walthamstow was almost completely wiped out when petrol was squirted through their letter box and ignited. Meanwhile two murders of Asians in Coventry, Satnam Singh Gill who was stabbed to death in a shopping centre by skinheads and Amil Dharry who was murdered when he stopped to buy fish and chips, provoked huge anti-racist protests (which were ambushed by white youths chanting *Sieg Heil*).

The police response

Arising out of this ten-year catalogue of racial violence, several charges are levelled at the police. They are accused of failing to provide protection to black people threatened by violence. At the height of the tension of 1978 in the Brick Lane area of east London, a saree shop owner phoned police to say that a gang of white youths was gathering at one end of the street. Half an hour later, 150 white youths rampaged down Brick Lane attacking people and property. Only after the violence had died down did police arrive.

Time and again police are accused of failing to accept the racial dimension of attacks on black people. This has been alleged in incidents ranging from the Altab Ali murder down to much less grave offences. In a case in Peterborough in 1979 in which a young Asian was stabbed to death, for instance, police issued an urgent call to interview two whites who were seen in the vicinity, at the same time as publicly denying that the killing had racial overtones. A classic example of this sort was reported in the London *New Standard* on 28 September 1981;

Six people were taken to hospital today after an arson attack on their Wembley home. Just before 2 a.m. a burning petrol-soaked rag was forced through the letterbox of a flat on the Chalk Hill estate. Mrs Jean Tudor and her four children were asleep inside. They managed to escape as flames spread through the flat. Antonio Tudor, 22, was taken to the Mount Vernon Hospital burns unit, suffering from burns to the shoulders, neck and face. The others, Mrs Tudor, 52, Cheryl, 23, Christopher, 16, Sonia, 10, and a friend, Alfred Jackobson, were all discharged from nearby Northwick Park Hospital after treatment for minor burns and shock. The family, of West Indian origin, was put up in emergency council accommodation for the night . . . A senior police office said: 'We are treating this as suspected arson, with no racial overtones. It is early days yet, but we discount any racial motive as a family friend who lived in the house was white.' Last week the lock-up rubbish cupboards outside the flat were set alight.

Even when they respond to reports of attacks, the police are frequently accused of delay and failure to follow up the report with adequate urgency. A case from Lambeth, reported by the 1981 working party on police–community relations, is typical. An Asian couple, owners of a side street store, suffered six months of harassment by local white youths. The shop windows were daubed 'Pakis go home'. The couple gave the names and addresses of the white youths to the police. One evening, the Asian wife was attacked in the street. She reported the name of one of her assailants to the police, and explained that witnesses were ready to give assistance. Police told her to take the case to a solicitor and bring a private summons. In another case in Newham, Ismaial Patel had insults shouted at him as he was going to his mosque. When he returned from the mosque he found that a brick had been thrown through his window. A fight broke out between the Asians and the white youths. The reaction of Chief Inspector Stephenson of the local police was: 'When we have so few resources, do we go and investigate a case in which an old woman has had her pension book and savings stolen, or do we investigate someone who has had his window broken?'[6]

Charges of police indifference are widespread. But Ismaial Patel can perhaps count himself lucky compared with some who have complained, especially when, like him, they defend themselves. Another Newham case reveals that the victim of a racial attack runs a serious risk of being treated as the aggressor. On 9 December 1978, Mr Uddin was serving in his Canning Town shop when three boys came in. These boys had already been banned from the shop because they were rude and stole. Mr Uddin chased the boys out, but as they went one was hit in the face by the door, which had a strong spring. A short time later three men entered the shop with the boy who had been hit by the door. They locked the door, seized some bottles and accused Uddin of hitting the boy. Mr Uddin picked up a small knife, which was on the counter for cutting portions of cheese. He asked the three men to leave but they did not, so he called the police. When the police arrived they took details from the whites, arrested Uddin and charged him with carrying an offensive weapon. When the case came on at Snaresbrook Crown Court in March 1980, Judge Percy directed the jury to find Uddin not guilty, and pointed out that he was defending himself when outnumbered three to one, in his own property. The judge said the prosecution should never have been brought and that if he had been in Mr Uddin's position he might have acted just as he did.[7]

Treating the victim as the aggressor is the most blatant of a number of hostile police sanctions which have been reported by black complainants. These include delay, inadequate note-taking, lack of attention to the victim's story and particularly in the case of Asians, questioning their immigration status. For example, during the investigation of Altab Ali's murder in 1976, relatives and witnesses were repeatedly asked by police questions for information about illegal immigrants.

Even with under-reporting in the press, it is clear that police were well aware of the growing problem of racial attacks in the 1970s. Several of the incidents were well publicized, and the Brick Lane confrontation between National Front supporters and the East End Asians received particularly extensive coverage. In the circumstances it is not hard to see why the Deptford fire of January 1981 had such resonance within the black community. It was an entirely typical event, in line with dozens of other arsons of black homes, except in the scale of the tragedy. But the reaction of white society, and in particular the reaction of the police, revealed nothing less than a complete failure of sensibility, as well as raising detailed issues about the police investigation of the tragedy. It took a sustained campaign in south-east London, a militant march and an uncompromising approach to the inquest on the dead to drive home the massive sense of threat and injustice under which black communities were by then reeling.

This made possible the successful lobbying of the Home Secretary, William Whitelaw, in February 1981, by the all-party Joint Committee Against Racialism. The JCAR lobby presented a report to the Home Office which detailed the rise in attacks, drawing on evidence from throughout the country. The Home Office's own survey was carried out from May to July 1981, in thirteen areas. When it was published in November, it was the most dramatic official confirmation that what the black community had been saying all along had been right. Whitelaw's introduction to the report made this plain: 'The study has shown quite clearly that the anxieties expressed about racial attacks are justified. Racially motivated attacks, particularly on Asians, are more common than we had supposed; and there are indications that they may be on the increase.' It was an unusually open recognition of past failures of Home Office and police sensitivity and response.

The survey found 2851 victims of inter-racial incidents in those two months alone. In a quarter of the cases, there was evidence of a racial motive. Blacks were thirty-seven times more likely than whites to be victims in such cases, and Asians fifty times more likely. The survey recognized that under-reporting meant that its estimate of 7000 racially motivated incidents during 1981 was certain to understate the correct figure. It agreed that police tended to play down the significance of racial incidents. However, although many incidents were the work of white gangs it concluded that these were not orchestrated by racist organizations. This judgement, which is in line with local studies, is in many ways more frightening and challenging than if the attacks could have been laid at the door of those organizations.

Racist organizations

The failure to provide the kind of policing which black people were demanding was also revealed in the police handling of racist organizations. Attempts to control racist propaganda have been part of the race relations laws since the first was passed in 1965. It is arguable that these laws have had some deterrent value in restraining certain public manifestations of racism. But neither the current version of the law against incitement to racial hatred nor the weaker version which it replaced in 1976 has had much punitive value. Under the 1965 law there were fewer than twenty prosecutions for incitement, of which a quarter were against blacks. The 1976 law was an attempt to make incitement easier to prove in the courts but it has so far notched just fifteen convictions out of twenty-one prosecutions. However, in January 1982, Joe Pearce, the editor of the Young National Front paper *Bulldog*, was gaoled for six months for incitement after an all-white jury had convicted him on a majority verdict. This may signal a change in the fortune of such prosecutions and hence in the readiness of prosecuting authorities to mount them.

Some libertarians dislike the 1965 law, seeing it as unacceptable restriction on freedom of speech. Attempts to tighten the law still further worry them more. But there is little doubt that effective prosecutions under the law would have had a reassuring effect on black people and anti-racists. The failure to achieve such convictions leaves the law with few friends. The police are reluctant to attempt to bring cases, not so much because they dislike the law (though the dislike does exist) as because they do not expect success. So too has the Attorney-General (whose consent is necessary for prosecution) shown a marked reluctance to authorize prosecutions. As a result, racist speeches and organizations go unchallenged and the police are made out to be accomplices in the failure.   This would be bad enough for the police were it not for the effect of their policies on marches by racist organizations. The growth of the National Front in the 1970s made this a major issue. In the middle of the decade, almost every time that this racist party, with established fascist links, chose to exercise the right to demonstrate, it was allowed to do so, even when those demonstrations were deliberately provocative on racist issues and through black community areas. Police leaders adopted a policy of massive protection of these marches. Thousands of officers, sometimes supplemented by police from other areas, were deployed. The paraphernalia of the highly technologized force was brought out to reinforce that protection; special reserve squads, surveillance squads, special protective clothing and shields, helicopters. This approach reached a climax in September 1977 when, in spite of a ban on all marches in the area, Greater Manchester police allowed Martin Webster of the National Front to mount a one-man breach of the ban through Hyde. The photographs of Webster's march, surrounded by ranks of police protecting him from counter-demonstrations, became the classic image of the policy of enforcing the National Front's right to demonstrate.

As with the problem of racist propaganda, the question

of racist marches raises very important civil liberties issues. In each case, however, the chosen solution created the impression that the police appeared to be protecting, or even supporting, the National Front in its hostility to black people. These suspicions reached a further climax during the 1979 general election campaign. By putting up candidates in black areas, the National Front was able to hold public election meetings in buildings to which they were denied access at other times because of local authority opposition. In a series of such meetings in Leicester, Islington, Southall, East Ham, West Bromwich and Bradford, the NF provoked local outrage which was strengthened by the enormous police mobilizations to protect those meetings.

These events all led to violence between police and counter-demonstrators. The worst violence was in Southall, with its large Asian population. Over three hundred people were arrested, the majority of them local Asian men. One person, an anti-racist schoolteacher, Blair Peach, was killed. Wild accusations were made by police that the whole protest was the work of outsiders and was premeditated. No public statement of sympathy was made by police to the people of Southall nor, at that time, to the bereaved of Blair Peach. In spite of detailed criticisms and complaints about police conduct – most seriously regarding the killing of Peach – no police officer was ever disciplined in any way, much less prosecuted, for any act committed at Southall. Police refused to offer any evidence or cooperation to the independent inquiry under Professor Dummett which produced an exhaustive examination of the events. These events were massively reported throughout the media.

The Dummett inquiry – which is far and away the most thorough, scrupulous and principled piece of research on any police operation in postwar Britain – concluded that white society was largely unaware of the wider significance of Southall. Black community trust in the courts and the police was deeply desired and deeply held, but the events of 23 April 1979 eroded that trust and, for some, shattered it:

No more catastrophic effect can be imagined. Those who belong to racial minorities and face repeated public and private expressions of hostility need some rock to cling to, some social institution they can trust to operate impartially, if they are not to be reduced to despair. Of all institutions, those whose impartial operation it is most important to maintain are the police and the law courts. Deprive people of the sense that they enjoy the protection of the law and of the agencies that enforce and administer it, and you destroy their whole feeling of security and any sense that they might otherwise have preserved that they are part of the society within which they live. It is this process which was begun in Southall on 23 April . . . The effect has not, of course, been confined to Southall . . . the repercussions of such events are felt among black people everywhere in Britain.[8]

In the aftermath of Southall, police continued their old policies. In April 1980, the National Front marched through the borough of Lewisham chanting 'The National Front is a white man's front' and singing 'Blair Peach's body lies a-mouldering in the grave'. More than 4000 police were deployed, at a cost of £500,000, after Lewisham council had failed to get a court order compelling the Metropolitan police to ban the march. In protest at the police's intransigence, the borough council threatened not to pay the £5.5 million levy due to Scotland Yard under the Metropolitan police funding arrangements.

In fact, by 1980, the Met's obstinate attitude was becoming overtaken by events. During the late 1970s the threat of a racist march ceased to provoke an automatic 'protect it at all costs' police response. Increasingly, police forces and local authorities began to change their tactics in favour of sweeping bans on all marches. This policy was undoubtedly more popular with black communities and anti-racists, but it was insufficient to undo the appalling effects of a decade of appearing to put white racists first and black defence second.

Black community events

The sight of thousands of outsiders in police uniform being specially bussed into black areas was a feature not just of National Front marches but of the policing of black community events. 'Overpolicing' – the police's own term – involves having a really large and visible police presence on the streets to make sure that there is no trouble. The problem is that overpolicing sometimes causes trouble rather than preventing it. The police cease to have a deferential attitude to the crowd. Instead they become more aggressive and self-confident. The more police officers engaged in a long overpolicing operation, the greater can be the risk of incidents.

Overpolicing is a very familiar aspect of the modern policing of demonstrations in London. It is important to remember that it isn't a miscalculation. Overpolicing is a deliberate tactic. One of the most important examples of it was in 1976 at the Notting Hill carnival. Previous carnivals had been generally peaceful, though large, noisy and crowded. In 1976 however a concerted local white campaign tried to get the carnival banned or penned into a stadium. A force of 1600 police ultimately patrolled the carnival, ostensibly to prevent the epidemic of pickpocketing which is a regular feature of the event. A confrontation was inevitable. An incident in which a white women's handbag was stolen and she was kicked and punched led to a full scale battle on a hot August night. A total of 500 people were injured, of which 150 needed hospital treatment. The more the police joined in, the more the violence went on. They refused to withdraw. When the dust had settled the carnival organizers criticized the high police presence as an insult, 'an unnecessary army of policemen which instilled fear in the revellers', who dissipated the psychological advantage of the organizers' own stewards.[9]

Black people's events have been overpoliced in other places. Similar accusations were made in Leeds in November 1975 when black youth rioted against police on Bonfire Night. But it has been the carnival in Notting Hill where the police have most consistently adopted the tactic. Police thinking about the carnival seems to be dominated by its public order implications. In the commissioner's annual report for 1978, for example, the carnival appears in a selective list of 'demonstrations'. Its inclusion on the list was dictated by an evident desire to bump up the apparent financial cost of policing demonstrations (the Met was worried about these costs). The cost of policing the 1978 carnival was put at £591,000, a fifth of the total listed cost of all 'demonstrations'. But the inclusion also reveals a police perception of the carnival as a category of crowd more akin to a political protest than to a holiday celebration.

'It is the citizens of London who suffer' from such costs and the diversion of police resources, said the report.[10] No such complaint is ever made by police about the 'cost' of policing state occasions, the Lord Mayor's show or big sporting fixtures. The wholly disproportionate police attention given to the Notting Hill carnival is shown by figures for 1979 and 1980. In 1979, 10,135 officers were deployed throughout the weekend with a further 1375 assigned to the simultaneous Finsbury Park carnival. In 1980, 11,022 police were on duty at Notting Hill and 1315 at Finsbury Park. This is equivalent to roughly half of the total Metropolitan police force (which totalled 23,691 at the end of 1980). The total of officers deployed made them by far the largest police operations in London in either year, involving over half as many police again as any other operation.

More intimate black social events and centres are also subjected to intensive policing. Black cafés and clubs are traditionally vulnerable. The policing takes the form of raids in search of wanted offenders, missing persons, drugs or illegal drinking, or complaints of excessive noise. The raids provoke aggressive resistance by the blacks, especially youths, the police call for reinforcements and a free-for-all ensues. The resulting arrests invariably arise from the confrontation rather than the suspected offence which had led to the raid. The arrested group then becomes a focus for community resentment against the police.

If this sequence of events seems familiar from the Bristol riot, it is also a pattern that has been repeated since the early 1970s. The first major raids on the Mangrove restaurant in Notting Hill took place in January 1969. Repeated police raids in search of drugs failed to find any. Nor was that all. The Mangrove's manager described what happened:

Besides the raids, there've been other visits, and people on their way home from here have been stopped and questioned: 'Have you come from the Mangrove? What's going on there? What are you carrying?' And because of the way the searches are carried out I've lost a lot of custom: people don't like being lined up against a wall, having flashlights shone over them, when they've come here for a meal.[11]

A demonstration was held to protest at police action against the Mangrove. Violence broke out and nine blacks ended up charged with riot, affray and assault (among them was Darcus Howe, now editor of *Race Today*). The case became a focal point. Police evidence was shoddy. In the event, after a ten-week trial at the Old Bailey, the nine were acquitted of riot, five were cleared on all counts and four were convicted of seven minor charges betwen them. After the trial, jurors bought the defendants drinks in a nearby pub.

The Mangrove's problems were not over, however. It was regularly raided during the 1970s and in 1979 a second Mangrove trial at Knightsbridge crown court ended in disarray for the prosecution just like the first, with the defendants, who included the Mangrove's owner, Frank Critchlow, being acquitted. The Mangrove, though, is only the most celebrated of such cases. In May 1971, sixteen black youths were arrested after a police raid on the Metro youth club in Notting Hill. Four were charged with affray. All were acquitted after the jury had considered its verdict for a mere thirty minutes. In August 1972, a North London black youth club was raided by one hundred police. In October 1974, following four visits in the previous fortnight, police entered the Carib Club in Cricklewood, north-west London, looking for a suspect who had stolen a vehicle. A battle ensued. Twelve blacks were tried at the Old Bailey for affray; all were eventually acquitted, after police evidence against the individual defendants fell apart under its own weight of contradictions and unsupported assertions.

Police action against other clubs and meeting places has been reported from many parts of the country. In many of the cases, the handling has been inept and insensitive, triggering off much more serious problems. Raids of this kind, whether or not justified in individual instances, have made a major contribution to instilling in the youths who congregate in these clubs the sense that they are under collective attack by police. Whatever other issues are involved, these raids have become tactically disastrous for police.

The point is recognized by some senior officers, though it doesn't mean they leave the clubs alone. Superintendent Webb of Handsworth, for instance stays: 'We don't go in for the stupidities of taking 100 police down to bust a café. You can close down places without a single protest if you go about it the right way.'[12] No better evidence for the effects of clumsy raids exists than the consequences of the one on the Black and White Café in Bristol in April 1980, which led to the riot there.

Police and immigration

For many Asians, restaurants are not only a social centre but a major source of employment. It is at such workplaces that a succession of 'passport raids' during the 1970s have served to increase anti-police suspicions among Asians in particular, as well as among other minority communities and black people generally. Passport raids are a direct consequence of the existence of tight immigration laws. The Immigration Act 1971 gives police and immigration officers the power to arrest suspected offenders against the controls, and from 1972 Scotland Yard has maintained a national intelligence gathering squad on entrants, the Illegal Immigration Intelligence Unit.

The first major police search for illegal immigrants under the new law took place in October 1973, in various premises in London. All those present were questioned about their immigration 'status' – that is, they were asked to prove that they had a right to be in this country and that they had gone through the correct procedures. A Camden rooming house was raided later that month. Eighty Asian men were questioned. One man was unable to produce his passport because he had sent it to the Home Office. Although he produced the Home Office's receipt and his employment voucher, he was taken to Marylebone police station for several hours until his status was confirmed. Since then, such passport raids have become common, and concern has mounted that they are little more than 'fishing trips' in which police, without reasonable suspicion that a particular offender is present, turn up in the hope of making a catch. Restaurants and rooming-houses are favourite targets, but factories have also been visited. The raids are normally carried out by a squad combining police and immigration officers, and normally take place in the early morning. Numbers vary, but the squad can exceed a hundred officers. Any black person on the premises can be caught up in the inquiries, whether or not police are looking for illegal immigrants of one particular ethnic group. Filipinos, Arabs and southern Europeans, as well as Asians, Africans and West Indians, are likely to have to prove their right to be in the country.

A survey by Paul Gordon, published in 1981, concludes that in each raid substantial numbers of people who were not in breach of immigration law, who may have lived long periods in Britain and who had not committed any offence are asked solely because of their colour to prove their 'innocence' by establishing their right to be here. Gordon believes that such 'operations' have 'helped create additional insecurity for the black community as a whole in areas where the raids have occurred'.[13]

Passport raids, it is important to add, are a particularly dramatic example of a growing practice of identity checks on black people in a wide range of circumstances. The police themselves have been accused of making such checks when they are dealing with black people as suspects or witnesses, as in the Altab Ali investigation. Other examples are legion. A Nigerian who went to volunteer bail for an arrested friend was himself arrested for failing to produce his passport. The same thing happened to a Spaniard who was foolish enough to go into a police station to ask for directions. In 1979 the Edinburgh police investigating the sale of alcohol to under-age drinkers demanded proof of immigration status from one black licensee. Identity checks are in danger of becoming a reflex practice in giving black people access to a range of state services. In December 1981, for example, the Department of Health and Social Security proposed that hospital treatment should be given subject to proof of immigration and nationality status. It is inconceivable that this practice could avoid being racially discriminatory and deeply humiliating. Such humiliations are already widely practiced by social security officers against black claimants, claimed a study by the Child Poverty Action Group in Leicester.[14]

Identity checks can be a precondition for schooling, too. In October 1981 Newham borough council instructed its head teachers to ask all immigrant pupils to produce their passports to show proof of their right to education. Not all these practices necessarily involve the police, but it is in the nature of the police's job that they are more readily implicated in the demeaning process of identity checks than any teacher or doctor is likely to be. This places the police officer in a different role in relation to blacks than to whites, because the legitimizing of such a system of identity checks compels the police to look on a black person with suspicion which would not be applied to a white. Conversely, it means that to black people, any police officer is necessarily a threat because any officer may demand proof of identity. If that is not a form of institutionalized racism it is difficult to see what else could deserve the name. In South Africa, the system is known as the Pass Law.

Police powers

None of the causes of antagonism between blacks and the police that has been discussed thus far – powerful though they are – has received as much publicity or caused such resentment as the everyday use of police powers of stop, search, arrest and questioning on the street and in the police station. The sheer number of police contacts with the public of this kind – and their visibility to others – ensures that this is likely to be the case. Moreover, it is from these incidents that allegations of police racial prejudice are most likely to spring. Scarman accepted that police do commit 'ill-considered, immature and racially prejudiced actions' in their street dealings with young blacks. He argued that some officers may react to a rising level of street crime by lapsing into the belief that all young blacks are potential criminals. Although he thought that such displays of prejudice are rare, and that they are not shared by senior officers, Scarman fully acknowledged the ripple effect of even an isolated incident. 'The damage done by even the occasional display of racial prejudice is incalculable. It goes far towards the creation of the image of a hostile police force.'

Complaints of direct racial abuse by police officers have been documented in several studies. 'Black bastard', 'black scum' and so on are among the terms complained of. The Institute of Race Relations speaks of 'the sheer volume' of such abuse. Maureen Cain's study of a city force in the 1960s found that 'immigrants, in particular the coloured immigrants, were subject to stereotyping and abuse'.

Robert Reiner's study of Bristol police unearthed frequent, spontaneous hostile views of blacks. One constable told him in 1974: 'The police are trying to appear unbiased in regard to race relations. But if you asked them you'd find 90 per cent of the force are against coloured immigrants.'[15] The police accept that there are racist attitudes in some of their recruits. One senior Scotland Yard race specialist has said: 'It is not a part of community relations training in the Metropolitan police to attempt to "convert" an officer to a particular point of view or to change personal or political opinions.'[16] The Police Federation believes that since the force is drawn from society as a whole and since society contains racists it is not surprising that there may be prejudiced officers.

The only published piece of detailed research on police attitudes was conducted by Andrew Colman, a psychology lecturer at Leicester University. He found that recruits and probationers had significantly more conservative and authoritarian attitudes than the population as a whole and that experienced officers also had markedly illiberal racial attitudes. One probationer told Colman: 'Fifty per cent of trouble caused today is either by niggers or because of them. Most of them are just dirty, smelly backward people who will never change in a month of Sundays. In my opinion, most Rastas should be wiped out of distinction [sic].'

Another probationer said: 'Coloured immigration into this country has brought with it a society of uneducated, troublesome people who come here only for the benefit that we provide such as social security and housing. The majority are disrespectful of the law and wish people in this country only harm.' And a recruit told Colman: 'The country is being taken over slowly but surely by coloured immigrants; if we continue like this there will be no white people left.'[17]

Anecdotal and impressionistic evidence of police mis-conduct against blacks is considerable. Much of this evidence from the 1970s was collected together by Derek Humphry, then a *Sunday Times* journalist, in his 1972 book, *Police Power and Black People*, and by the Institute of Race Relations in its 1979 pamphlet *Police Against Black People*. Humphry dealt in some detail with a small number of cases, using each to illustrate a more general injustice. He commented – and note that this was as long ago as 1972; 'To many blacks in our inner cities, police harassment has become a way of life. The police are viewed as the army of the enemy, which is the immigra-tion-controlling, arms-to-South-Africa-selling, friend-of-Ian-Smith British government.'

The IRR study, submitted as evidence to the Royal Commission on Criminal Procedure, drew out a number of themes from a collection of publicized cases and private reports. It argued that police misconduct towards black people had become 'an everyday occurrence, a matter of routine'. The institute identified seven ele-ments of this misconduct: stop and search without reason; unnecessary violence in arrests; particular har-assment of juveniles; danger of arrest when suspects asserted their rights; risks to witnesses and bystanders, repeated arrests of individuals; black homes and prem-ises entered at will.

A partial boycott of both the Scarman and Hytner inquiries meant that neither received a large amount of first-hand information on such abuses. Whoever else gave evidence to these inquiries, it was not those who rioted. So claims that all the rioters had grievances arising from direct personal experience with the police are unprovable.

Statistical studies of the use and abuse of police powers have been rare in Britain until quite recently. As is well known among academic researchers, such exercises are beset with problems of interpretation. As Lord Scarman observed, such statistical material has both strengths and weaknesses. It is certainly true that no comprehensive and systematic study of policing the black communities of Britain exists.

However, some relevant research findings have been produced. A Home Office study of arrests in the Metropolitan police district in 1975 indicated that blacks (but not Asians) are arrested far more often than would be expected from their numbers in the population. Arrest does not necessarily indicate that an offence has been committed. Clearly, if police believe blacks to be more crime-prone or patrol more in black areas, this can affect the rate of black arrests. Allowing for age and socio-economic factors that could affect the figures, the Home Office study found that blacks were still most heavily arrested in offences where there was particular scope for suspicion to be aroused from preconceived views. In these offence categories – wallet and handbag snatching and the 'suspected persons' law (see page 91) blacks stood a fourteen or fifteen times greater chance of arrest than whites.[18] A more recent study found that London black juvenile suspects accused of crimes of violence, burglary or public order offences were more likely to be harshly treated than their white counterparts.

Studies in other areas give a different picture. A Home Office study of south Manchester (including Moss Side) found an overall similarity between West Indian and white experience of stops, searches and arrests. Even among young people it happened to the same proportion – eighteen per cent – of blacks and whites. This is, of course, a high frequency. Allowing for the fact that more men than women were stopped, the researchers found that about a third of all young males, black and white alike, had been stopped, searched or arrested during one year. The study concluded that West Indian and white experiences of crime and police generally were very similar and did not support a picture of massive police discrimination.[19]

Figures supplied by the police to the Scarman inquiry showed that blacks accounted for 32 per cent of police stops in the borough of Lambeth in the two years

1979–80. There were 14,109 stops of blacks, 26,004 stops of whites and 4305 of other groups (including Asians). Blacks accounted for 35 per cent of all arrests in the borough in the same period (2458 out of a total of 6952 arrests). In the Brixton division of Lambeth blacks accounted for 41.4 per cent (7351 out of 17,729) of all stops in 1979–80 and 49.9 per cent (1315 out of 2636) of all arrests. Scarman says that (on 1978 figures) 25 per cent of Lambeth's population is non-white, rising to 29 per cent among 15–24-year-olds and 39 per cent among under-fifteens. Comparing the stops and arrests with the population of the borough, it would therefore seem that blacks are stopped disproportionately to their overall numbers and that, once stopped, they are more likely to be arrested than whites are. A more thorough analysis cannot be made from the available material but it certainly suggests that there is statistical backing to the complaint that stop, search and arrest were applied disproportionately to blacks in Lambeth and it is strange that the Scarman Report failed to investigate the matter further when it had the opportunity of doing so.

As the Home Office researchers pointed out, stops and arrests are not necessarily an accurate pointer of criminality. The police however argued that black crime rates in Brixton were disproportionately high. In the Met's words, 'Brixton is unique in terms of its violent street crime and the fear it generates.' The police recorded a 13 per cent increase in serious offences in Lambeth between 1976 and 1980, and a 66 per cent increase in robbery and violent theft. In those five years, 30 per cent of all those arrested for serious crimes in Lambeth were black, as were 39 per cent of those arrested in Brixton. Among juveniles, the proportion of blacks were even higher, with 40 per cent of Lambeth arrests and 38 per cent in Brixton.

Blacks and crime

Whether the black crime rate is disproportionately high

in general throughout the country is an emotive question. Home Office researchers have argued that the incidence of indictable crime in 1971 in major urban areas was not related to the proportion of blacks who live there. The conurbations with the highest crime rates were places like Tyneside, with low numbers of West Indians. The same was true for police divisions within the conurbations. In London, boroughs such as Camden and Tower Hamlets had higher crime rates than boroughs like Lambeth or Hackney, where there were large numbers of West Indians. This conclusion could be out of date. Another objection is that it does not differentiate between different offences, leaving open the possibility that different ethnic groups may commit particular offences disproportionately. Given the different socio-economic and age compositions of the different ethnic groups, such a conclusion would not be surprising.

This is the argument which underpins the mugging controversy. White society has a tradition of associating blacks with particular sorts of crime. In the 1950s they were supposed to be living off immoral earnings. Later, drug pushing became the vogue accusation. In the 1970s, the stereotype of the black mugger was created. Newspapers and the police themselves did much to encourage this 'moral panic', that Britain was catching an American disease and that the perpetrators were black. The sheer emotiveness that the subject acquired, the caricaturing and insensitive selectivity with which it was bandied about, and the vicious use made of it by white racist organizations combined – with some success – to rally black activists and their allies behind an exclusively defensive attitude on mugging. For reasons that were entirely correct, the problem of an increase of mugging (robbery of personal property in the open following sudden attack by an assailant not previously known to the victim) was largely ignored. In fact, a study of London mugging found in 1980 that this type of robbery has increased tenfold over two decades, with the figure doubling every four or five years. The typical victim was male, not female as popular mythology would suggest. The typical attacker, the study found, would be male, acting alone or in a group of two or three, under twenty-one and 'more often than not he will be black'.[20]

So there is some evidence that blacks are more heavily involved in some types of crime, even taking into account socio-economic and age factors and any effect of police discrimination. The true level of disproportion and whether it is higher in some black communities than others are both unknown. Whether that disproportion justifies the kind of policing to which areas like Brixton have been subjected is another question altogether.

'Sus' and 'sas'

One particular 'crime' came, in the 1970s, to be seen as proof that blacks were being picked on by police. This was the infamous 'sus' offence. Section 4 of the Vagrancy Act 1824 allowed police to arrest a person on suspicion of loitering with intent to commit an arrestable offence. No other crime had to be committed, there was no need for a victim, no need for any witnesses beyond two police officers. The offence could be tried only in the magistrates' court, so there was no right to trial by jury and the 'sus' charge put the onus on defendants to prove that they were not acting suspiciously. The figures showed what black communities knew from experience, that they were more likely to be regarded with suspicion by the police. Some areas of the country – notably the centre of London – became regarded as unsafe for blacks because of the risk of sus arrest. One magistrate told a young black who had just been acquitted on a sus charge that black youths who came into the West End to shop were asking for trouble.

Sus was used very unevenly around England and Wales (and was only rarely used in Scotland). Three quarters of all sus charges in 1978 were in three police force areas: the Met, Merseyside and Greater Manchester. Within London use of sus was concentrated in four areas: Westminster (West End), Kensington and Chelsea, Camden and Lambeth. It was little used in other boroughs, even including some with high levels of street crime. Black arrests accounted for 44 per cent of London's sus arrests in 1978 and 40 per cent in 1979. In Lambeth, 77 per cent of those arrested for sus were black. A select committee inquiry of April 1980 concluded that neither total black sus arrest rates nor in particular some divisional figures accurately reflected black involvement in street crimes.[21] The report brought to a head a growing campaign against sus (a campaign which long predated its use against black people).

In spite of police denials that sus was used discriminately against blacks, and in spite of police claims that it was essential to retain the law, the enormous damage which sus was doing to police–black relations compelled the government to repeal the law in the Criminal Attempts Act of 1981. It was not, however, an unmitigated victory for the opponents of sus. The new act created an offence of interfering with a motor vehicle in a public place which many lawyers regarded as equally open to abuse. The legal correspondent of *The Times* called it 'an unsatisfactory law which can have only the most marginal effect on the fight against crime'.[22]

It may be argued that this is an unproven objection and that the repeal of sus may have lessened tension between blacks and police. This argument ignores both the legacy of sus in individual cases and the colossal agitational power of the sus issue in harnessing a range of resentments against the police. In addition, the repeal of sus did not mean that blacks were in any general way less likely to be stopped in the street. Repeal may have lessened the likelihood of stop and search in particular places, such as shops, but it also removed a power whose use was declining. In 1980, for instance, a total of 1469 people – black and white – were arrested for sus throughout London, equivalent only to about one third of the number of police stops of blacks in the Brixton division alone in the same year. Police have many alternative stop and search powers other than sus, ranging from local enactments (such as section 66 of the Metropolitan Police Act 1839) to their general power of arrest. Research in Liverpool has shown that in 1978 police were already preferring to use stop and search powers in place of sus. As one black youth quoted in that study puts it: 'It's not sus that leads to hassle with the police, but the number of times that we're searched on the street.'[23]

By 1981, stop and search powers were being used in Liverpool on an extremely high level. In the four police subdivisions in and around Toxteth 3482 people were searched in the first seven months of the year. Of these only 179 were arrested. The Merseyside police committee interim report on the riots highlighted this issue: 'Harassment is the allegation expressed most vociferously and most often'. It called for a greater level of police discrimination in the use of stop and search powers.

Saturation policing

As the Brixton example graphically showed, police responded to their judgement of the district as a 'high crime area' by occasional saturation policing exercises such as Swamp 81. Saturation policing is a practice which is carried out disproportionately in black residential areas. It necessitates the drafting in of extra police, which often means bringing in the Special Patrol Group. The SPG has been repeatedly used in such operations in Brixton, Peckham, Lewisham, Tooting, Stoke Newington, Kentish Town, Hackney and Notting Hill – all areas of black residence. Its burgeoning reputation as an élite, aggressive, unaccountable squad, known for its involvement in public order confrontations, combined with the actual experience of its stop, search and arrest tactics during such operations, makes the SPG a byword in hostile policing – what the Institute of Race Relations calls 'policing against the community'.

Special Patrol Group operations in Lewisham in 1975 involved 14,000 stops and 400 arrests. The main targets of such stops were black people. The operation drew repeated complaints of abuse, maltreatment, violence and denial of rights. Similar accusations were made in Brixton in 1975 and 1978 when the SPG were brought in. The tactics of random street checks, early morning raids and road blocks served only to alienate the black community still further. In November 1978, 430 people were arrested during the SPG operation, forty per cent of them black. Their activities were centred on four housing estates with black populations. Study of these operations leads to the conclusion that the number of stops was out of all proportion to the reasonable suspicion of criminal offences and that the operations were a form of harassment.[24] They were certainly perceived as such.

The effect of such blitzes on local police–community relations can be disastrous, as some police now recognize:

They [the SPG] might apparently solve one problem but in its wake create another of aggravated relationships between minority groups and the police in general. It is then in this atmosphere that the permanent beat officer is expected to continue his work, often finding that his task, which was always difficult and delicate, has now been made almost impossible.[25]

That was the view of the then assistant chief constable of Nottinghamshire, Geoffrey Dear. Dear is now in charge of training in the Metropolitan police and was one of the two principal police witnesses in the second phase of the Scarman inquiry.

Breakdown

This breakdown of police relationships with communities results from many of the factors discussed in this chapter. A final cause must be added. Police liaison with black communities is dependent upon some degree of trust and confidence. It is clear that this was absent in several of the communities where riots took place in 1981. While trust is obviously influenced by the way that areas are policed, it is also strongly affected by the visible degree of commitment to good relations with the community, a readiness to listen and accept the grievances of those communities and a proven prioritization of responsiveness to racial issues. The police have a very dismal record in this field, which is not made any easier by the monolithic disciplined nature of the force decision-making process. In the case of Brixton, the police reached a point where they were exceptionally reluctant to discuss issues with the local black population. Commander Adams' explanation of why he had not told the Lambeth liaison committee of the forthcoming SPG saturation of Brixton – 'No good general ever declares his forces in a prelude to any kind of attack' – spoke volumes on senior police attitudes. The failure to consult before Swamp 81, condemned by Scarman, was yet another in a long series of such snubs.

For all their professed commitment to good liaison police have a history of refusing to credit those who speak on behalf of black communities with any real authority. Robert Mark spoke disparagingly in one breath of 'black activists, white left-wing opportunists, people employed in the race relations industry'.[26] His successor, Sir David McNee, made another revealing remark in his evidence to Scarman when he said: 'In policing the community it is necessary to listen to the voice of the community. The difficulty is to select which voice is more representative of the community.' The reluctance to accept criticism was shown in the closing speech of the Met's counsel at the inquiry, who said that 'in situations like this it is not the responsible voice of the community that is heard, but the extremist voice'. Police objections to Scarman's proposed statutory liaison machinery are based, in the words of the Association of Chief Police Officers, on the view that 'There are community leaders who are not in fact community leaders. They do not represent the people at grass roots level in the way they think they do.'

This police refusal to accept the black community on its

own terms reached its peak in a speech by the chief constable of Greater Manchester, James Anderton, in September 1980. Speaking in the extraordinary forum of a meeting of animal rescue organizations at Troutbeck Bridge in the Lake District, Anderton claimed the original good intentions of race relations workers had been subverted by people bent on disharmony. 'They have been infiltrated by anti-establishment factions, one of whose aims is continuously to impede the police,' he said.[27] By no means all police agree with Anderton, but police culture is so protective that no voices were raised against his statement from within the force.

The idea that communities must be 'liaised' with is significant in itself. It indicates the need for some mediation between two essentially separate entities – the police and the community it polices; a go-between where accountability in any meaningful sense is lacking. While liaison committees and liaison officers were first created to deal with the mistrust of immigrant communities, now they are seen to be necessary on a more general scale. Looking at it in this light, liaison can be seen as a recognition of failure, not as a hallmark of enlightenment.

Such selectivity has emboldened police in various parts of Britain to refuse to participate in local inquiries into policing unless the inquiries are statutory, as Scarman was. These wider issues of accountability are dealt with elsewhere, but refusals have included the South Yorkshire county council inquiry, the Dummett inquiry on Southall and, not least, the Lambeth borough inquiry. If there were no other factors threatening the police's credibility, such refusals might be understandable. But the inquiries were genuine attempts to improve local policing. The refusals to cooperate only hardened local views that policing was seen by police as a one-way contract and that community liaison was a marginal aspect of police work, to be entrusted to soft-hearted specialists whose influence over general policing policy and attitudes was negligible.

By the middle of 1980, relations between police and

black people had reached a new low. At a meeting in London, a hundred leaders of between forty and fifty black organizations, including large bodies like the Indian Workers' Association and the Standing Conference of Pakistani Organizations, called on all black people in Britain to withdraw cooperation from the police. The call included specific injunctions to blacks to have nothing to do with liaison schemes, for blacks not to join the police and not to take part in identity parades. In retrospect, perhaps the warning should have been taken more seriously. While the call had little effect, and was not in any direct sense a cause of the riots of 1981, it was indicative of the state of profound mistrust which now consumed black–police relations. Instead, the establishment response was to wax indignant at such impertinent proposals and to disparage the credibility of the meeting.

No single aspect of the policing of the black community was alone responsible for the collapse of the police's standing. Each of those aspects that has been discussed contributed to the situation which existed in many British cities by early 1981. What happened in Brixton and then in several cities in July was an explosive intensification of a series of confrontations which had been developing over several years. What Scarman said of Brixton held good in many other places:

The young, particularly (but not exclusively) the young of the ethnic minority, had become indignant and resentful against the police, suspicious of everything they did. Whatever the reason for this loss of confidence, and whether the police were to blame for it or not, it produced the attitudes and beliefs which underlay the disturbances, providing the tinder ready to blaze into violence on the least provocation, fancied or real, offered by the police.

4 The Explosion: The Brixton riots of April 1981

> When Bristol happened, everyone was saying, 'Brixton next'. We were living in anticipation, in a way, of exactly this happening. And everyone said, 'When it happens, it will be a lot bigger than Bristol.'
>
> Herman Ouseley, former principal race relations adviser, Lambeth[1]

Friday 10 April 1981 had been an unusually warm day with blue skies and almost unbroken sunshine. In Brixton, south London, this had the effect of bringing the black population out on to the streets in bigger numbers than usual. But for police constable Stephen Margiotta, a uniformed officer who was on duty that evening, there was nothing else out of the ordinary. As he walked along Atlantic Road he noticed that most of the shops had shut or were closing, and Brixton's bustling multi-racial crowds were on their way home.

His attention turned to a traffic hold-up in front of him at the junction with Coldharbour Lane. He noticed some movement – a black youth was running across the road towards him pursued by two or three others. Margiotta was immediately suspicious. The young man looked very upset and Margiotta thought that he might have committed an offence. He made two grabs for him; the second was successful. The two men ended up wrestling one another on the ground and when the black youth, Michael Bailey, aged nineteen, got up, Margiotta found that his own arm and shirt and the back of Bailey's shirt were covered in blood.

He asked Bailey what was wrong but he received no

reply. Instead Bailey broke away only to be caught again and asked again what was the matter. In reply he took off his shirt, revealing a three- or four-inch-long stab wound in his back between his shoulder-blades. There was a lot of blood and the youth was clearly suffering. But he did not want to remain with Margiotta, who had by then been joined by PC Saunders, and he put up a great struggle.

The two police officers found they were joined by three other young blacks angrily shouting, 'Leave him alone.' They tried to explain that they only wanted to help but the youths jostled them and Bailey was able to escape again. At this point Margiotta got out his radio and asked Brixton police station for help. In the meantime Bailey had fled to some flats in nearby Rushcroft Road where he staggered up three flights of stairs and knocked on the door of the home of complete strangers. The occupants were white. They took the youth in, bandaged his wound with kitchen roll and asked who was responsible for the stabbing. Bailey simply replied, 'Blacks.' A minicab was called to take the injured youth to hospital; Bailey was bundled inside and the car took off.

As it left it was spotted by police in a transit van who had arrived on the scene in reply to the call for help. They followed the cab, stopped it and examined Bailey's wound. Almost simultaneously an officer with a first-aid kit arrived and the officers dressed the wound, pressing down on it to try to seal it because they believed Bailey's lung might be punctured. The injury looked very serious; it was frothy and bubbly as if air were being lost and the youth said he was having difficulty in breathing. For this reason and in line with their training the officers radioed for an ambulance.

Meanwhile a large crowd of about forty or fifty black youths clustered around crying, 'What are you keeping him for?', 'Why don't you try to get an ambulance', and 'Look, they're killing him.' An officer explained that they thought it would be dangerous to move Bailey in his condition but the crowd would not listen. The police were pushed aside, the youth was pulled out of the car and spirited away to shouts of 'We will look after our own.' A passing car was hailed and the driver asked to take Bailey to hospital, which he did. The ambulance arrived shortly afterwards.

This fairly minor but revealing incident was the trigger for two days of the most serious violence and disorder Britain has witnessed this century. The Brixton riots led to £6.5m of damage, 158 people injured, and the first widespread use of petrol bombs on the British mainland. Although it did not cause heavy violence to break out that Friday night, it set the scene for a big police presence the next day when black youths were still simmering with anger and suspicion from the night before. It needed a small incident the next day to set off a major battle, exactly one year after the Bristol riot. As Herman Ouseley made clear in his comment at the beginning of this chapter, Brixton's blacks were almost waiting for an opportunity. Lord Scarman, in his report on the riots, agreed:

The inference is irresistible that many young black people were spoiling for a row as a result of their frustrations, fancied or real, and of their beliefs as to what happened on Friday. The young people who crowded the streets believed Friday's events to be yet another typical instance of police harassment of young blacks. And many of them were deceived by rumour into thinking that police callousness on the Friday had actually led to the death of the wounded man.

Conditions in Brixton

The problems faced by British blacks are perhaps nowhere as acute as in Brixton, a small area of the London borough of Lambeth. It is not the black ghetto of some popular mythology. Many of its inhabitants are white. In the wards where blacks are most concentrated they form forty-nine per cent of the population or perhaps a little more; in Lambeth they make up about one quarter of the whole, less than the number of blacks in the London boroughs of Hackney, Haringey and Brent. The difference is that in these local authorities the black people are very spread out; in Lambeth they are bunched together, giving even greater visibility to their presence by spending much of their day on the streets. The younger age groups have much higher proportions of blacks – 40 per cent of those aged nineteen and under in Lambeth are black – and it is these young people, many of whom were born here, who are suffering most from Britain's economic recession. It is estimated that 55 per cent of black male youths under nineteen are registered as unemployed at the Brixton Employment Office.[2] No one knows how many more do not bother to register. Unemployment for blacks is three times as high as that for whites.

Economically the area has been declining for the past sixty years and this decline has perhaps been hastened by the influx of blacks and corresponding exodus of whites. Its population is still falling and its shopping centre continues to decline. There is a big housing shortage, with a high proportion of homeless families and overcrowding. More than 12,000 homes in the borough are designated 'unfit' with a further 8250 lacking one or more basic amenities. The greatest physical blot on the landscape, however, is the area around Railton Road, which is known as 'the front-line' and runs like an artery through a wasteland of corrugated iron and boarded-up houses. As the front-line (the term is variously used to describe a battle front or a meeting place) Railton Road was the centre of the rioting. On most days it is a focus like Grosvenor Road in Bristol's St Paul's area. Although it is not a red-light district, it does contain the familiar social activities – shebeens, gambling dens and cannabis dealing – of black working-class life. The street is rarely empty, especially in the evening. The presence of street crowds often appears deliberately aggressive to whites. Black youths flock to the front-line for want of anything better to do. There is a marked lack of social provision for them unless they are willing to go to one of the youth centres, of which there are now quite a number. The commercial centre of Brixton contains merely two Wimpy bars and a range of pubs, and is dead after 6 p.m. This, together with very high unemployment and the social problems faced by black youth (one in six of Lambeth families has only one parent and 2.3 per cent of youth have been in care), goes some way to explaining Brixton's crime rate. The Railton Road Youth and Community Centre told Lord Scarman's inquiry:

Young people around in the streets all day, with nothing to do and nowhere to go, get together in groups and the 'successful' criminal has a story to tell. So one evil has bred another, and as unemployment has grown in both older and younger generations crime has become more commonplace and more acceptable. This is a vicious circle to which there is no present end in sight.[3]

During the Scarman inquiry there was much debate about the crime statistics locally, and the police response to them. Senior officers are fond of describing Brixton crime levels as 'unique', and did so frequently to Lord Scarman. He commented that this might be indulging in hyperbole, but it is quite clear that certain types of crime (commonly known to the police as black crime) have increased dramatically in Brixton. Between the five years 1976 to 1980 offences of robbery and other violent theft recorded by the police increased by 138 per cent in Brixton compared with 66 per cent in L district as a whole and 38 per cent throughout London. This frightening statistic should, however, be seen in its context. Crime statistics are notoriously unreliable in certain respects, and differences can reflect different degrees of police attention as well as different levels of crime commission. Moreover, serious crime, as defined by the Metropolitan police, went up by only 13 per cent in Brixton in those five years compared with a 15 per cent increase in London as a whole. The so-called black crimes – muggings, snatch-thefts and pickpocketing – formed only a small proportion of the total crime picture. During those five years robbery and other violent theft made up only 2.2 per cent of all serious offences recorded in London, 5.1 per cent of serious offences in L district and 7.2 per cent of all such offences in Brixton.

Whether or not there were higher levels of street crime in Brixton (and the evidence is that there were) the police reacted as if there was no doubt about the matter. They dealt with 'high crimes areas' in the only way they knew — by saturating the area when things got really bad with an outside mobile force, the Special Patrol Group. Between January 1978 and September 1980 Commander Leonard Adams, the former head of the local force, brought the SPG into the area on four separate occasions. It is not difficult to see why SPG officers were so unpopular: their job was to stop and search people, many of them innocent, on the streets. Their activities had the effect of driving the crime away but as soon as they left the crime curve was soaring again. Moreover they left behind them an ever-increasing residue of bitterness among innocent black youth and their parents who usually received no redress when they complained. The resentment was to have a dramatic effect on the formal police–community relations machinery.

In late 1978 a liaison committee had been set up by the police and the Council for Community Relations in Lambeth (CCRL). Three days after the first meeting of this new body the SPG arrived in the area for one of its crime-busting operations. Community representatives on the committee were furious at not being told, but they became even angrier three months later when three members of CCRL's staff were arrested and detained for between one and five hours in what became known as the 'sheepskin coat affair'. The community representatives withdrew immediately from the liaison work, a decision which Lord Scarman condemned, the committee folded and formal police–community relations were left in tatters.

The skeepskin coat affair was important because it involved the arrest of three of Brixton's best known black citizens — race relations workers who had heard a great deal about so-called 'police harassment' but had not been on the receiving end before. The police were looking for a black man with a sheepskin coat who had allegedly been involved in an assault in a pub. The race relations workers also wore sheepskin coats but they were totally innocent. For the CCRL it was the last straw. (Civil action is now being taken against the police.)

All police attempts to get liaison going again failed, though there was informal contact between the two communities. Formal relations deteriorated even further when Lambeth council set up an independent inquiry, chaired by David Turner-Samuels QC, into policing in the area. The police refused point-blank to give evidence to it. The subsequent report, published in January 1981, contained a mass of verbatim allegations. Some were unsubstantiated, as the police were quick to claim. But these claims would have carried more weight if the police had been more cooperative towards the inquiry. The Lambeth report was bitterly and emotively written but Lord Scarman was later to recognize that 'it reflected attitutes, beliefs and feelings widely prevalent in Lambeth since 1979.'

Swamp 81

This then was the background to the events of April 1981. One in four of Brixton's blacks between the ages of thirteen and twenty-four have said they have been in trouble with the police through being stopped and searched or charged with 'sus'.[4] Their resentment was intense, much greater than existed elsewhere, and led to the feeling that Brixton was a time-bomb which was bound to explode sooner or later. (Bristol, by contrast, was felt to have been a harmonious community, and its riots surprised everybody, the black community included.) The week before Brixton's riots there had been greatly increased police activity in the streets. This was caused by Swamp 81, a police operation which flooded Brixton and other parts of Lambeth with officers hunting muggers and robbers. It was an extraordinarily inept name to choose (quite apart from any other criticisms which can be made); the political echoes were of the jungle and of Margaret Thatcher's notorious pre-election comment about white communities which feared swamping by blacks. No wonder the police kept the name quiet.

Swamp 81 was devised by Chief Superintendent Jeremy Plowman, who had taken over crime operations in the district two months before, and it involved 112 uniformed officers being put into plain clothes. It was a novel scheme, not least because it was conducted by L district officers operating in pairs, and not by outsiders – an implicit recognition of the political danger of using the SPG, as in the past. The police, as was their practice, did not consult community leaders beforehand, a failure which was criticized by Lord Scarman. But the community liaison officer was sounded out, though Scotland Yard's headquarters community affairs branch was not. The new local commander, Brian Fairbairn, gave the operation his blessing. They foresaw no problems.

Lord Scarman commented in his report on the riots that Swamp 81 had been a 'serious mistake' because of its timing. It was preceded by a drugs raid on the front-line – always a potentially explosive action – and Courtenay Laws, who runs the Brixton Neighbourhood and Community Association, said that tension was high in the area for several weeks before the trouble. He had tried to alert the police to this three times.

Operation Swamp began on Monday 6 April and was considered by the police to have been a resounding success because they thought it flattened the crime curve and improved police morale. It led to 943 people being stopped, of whom just over half were black, and 118 people being arrested. Seventy-five charges followed. It is difficult to escape the conclusion reached by Louis Blom-Cooper QC, one of the barristers involved in the Scarman inquiry, that Swamp 81 created its own crime. Few people were charged with robbery or burglary which was the whole purpose of the exercise and in the Brixton area, one of the four divisions saturated by Swamp 81, eight of the offences were directly related to the police stopping people. These were assaults on and obstructions to police officers and one involved a 47-year-old Jamaican woman. It is equally difficult to understand how the police can claim that offences of burglary and robbery declined by fifty per cent during the swamp. Scarman's criticisms were not confined to the tactical side; he too thought that the whole operation was of doubtful efficacy.

While the operation cannot be seen as the direct cause of the riot, it undoubtedly added to the tension and it was two Operation Swamp officers whose actions led to the devastating violence on the Saturday. Also the day before the incident with Bailey, the stabbed youth, an incident occurred close by the front-line which worried Railton Road's home beat officer, John Brown. A group of twenty black youths started to play football in 'the triangle', the patch of road at the junction of Railton and Mayall Roads. This meant traffic could not get by. When the young men were told to stop they refused and instead challenged a police officer to a fight. John Brown did not recognize any of the youths as locals. The potentially explosive situation was defused pretty quickly but it was a sign perhaps of the temperature in Brixton.

The final spark

The following night, after Bailey had been whipped off to hospital, violence broke out and it quickly became clear that a fairly commonplace clash, by Brixton's standards, had turned unusually nasty. The crowd of youths which had seized and disposed of Bailey ran off pursued by officers who had answered the call for help. Bricks and bottles were thrown at the police and riot shields were then brought out. A crowd of about one hundred faced thirty to forty policemen, two with dogs. Arrests were made, the windscreen of a police van was smashed and there was more missile throwing.

At 7.30 p.m., about one hour and twenty minutes after it had begun, the violence ended. The crowd dispersed and most of the officers retired. But it was decided that because of what had happened ninety-six extra officers should be posted to Brixton indefinitely and that foot patrols should be stepped up to twenty-eight officers patrolling in pairs. (The rest would be kept in reserve.) Van patrols were reduced.

Chief Superintendent Sidney Nicholson who was in charge that night also decided to continue with the Swamp 81 operation ('an unwise decision', said Lord Scarman) and made efforts to quash the rumours circulating about the Bailey incident. There was gossip that the injured youth had died, that he had been attacked by police, and that the police had tried to prevent him from receiving treatment. Five community representatives were contacted and agreed to try to dispel the rumours, but this did not seem to have much effect. On Saturday Brixton was seething with rumour and excitement and the atmosphere can only have been heightened by the presence of all the extra bobbies on the beat – twenty-three in central Brixton on top of the usual eight patrolling throughout the division. Lord Scarman has commented that the reinforcements were a wise precaution and that the police had to take a risk here; community leaders said the police were asking for trouble.

On Saturday afternoon the forty-eight Swamp officers operating in the Brixton division of L district, dressed in plain clothes, began their hunt for thieves. Two of them, PCs Cameron, aged twenty, and Thornton, aged twenty-four, decided to question a minicab driver outside the office of S & M Car Hire in the triangle area at the top of Railton Road. They had seen him put wads of paper in his right sock and thought this might be drugs. (Again, a search for drugs was to be the spark for violence.) The driver was questioned, said it was his habit to put bank notes in his sock, but agreed to be searched. The officers found that the paper was indeed money, as the driver had said. But they did not stop there despite a growing number of hostile young blacks gathering round the car on the pavement. They proceeded to search his car as a matter of routine practice, they told the Scarman inquiry. There is some dispute about whether the driver gave his permission. By this time the crowd numbered between thirty-five and forty and was getting noisy. There were cries that the driver should be left alone and suggestions that the officers were planting cannabis inside the car as they searched. A very ugly situation had developed, but instead of beating a quiet and hasty retreat the officers dragged out the incident further. They had found nothing incriminating in the car but they decided to take the driver's particulars on the grounds that the money in his sock might be the ill-gotten gains of drug-dealing.

While PC Cameron wrote down the man's details at the back of the car, PC Thornton strolled round to the front and attempted to pacify the crowd. He then tried to return by way of the pavement but found his path blocked by a young black. There is dispute about what took place here and the evidence to the Scarman inquiry was held in secret at that point to protect the youth who had been arrested by the police and faced charges. PC Thornton claimed that the young man abused him and pushed him in the chest. According to the young man, the constable threatened him and trod on his foot. Whatever happened, the young black was arrested for obstruction, allegedly struggling violently, and taken away in a police van. (The officers said that during the incident a number of youths were taking photographs from the roof of S & M Car Hire, a matter which made them deeply suspicious). Violence broke out immediately.

There is little doubt that the two constables handled the incident very badly, though their conduct was lawful; as Robin Auld QC, counsel to Lord Scarman's inquiry, put it, they 'must bear a great responsibility for the start of Saturday's disturbances'. In his summing up of the inquiry Auld accused the officers of folly and insensitivity: 'It was a needless display of authority, just another of the many examples of needless police harass-

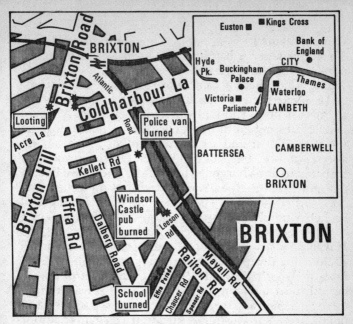

ment to add to many.' Lord Scarman in his report merely criticized them for a lack of 'discretion and judgment which maturer years might have brought'. He said the tinder for a major conflagration was there in the history of police–black relations; 'the arrest outside the S & M Car Hire office was the spark which set it ablaze'.

The blaze begins

The crowd watching the van move off had by then grown to about 150, traffic was at a standstill and bricks were thrown at the departing van and at policemen. There were scuffles and a number of arrests but mostly the crowd was yelling abuse, complaining about police harassment and alleging that some police officers had been wearing National Front badges. A plastic carrier bag was produced, corresponding to one PC Thornton had lost, and the inspector in charge was told to examine it and those of other officers on the scene. Black youths said they contained iron bars. The inspector refused. Thornton said his bag had contained a truncheon, his personal radio and a jacket.

The atmosphere became more and more highly charged as police poured in from all over London in response to calls for help. Suddenly the crowd erupted. A hail of missiles descended on the police, and a police dog van was turned over and set alight. Another police car was also set on fire. The riot had begun. Officers drew their truncheons and charged. This worked, the crowd departed and Atlantic Road was cleared, but the action had only shifted and reports soon came in of looting and broken windows. Meanwhile a large crowd had gathered down in Leeson Road, which runs between Railton and Mayall Roads, and a group of twenty officers confronted it, clutching dustbin lids and coming under a heavy barrage of flying objects. The first of many petrol bombs were thrown and many officers injured. A private vehicle was overturned and set alight. The pelting continued and police, armed now with riot shields, tried again to scatter the crowd. They failed and the injuries were serious, partly because petrol ran under their shields and set fire to their clothes. Eventually that little force, which had been joined by officers from the Special Petrol Group, had to withdraw, followed by the crowd which stoned them with anything they could find – bricks, stones, bottles, pieces of iron and paving stones. A police van was left behind. It was overturned and set alight along with two other cars. The Windsor Castle pub was also set on fire; by the end of the evening it had been reduced to a heap of rubble.

Meanwhile another crowd had gathered in Railton Road where a No. 2 bus was hijacked, and the conductor assaulted and robbed of his takings. According to one witness the atmosphere was fairly 'light-hearted' and reminiscent of a carnival.[5] The bus was driven by one of the crowd north up Railton Road towards a thin cordon of police. As it advanced, people shouted at the officers, who were without shields at the time, and coming under a hail of bricks and pieces of wood. To stop the bus a policeman threw a brick at the windscreen, which smashed, and the bus came to a halt against a wall.

The battle lines were being drawn up. After the bus incident rioters created a barricade across Railton Road out of an upturned car and corrugated iron which they ripped from the boarded-up sites. The police meanwhile, severely undermanned and under-equipped, were gathering at a cordon at the top of Railton Road. For almost the next three hours the police were to stand at the cordon, holding the shields which had by then arrived, and 'looking a bit like targets in a coconut shy', according to another witness,[6] waiting to be told what to do next. Between 7 and 9.30 p.m. about twenty policemen were struck, a number simply collapsing after being hit on the head. The same witness said: 'The cordon was like some ghastly scrum and every so often, instead of a ball coming out, a policeman would be dragged out by his colleagues.'

'Commander Fairbairn had arrived on the scene at 6.15 p.m. and quickly realized that he did not have enough men to put down the riot. Hence the long wait for reinforcements during which time the officers were sitting targets. Rioters even poured whisky at one stage over shields to provide fuel to set alight. At some point too, around this time, a military liaison officer, (a naval officer in plain clothes) was drafted into Brixton police station (codenamed 'Lima Control') in case troops needed to be called in to maintain control.

At about 7 p.m., when it was getting dark, four people asked the commander to withdraw his forces to prevent further trouble. They were two Lambeth councillors, John Boyle and Stewart Lansley, the Reverend Nind of St Matthew's church in Brixton and Tony Morgan, who had tried to persuade the police to withdraw two hours earlier. Commander Fairbairn refused, saying that he was not prepared to tolerate a no-go area and that anyway the destruction was likely to get worse. The four were, however, given a police loudhailer and set off to talk to the rioters. They made their way under a hail of missiles towards the barricade where they were seized by some of the crowd and given three conditions which would have to be met before the rioters dispersed: the police would have to withdraw, there should be an end to police harassment and those arrested that day and the night before should be released. None of these was acceptable to Commander Fairbairn, who said the police were not going to do what they had done in Bristol and that he did not believe the group behind the barricade was controlling the crowds. There is little doubt that things had gone too far for withdrawal.

As disorder raged around the front-line, black and white people of all ages took advantage of the chaos to smash shop windows and help themselves quite freely and casually to what was on offer in Brixton's commercial centre. Witnesses saw a youth carefully trying on pair after pair of trainer shoes in a sports shop until he found what he wanted and cars drawing up and shovelling two or three television sets into the boot. Many looters were white, some of them wearing gloves, according to one witness, and their ages varied enormously, from seven- and eight-year-olds to middle age. They were not the same people as those battling with the police – who, incidentally, were too few in number to control the looting.

Also during this interval the rioters, who were predominantly black but included some whites, turned their attention to houses, shops and two pubs in Railton Road. Wearing masks and brandishing vicious looking weapons, they raided buildings and set fire to them, with the result that some people lost not only their possessions but also their homes and their livelihoods. The attacks were selective: some buildings, such as the anarchist bookshop, which sported a poster depicting the Bristol riot in its window, were untouched. The George pub was razed to the ground, allegedly because it had refused to serve black people. By about 8 p.m., it looked as though the whole of Brixton was on fire as the flames roared, buildings crashed to the ground and a pillar of smoke rose into the darkening sky. The extent of fire damage and injuries was a great deal worse than it should have been because fire and ambulance men were prevented from getting through to buildings. As in Bristol – and as has often been the case in Northern Ireland too – these officers were attacked and their vehicles and equipment stolen or damaged.

The most ferocious battle of the night came when Chief Superintendent Robinson moved with his men to protect the fire brigade in Effra Road, halfway down the front-line. It quickly became a desperate struggle between sixty to seventy officers and three to four hundred rioters with a new weapon – flying plates – being hurled at police. At one point a car was pushed as a battering ram into the police line. At about 9 p.m. Robinson's men, who were by then down to at most thirty in number because of injuries, came under intense pressure and were temporarily overwhelmed. This was because they were caught between two armies of police moving in from both ends of Railton Road in a pincer movement, a manoeuvre which was to end the serious rioting. But for those minutes Robinson's men came under fierce attack and he feared some might be killed.

'We are getting a good hiding and we can't hold out any longer,' Robinson said desperately into his radio. He wanted reinforcements but no one heard him because communications had broken down. In the end the chief superintendent and his men took the hoses from the firemen and turned them on the attacking crowds. Soon after they were relieved by more officers, and by about 10 p.m. the main riot was over. Hundreds of police, called into Brixton in the previous three hours, had stormed north and south down the front-line, some beating on their shields with their truncheons and yelling as Lord Scarman put it 'in a manner reminiscent of ancient warriors going into battle'. This cannot have been an edifying sight. It was done, so the police said, to keep their spirits up.

By 11 p.m. Brixton was quiet. Left behind was a scene

of utter devastation, burnt-out, looted and damaged buildings, burnt-out cars and many people injured. On Sunday Brixton was bristling with policemen as William Whitelaw, and Sir David McNee, Metropolitan police commissioner, strode around surveying the damage. Youths greeted Whitelaw with shouts of *Sieg Heil*. Violence broke out again in the late afternoon with isolated attacks on police, and looting. This intensified later. Much of the action was concentrated on the town hall and there were heavy police injuries. In many ways Sunday was more frightening than Saturday because of the number and spread of the disturbances. There was more trouble on Monday evening but it was relatively minor compared with the previous days and by 11.30 p.m. the April riots had burnt themselves out.

Over those three days more than 450 people, many of them police, had been injured; 207 vehicles were damaged or destroyed; and there were 354 arrests. There were also nineteen formal complaints lodged against the police. On Saturday one ambulance man and fourteen fire officers were reported injured and four ambulances and nine fire engines were damaged. There were 145 buildings damaged, 28 by fire, and a total of 7300 police were eventually called in – most from outside Lambeth – to put down the riots.

The allegations

Hours after the serious violence on Saturday night, police leaders were suggesting the rioting may not have been a spontaneous local action. Sir David McNee said in a statement for Sunday's newspapers that unconfirmed reports indicated that 'troublemakers from elsewhere' may have gathered in the area. It was a year after the Bristol riot and there could be a connection, he added.

The police did not provide convincing evidence to support this allegation that the rioting was planned and organized by outsiders, either at the time or during Lord Scarman's inquiry. And it was vigorously denied by black representatives. Rudy Narayan, convenor of the hastily assembled Brixton Defence Committee, said: 'The only outsiders were McNee's storm-troopers, the Special Patrol Group, some armed with guns, who came to attack and terrorize our community.' Others said there was little doubt that white and black agitators came into the area once violence had broken out but that it had not been inspired by them. The only newspaper which claimed to have established planning of the riots was the *Daily Star* which said that black youths 'had schemed to take to the streets over Easter weekend. But police involvement in a stabbing indicent sparked off the violence early.' *Daily Star* journalists said they had talked to young people in squats, illegal drinking clubs, derelict houses, drug dens and illicit gambling clubs 'where the air is so thick with marijuana smoke they gasped for breath'.

It was hot stuff but Lord Scarman did not seem to give it much credence. He was satisfied that the disorders originated as a spontaneous crowd reaction to police action and were not premeditated. However the judge did conclude that there was evidence of leadership and 'outsider participation', and he referred to evidence given to his inquiry in support of this: a woman with an American accent who at one point asked the police to withdraw; the presence of a white man and a black youth who, according to one policeman, were directing operations; the terms offered by the rioters for police withdrawal; a 'grimly determined' group of black men who told the Vicar of St Jude's that they were attacking the George pub and a newsagent's because the police had been harassing blacks and homosexuals; the evidence of a policeman that many of the black people opposing him were strangers; and, finally, 'clear and credible evidence' given to Lord Scarman in private session by two Brixton residents that they saw white men making, stacking and distributing petrol bombs. Lord Scarman admitted that this was a shadowy area and that the evidence would not stand up in a court of law, but he considered it important enough to devote more than a page to in his report.

Most newspapers in the days after the riots ran the same picture of a London bobby with blood streaming down his face as a result of riot injuries. 'The Bloodied Face of Brixton', was how the *News of the World* described it in banner headlines. 'The despair shows. And the shock.' Months later, during the inquiry, it was revealed that the man had not been seriously hurt at all and that Caroline Tisdall, a freelance journalist who gave evidence to Scarman, had taken a picture of him grinning broadly through the blood. There was much sympathy and praise for the police, particularly from the Conservative government and from many members of the public who had watched with shock the collapse of law and order on their television screens. The police's strategy and tactics during the riot were vindicated by Lord Scarman who said they should be commended not criticized and, if they were at fault, it was because they were insufficiently equipped and prepared. But criticism of the police was also made loud and clear: allegations of police harassment, which in national terms had previously been the province of the extreme left and the black community, were now accepted by people of other persuasions.

A particularly nasty incident, which was corroborated by a number of witnesses, involved the ferocious beating by police of a freelance photographer, Neil Martinson, who took a picture of the police arresting a black man. According to John Clare, the BBC's community affairs and education correspondent, three officers jumped on Martinson, his camera was wrenched away, thrown into the gutter and stamped on. Martinson was severely beaten up with the police aiming at his groin: the motorbike he had been riding when he took the picture was dragged along the road and its petrol tank ripped open. There were one or two other reports of people apprehended being beaten up and John Clare said he saw two Rastafarians being dragged along by their dreadlocks. He and others also saw police carrying unauthorized weapons. Caroline Tisdall saw two men moving with the police line carrying iron bars. She told one that it created a terrible impression and he allegedly replied in a state of some excitement: 'It's great, it's like Notting Hill.' Others were reminded of the death of Blair Peach in 1979, probably struck by police with an unauthorized weapon. John Clare saw men in plain clothes, one carrying an axe handle, another a three-foot-long stave and the third a solid rubber pipe. He was in no doubt they were policemen because they were carrying riot shields and associating with the police. He approached the one with the axe handle and asked if he was a policeman. 'He said "yes" rather abruptly and gave me a hard stare,' said Clare. 'The conversation didn't seem worth pursuing.'

While Lord Scarman found generally that the police did not over-react, he was concerned about instances where they behaved aggressively and used excessive force. The allegations about unauthorized weapons should be examined, he said, and 'if verified' stringent action taken. He was confident that the Metropolitan police commissioner could handle these matters.

The political fall-out

National politicians and black representatives responded fast to the disorders: the government realized that it had to do more than it had done after Bristol 1980. On Monday, before the violence had finished, the Home Secretary announced he was setting up an urgent inquiry headed by Lord Scarman under section 32 of the Police Act 1964. After some complaint from the Labour opposition that this would be too narrow an investigation, neglecting the 'deep-rooted and fundamental causes' of unemployment and housing, the Home Secretary said it could look at these matters too. The important thing was to get a quick inquiry, he said. The House of Commons Home Affairs committee was now completing its report on racial disadvantage – the same one that Mr Whitelaw referred to after the Bristol riot – so 'it was wrong to cross the wires of the two inquiries'.

Both sides of the House condemned the violence, though the Conservatives tended to see it as criminal in origin, and Labour as social. Like a loyal government minister in a monetarist cabinet, Whitelaw reminded the country that Britain could not buy its way out of these problems. He refused to respond to the bomb which Enoch Powell lobbed over the chamber: 'In reflecting upon these events, will he and the government bear in mind in view of the prospective future increase of the relevant population, that they have seen nothing yet?' The Prime Minister later went on television to say that she did not think unemployment was the primary cause of the disorders and that 'nothing, but nothing, justifies what happened'.

Down in Brixton the defence committee, set up within hours of the first rash of rioting to advise those charged with offences, was holding some large and angry meetings where it was decided to boycott the Scarman inquiry. This group eventually fell apart after squabbles about who was to be their spokesman and whether whites would be admitted. This was a sign of the deep divisions – and of the balance of power – between the black separatist tradition in Brixton (and elsewhere) and those who argued that reforms could be won from 'the system'. It also signalled divisions within the left and between generations. And it revealed, for whatever reasons, just how little organizational and representative purchase black Britain has upon the working of the political process.

There was deep suspicion of attempts at leadership. First Rudy Narayan and then the poet Linton Kwesi Johnson were rejected before the committee broke up. After the riots (or 'insurrection' or 'uprising' as they were called by black radicals) there was a great deal of playing out old battles between Brixton's self-appointed spokesmen. Most of the more establishment groups, run by older blacks, decided to cooperate with Lord Scarman's inquiry, particularly because he said he would be looking at underlying causes.

It seemed as if the lines were clearly drawn and that Scarman was going to get at least some cooperation from Brixton. He had given immunity from prosecution to witnesses, he was prepared to hold secret hearings to protect their identity, he would accept hearsay testimony and said that independent legal help would be given to those making statements.

Less than two weeks before the inquiry opened a new Brixton defence campaign, which had arisen out of the ashes of the old committee, drew up a statement outlining why Scarman should be boycotted. The campaign operated with great secrecy, refusing to talk to the press, and claimed the support of thirteen community groups, including the three established organizations – the Melting Pot, the Brixton Community Neighbourhood Association and the Council for Community Relations in Lambeth. These groups, however, had all decided to give evidence to Scarman and seemed unaware of the defence campaign's claims. The campaign, which operated out of Brixton law centre, was not particularly representative and, as events were to prove, not so powerful as at first appeared. Its most active members were the young black left, members of the Black Women's Group, Blacks against State Harassment, and the Socialist Workers' Party. Whites were excluded. The hand of law centre workers was evident in the statement which said that the inquiry represented a danger to people charged with offences after the riots and that no black person or organization should give evidence to it. It concluded:

The Brixton Defence Campaign is satisfied that Lord Scarman is disposed to be used by the state to provide it with a basis for rewriting the Riot Act and to provide justification for dramatically increasing repressiveness in policing methods, which are already massively racist, lawless and brutal as well as substantially uncontrolled.

In the event, Scarman gave the lie to such wishful thinking. But the statement rattled the other local groups and Scarman took it sufficiently seriously to issue an appeal for cooperation. He rebutted points in the statement and for the first time said he would be holding private meetings with black youth. It had been made clear to him that otherwise he would not hear from the young generation, some of whom took part in the riots and would be afraid of being beaten up by police if they came forward to the public inquiry. Local community groups thought again about their decisions to give evidence. After long discussions, they decided to go ahead and cooperate, some by slim majorities.

The inquiry opened in Lambeth Town Hall on 15 June, in an atmosphere of uncertainty. Outside, there was a large picket from the defence campaign and the so-called Labour Committee for the Defence of Brixton, a new group which was thinking of setting up an alternative inquiry. It was two months after the rioting and all eyes were now on Lord Scarman. Yet there were some who felt that the longer he sat and the more distant the Brixton events became, the less relevance the inquiry would have. Events, though, were about to prove them wrong.

5 Deprived and disadvantaged?

Round our way, we've got a Youth Opportunities Programme: we call it rioting.

Alexei Sayle

The riots took place during an economic recession which was widely perceived as the worst since the 1930s. Like the previous Depression, that of the early 1980s was international and not confined to Britain. From 1974 onwards the western capitalist nations suffered a common crisis triggered largely by the rapid rise in oil prices. These rises helped to drive up the rate of inflation, increase the cost of borrowing and thus to create a recession in which unemployment rose throughout the West.

Britain's economic decline, however, was already well under way before the oil crisis gave it such a violent push. British industries were finding that they were uncompetitive in world markets. The products which had traditionally made this country self-sufficient, even after the Second World War, were being produced more cheaply and better elsewhere. Manufactured exports went into decline and British industry soon found itself facing serious battles in domestic markets. When such battles were lost, whole sectors of industry were wiped out. Motorcars, shipbuilding, steel and textiles took most of the battering. And as these industries were forced to cut back, dependent suppliers went out of business too.

Britain was slow to invest in new industrial processes. As a result, the economy failed to expand fast enough through the 1970s to make use of the people that were losing out from the closures and cuts. In some places –

Consett in the north-east of England, or Corby in North-amptonshire – towns and communities which were especially dependent on one type of industry suffered specially hard.

Inflation made the recession seem particularly cruel. In the 1970s, people talked as if inflation was a special torture invented by Arab oil sheikhs. In reality, inflation has been a fact of postwar economic life. The difference was that in the 1970s it stopped being gradual. A pound in 1950 was worth 72 pence in 1960. A pound in 1960 was worth 68 pence in 1970. These were big reductions in the value of money over fairly short time spans, but they were *steady* reductions. Now compare 1970 and 1980; a pound in 1970 was worth only 27½ pence in 1980. By any standards this was much more alarming – not just because it was a big fall but because it went on falling and many people could remember a time when it didn't. The fears and insecurities brought on by inflation – the tough, unsentimental struggle to preserve a standard of living and levels of expectation – were part of the daily experience of all communities.

Unemployment and the cuts

Unemployment had a long reality, too. Ever since the Second World War the number of unemployed people was never smaller than the total population of Southampton. But from 1966, the total began to creep upwards. A new postwar record of 587,000 was reached in the spring of 1970; the million mark was passed late in 1975. By early 1981 the total was over 2.5 million and by the autumn – just after the riots – the emotive three million figure was in sight. By the time the riots took place, unemployment had more than doubled since the election of the Conservatives in May 1979. More than one in ten people were registered unemployed. No region escaped. Worst sufferers were Northern Ireland, Wales and north-east England. But by the end of 1981 even the relatively prosperous south-east of England was registering 8.4 per cent unemployed. This was a higher regional rate than even the worst hit British region had ever recorded postwar before 1980.

The rises affected all age groups but particularly the young. When the Brixton riots broke out in April 1981, there were over 917,000 registered jobless under the age of twenty-five, of whom 60,000 were under eighteen. Young men were specially hard hit. Official unemployment among men under twenty-five rose by around 150 per cent in the two years from October 1979. These figures, moreover, were widely recognized as optimistic. Some young people failed to register at all, while large numbers – 180,000 in July 1981 – were 'employed' on the government's Youth Opportunities Programme, which took them out of unemployment without giving them full-time employment. YOP had a poor reputation – perhaps undeservedly. However, whatever the rights and wrongs of it, few far-reaching claims could be made for YOP. As one not unsympathetic observer wrote: 'It is a holding operation, and will remain so while the training component is limited and the job opportunities so pitifully few.'[1]

Faced with such severe and deteriorating economic conditions, it is not surprising that many people blamed them for the riots. But as Lord Scarman among others pointed out, to say there was a connection is not to say that such factors *caused* the riots. Indeed, as we have just seen, two of the areas of Britain with the worst rates of unemployment were Wales and the north-east of England and yet (save for one or two very isolated incidents) these areas were almost untouched by the riots. There was no riot in Consett or Corby, for example. So, while recognizing that what David Donnison, former chairman of the Supplementary Benefits Commission, called 'the brute fact of three million unemployed' and the social and psychological implications of that brute fact were central issues of ordinary life in 1981, it is necessary to look further at their relevance to the riots.

The effect of cuts in public spending is even more

difficult to assess. The Labour government of 1974–9 started the process. But it was the return of the Conservative government in 1979 that ushered in the toughest modern policy on public spending controls. The theory of Conservative economic policy makers was that reductions in public spending would help to cut borrowing and monetary growth and hence inflation. Tax cuts would create incentives and productivity would rise.

In practice the picture is different. Public spending under Margaret Thatcher increased, monetary targets were overreached, inflation continued to rise at higher levels than when the Conservatives took over. The tax burden rose rather than fell and the recession deepened. At first, it had looked as if the monetarist policies were working. The first budget of the new government cut existing programmes, sold off government assets and stuck to rigid cash limits. Spending was held level in 1979–80. The 1980 budget appeared to drive home the policies. Spending, said Chancellor of the Exchequer Sir Geoffrey Howe, would fall by four per cent by 1984 against the 1981 level.

It didn't work out. Instead of a planned fall in spending in 1980–1 of one per cent there was a two-per-cent rise. There were many reasons. Higher unemployment meant higher spending on benefits and special employment programmes. 'Lame ducks' got reprieved. Defence spending rose faster than planned. Nor did the tax programme work as intended. In 1981 Britain paid more of its national income in tax than it did in 1979. More people were paying income tax in 1981 than when Labour left office.

Local authorities were hard hit, however. While central government spending rose, local spending fell by three per cent between 1979 and 1981. When Labour local authorities tried to raise rates to compensate for the drop in central funding the government gave itself new powers to dragoon local spending into line with Whitehall's budgets.

Inner-city policies before 1979

These cold economic winds hit the old industrial cities and towns hardest. The Victorian cities that had been the powerhouse of the world's first industrial nation fell gradually into decline. Their economies waned. Manufacturing employment in the old cities fell by around a quarter between 1971 and 1976 and faster after that. Firms moved out to more attractive sites, but many simply closed. The cities became increasingly dependent not on productive industry but on service industry. When this too went into decline under Labour, and then into even faster decline under Margaret Thatcher from May 1979 onwards, the recession in the cities became acute.

But the decay of the cities had a long history. The 1960s and 1970s witnessed a slow but sure procession away from the old centres of population. Overall, the number of people in Britain wasn't declining – indeed it rose slightly. The big cities, however, got smaller. Only two of the twenty largest towns in England and Wales outside London had more inhabitants in 1981 than in 1971. They were Plymouth and Dudley. For the other eighteen, and for many more besides, the opposite was true. In many of the biggest cities numbers fell dramatically. Birmingham, Liverpool and Manchester each lost about 100,000 inhabitants over the decade. The number of people living in Greater London fell by more than three quarters of a million in the same ten years. Planners and demographers expect the trend to continue into the 1990s.

The irony is that for much of this century, and particularly in the postwar period, this shift has not only been recognized, it has been encouraged. Indeed, some experts would argue that 'anti-urban' moves began almost at the same time as the towns themselves began to grow during the nineteenth century. The vision of decentralized, low-density, land-based living captured the minds of Victorian social critics of industrialization. Utopian communities for town dwellers were being set up in the 1830s. Model industrial towns like Saltaire, Port Sunlight and Bournville were more lasting. In 1903, the first 'garden city' at Letchworth was begun. By the Second World War, planners were determined that the old, crowded urban environment had to be replaced.

The destruction of so much of these cities by the German bombing raids gave these ideas both a stimulus and an opportunity. A royal commission in 1940 on the distribution of the industrial population called for congested urban areas to be redeveloped and for industry and the working population to be redistributed in a planned manner. The demands of wartime suited this emphasis on planning and coordinated programmes. The Ministry of Town and Country Planning was established in 1943 and planning control was extended to cover all land.

The model for postwar urban planning policy was Patrick Abercrombie's *Greater London Plan* of 1944. This envisaged moving up to one million Londoners out of the congested inner areas of the capital into outlying communities centred on eight new towns and the expansion of country towns beyond the green belt. By 1949, the new towns (Basildon, Bracknell, Crawley, Harlow, Hatfield, Hemel Hempstead, Stevenage and Welwyn) were under way around London. In Scotland, East Kilbride and later Cumbernauld were designated for Clydeside. Aycliffe, Corby, Cwmbran, Glenrothes and Peterlee followed in other parts of the country.

In practice, things didn't work out so neatly. The cities began emptying their inner areas but the build-up of the new towns was uneven. Nonetheless, during the 1960s, the designation of new towns went on and existing county towns were expanded (Peterborough and Northampton, for example). Further impetus was given by arrangements made between the big cities and various towns for transfer of population. By 1970, Greater London had agreed thirty-one such schemes involving 90,000 dwellings. Birmingham had fifteen and Glasgow's negotiations ranged as far as Wick.

This movement went hand in hand with the postwar

slum clearance programme. Between 1955 and 1974, 1,165,000 houses in England and Wales were demolished or closed. Scotland got rid of a further 296,000. As a result, more than three and a half million people were moved out of their homes. During the 1960s the annual figure was never less than 100,000 people, rising to a record 189,000 in 1968.[2] All the great nineteenth-century cities have seen this process. Writing of Glasgow, the economic historian S. G. Checkland summed it up like this:

It is almost as though the economy and society, by a kind of consensus, wished to abandon, as places of work and living, its older focal urban centres, with their intimacy and congestion, and substitute something different – a kind of writing off of the past and an entering upon the new.[3]

The problem with this whole process was that it was one thing to abandon the old but quite another to construct the new at the same time, especially in the storm-tossed economic situation of the 1970s. London, for instance, may have lost three quarters of a million people in the decade before Brixton. Nearly seven million still live there and more still come in each day for work. The same, on the smaller scale, is also true of the other cities.

Public opinion and planning orthodoxy had begun to get alarmed with what was being done with the cities in the late 1960s. Reports in the 1960s highlighted the uneradicated deprivation that existed amid city affluence. Inner-city riots in the United States added to the unease. The partial collapse of the Ronan Point tower block in east London in 1968 was both a real tragedy and a metaphor for the failure of postwar city planning. The emphasis began to shift towards the conservation and improvement of the inner cities. Housing policy marked the change in 1969 with the creation of General Improvement Areas and in 1974 with the introduction of Housing Action Areas and Priority Neighbourhoods. Educational and social ventures financed through the Urban Programme introduced by Labour in 1968 followed suit.

The trouble was that these were small-scale, unevenly implemented local answers to a problem that was already full of half-completed restructurings. In some ways the new recognition of inner-city needs meant that government found themselves getting the worst of all worlds. Resources were diverted from the new towns to the inner cities, from the shire counties to the metropolitan counties and Greater London. At the same time, the continuing drift away from the towns meant that the shires and new towns needed more resources rather than less.

The 'inner-city problem' of the 1970s was therefore a combined problem of low employment, low wages, low investment and the physical decay of much of the domestic and working environment. Local authorities were faced with the problem of having to spend more and more merely to maintain the cities at a doubly unfavourable time – industrial investment was leaving the cities and public spending was being squeezed hard. As Labour's White Paper in 1977, *Policy for the Inner Cities*, saw it, there was a 'mismatch' between labour and industry in the inner cities – too much of the one, not enough of the latter. It concluded: 'The inner parts of our cities ought not to be left to decay. It would mean leaving large numbers of people to face a future of declining job opportunities, a squalid environment, deteriorating housing and declining public services.'

In 1978, the Labour government tried to turn the trend round in favour of the cities. The Inner Urban Areas Act aimed to strengthen inner-city economies, improve the environment, tackle the special social problems of the cities and to stem the flow of people and jobs to other areas. The special measures that had earlier been applied to the regions were now applied in the cities – investment incentives, relaxation of planning controls, special job training and so on. The principal weapon in the new programme was the 'partnership' scheme – under which local authorities could act in concert with central government approval to tackle the worst problems in their areas by assisting the local economy through grants, loans, site clearance and factory provision. Seven partnership programmes were set up. Four were outside London: Birmingham, Liverpool, Manchester–Salford and Newcastle–Gateshead. Three were in the capital: docklands, Hackney–Islington and Lambeth, the borough of Brixton.

The individual partnership plans were strongly criticized by the planning expert Professor Peter Hall for being so heterogeneous and ill thought out: 'The primary impression emerging from these programmes is that they represent less a coherent strategy for the regeneration of England's decaying inner cities and rather more a list of projects that have long been on departmental and committee shopping lists.' All the partnership areas were selected for their high levels of unemployment. Most of them spent their money on industrial investment, loans to firms, conversions, development grants, advance factories. Others, though, preferred to spend on education, transport and recreation. Lambeth, in particular, chose this course – the Lambeth Walk swimming pool got £575,000 and the Kennington lido £870,000. It may make sense, Hall argued, for post-industrial society to invest in leisure like this, but he was doubtful. 'At the programme's end,' he said 'young workers in Brixton may still be unemployed but at least they'll be able to swim for their supplementary benefit.'[4]

The partnership programme was still secondary to the amounts of public money that were already flowing into local authorities through the block grant and rate support grants. In the docklands partnership area, for example, sixty-eight per cent of programmed capital spending came from these two sources. The total available nationally through partnership was only around £100 million a year.

This was one of the reasons why the effects of the programme, expecially in job terms, were modest. The emphasis on labour-intensive industry was unattractive to the private sector and the Labour government's National Enterprise Board (closed down by the Conservatives in 1981) was also reluctant to steer its clients into the inner cities. The emphasis in the partnership schemes on help for small businesses meant that any employment effects were also small. Only a few big firms – Tesco's supermarkets were an example – showed much interest. Private sector service industries, like those in the public sector, were still cutting jobs rather than creating them. In short, the partnership programme was a recognition of the right question rather than a provision of the right answer.

The Conservatives and the inner cities

Around the 1979 general election, Conservative Party thinking on inner cities was dominated by the free enterprise economic principles which underpinned so much of the strategy of Margaret Thatcher's wing of the party. In June 1978, Sir Geoffrey Howe set out the proposal of 'enterprise zones' for the inner cities. The next year Howe became Chancellor of the Exchequer and the plan was incorporated in the 1980 budget. The enterprise zone idea is based on the theory that the root cause of inner-city problems is government interference which frustrates the working of market forces. Government owns the land, makes the planning decisions, levies the taxes, controls the pay rates of much of the workforce. The blame was shifted from capitalism to the state.

Howe originally expected around six enterprise zones to be set up. While in opposition, he had envisaged a wholesale liberation of the zones from state intervention for a 'stated and substantial' number of years. Firms would be freed from detailed planning controls, from some health, safety and pollution controls, from some of the constraints of the employment protection legislation and perhaps also from price and wage controls. Financial incentives would encourage firms into the zones; they would not have to pay rates or development land taxes.

The scheme which was eventually announced in the March 1980 budget was watered down. The Health and

Safety Executive prevented decontrol in its sphere of responsibility. The Department of Employment stopped exemptions from employment protection law. The criteria for a zone were more restrictive than Howe had envisaged in 1978; zones had to be relatively derelict, should not require major new infrastructural development, and should be around 500 acres in size. Eight concessions would be allowed over a ten-year period: full capital allowances on industrial and commercial building; relief from Development Land Tax; full de-rating on industrial and commercial property; simplified planning requirements; exemption from industrial training obligations; accelerated customs-free warehousing; exemption from industrial development procedures; minimal demands from government for statistical information.

In the process from announcement to implementation, the enterprise zones changed even further. Some local Labour authorities in earmarked zone sites refused to have anything to do with the scheme. In Sheffield, for example, Labour opponents argued that free enterprise had caused the problem and so could not be the solution. Boundaries were chopped and changed under pressure from local authorities and regulations were adjusted in individual zones. In Manchester, local business interests fought a successful campaign to prevent rating concessions to a new hypermarket. The result was the creation of eleven enterprise zones in 1981, in Corby, Dudley, Swansea, Clydebank, Hartlepool, Newcastle–Gateshead, Salford–Trafford, Speke, Wakefield, Belfast and the Isle of Dogs. By no means all of these are inner cities. Stan Taylor, a politics lecturer who has made a special study of the zones, says:

The Enterprise Zone scheme in its final form was markedly different from that originally envisaged by Sir Geoffrey Howe. It was transformed from a radical attempt to provide a market-based alternative to interventionism in solving the apparently intractable problems of the inner cities to a miniature version of regional policy whereby mainly financial incentives were provided, to lure firms into areas selected on the basis of 'ministerial whim' in specifying a site size and political factors as much as economic and poverty-related ones.[5]

Other critics have been even harsher, regarding the zones as little more than glorified industrial estates, draining off business investment from the areas immediately surrounding the zones. If this is proved a valid fear, the enterprise zones could actually siphon money away from the inner-city areas without the compensations originally envisaged from the partnership schemes. Indeed, the emphasis within partnership is now strongly on economic investment and, to that extent, the two sets of projects are to some degree in direct competition.

The final verdict on enterprise zones remains to be written. But in no sense were they a mass issue in 1981. Nor were any of the alternative inner-city programmes. Nobody rioted in Toxteth because they weren't being made an enterprise zone and Speke was. Nobody went on to the streets of Brixton to demand more government investment in the partnership scheme. It is very doubtful whether more than a handful of people in Britain are at all familiar with the intricacies of the urban programme.

Lee Bridges, writing in autumn 1981 in the journal of the Institute of Race Relations,[6] saw the riots as in part a repudiation of all that had gone on over the previous fifteen years in the name of British urban social policy. This statement is so broad as to contain some truth. But the problem is that it attributes too great a direct political rejection to the rioters. The truth is that the riots marked a great failure of these policies to make an economic and – at least as important – a political impact upon those whom they have been designed to benefit.

This failure to win hearts and minds, for whatever policy, has bred a sense of fatalism and defeatism among planners which the riots encouraged rather than discouraged. It has also led to a gimmicky approach. It could be seen in the government's response to the riots, dressing Michael Heseltine up as 'Minister for the Cities', packing him off to Merseyside and then rejecting his plan for a government-led programme of campaigning and spending on the cities. A similar trend had been seen in the United States. It was described by one economist, Anthony Downs, as 'the law of inescapable discontinuity' and 'the law of compulsive innovation'.

Michael Heseltine's 1981 experience fits those two phrases rather well: he was appointed to show that something was being done. A month later he announced his plans to the Cabinet. Again the accent was on innovation. Individual ministers would be put in charge of specific run-down areas. Their brief would be to coordinate state spending programmes in each urban area. An official committee in London would ensure that spending was being directed into private sector projects. The emphasis on the private sector and on central control of local responses fitted well with the government's existing priorities. But the plans were rejected. The reason, said *The Times*, was that the Treasury regarded the Heseltine package as 'nothing more than a well disguised blank cheque'.[7] There was more to it than that, for the measures added up to a slap in the face for Geoffrey Howe's enterprise zone approach to inner-city regeneration. In spite of the fact that the ultimate enterprise zone package was less pure market medicine than Howe intended, the Heseltine measures were a subsidizer's recipe, and as such had to be opposed. But they showed Heseltine's appetite for both innovation and discontinuity along American lines.

In the event, Heseltine's measures for inner-city expansion were much less dramatic and creative than had been whispered (or hoped). They added up to a quango on the quiet and an increase in direct spending (offset by other measures) – very much the traditional 'spending ministry' approach. In October at Heseltine's suggestion, banks, building societies and finance houses nominated twenty-five 'socially concerned capitalists' who were to become temporary civil servants, to visit American and British cities and come up with bright ideas on private–public projects in the inner cities. In December Heseltine announced a further £95 million would be spent on job creation and environmental measures in the cities. The urban programme got the lion's share – £55 million – taking its total budget in 1981–2 to £270 million. A further five million pounds went to the derelict land reclamation programme, with an extra £35 million going to the two urban development corporations in London and Merseyside. But the net effect of these measures was less impressive when compared with the cuts in central government funding to local authorities under partnership schemes.

Inner-city policy offers no bright vistas of progress to plenty. Nor did it do so in the 1970s. The policies changed, but the reasons for their failures did not. Those reasons include unrealistic expectations of early results, power struggles between local and central government and, above all, the contradictions between the interests of government, and the community and industry. Government calls loud for regenerated inner cities but tries to put industry's money where it own mouth is. Industry cannot be tempted because the prospects of a return are not attractive enough. Government is left with the problem but is unable to deliver the answer. Communities meanwhile cannot afford to wait. Communities lose confidence in both industry and government.

However, as with unemployment the direct connection between inner-city deprivation and riot is not clear-cut. To put it simply, inner-city problems appear to be a necessary but by no means sufficient precondition for riot. To take the most obvious and important example which supports this view, it is necessary to look at Glasgow. By almost any index of urban deprivation, Glasgow is amongst the most deprived cities in Europe – the Naples of the North. In the summer of 1981 one in every six Glaswegians had no job (and one in three of the young), forty per cent of the population was poorly housed, the population had slumped by a third, old working-class communities had been torn out of the city centre and redeveloped to suit the planners' favoured preconceptions. Glasgow had a militant left-wing history and culture, a tradition of police–community hostility and 20,000 black inhabitants, mainly Pakistanis. Yet Glasgow had no riot. An article in the *Observer* in September hinted that the explanation may have been the lack of a West Indian population.[8] True or false, Glasgow at least confounds simple cause and effect theories on the relationship between socio-economic conditions and the outbreak of riot. Nor was Glasgow alone in its riotlessness. Cardiff and Southampton were other major towns which remained quiet.

So any attempt to understand the riots needs to keep an open mind and adopt a flexible approach towards these connections. Obviously, the question of race now needs to be assessed. It is one dimension – perhaps the most important one – of this more sophisticated approach. In short, does the racial dimension of unemployment or deprivation provide a more convincing explanation? Does race supply the connection that turns socio-economic grievances into street riot?

Racial disadvantage

The problems of the recession have hit the black population of Britain with special force. Britain's blacks are not evenly spread throughout the country geographically. Nor are they evenly spread throughout the economy. They are concentrated in particular places, in particular trades and at particular levels in those trades.

Unlike the white population, though, most of Britain's black people live in towns. Three quarters of all West Indians in Britain and almost two thirds of Asians in England and Wales live in conurbations. By contrast, these towns account for only a little more than a third of the total population of the country.

But the distribution of the black population among Britain's towns is very uneven. It reflects, to a very large extent, the pattern of the demand for labour that existed between the mid 1950s and mid 1960s. So London and the south-east, the west Midlands and the north-west all have particularly well-established black communities. Some forty-five per cent of all Asians and West Indians are now in the south-east of England, and a further twenty-five per cent in the west Midlands. On the other hand, the towns of north-east England, lowland Scotland, the south coast and South Wales do not have large black populations.

The concentration of the black population in particular places is very relative. Over the country as a whole, the black population only comprises around four per cent of the total. And even in those towns that have large numbers of blacks, the white population massively outnumbers them. There is no London borough with a black majority, and very few wards.

The sheer smallness of the black population is a very important factor. It greatly limits the political clout of the black community. Nor is this disproportion likely to change. This contrasts dramatically with the United States. There, several cities, including Washington DC, are majority black cities. Dozens more cities have very large black minorities of well over a third, for example. Projections of population change suggest that several of these will become majority black cities by the end of the century. Britain's blacks have nothing to compare with this. One of the greatest problems facing the black population in its attempts to gain equality is the fact that it is so small.

The internal balance of the black population, however, differs from that of the white population in Britain. The young are more heavily represented among black people than among whites, while the old form a smaller proportion. The sex ratio among blacks slightly favours men – by contrast with the white population, where there are more women. These differences too reflect the fact that the immigrants among the black community were initially mainly men of working age. But these differences in age and sex structure among blacks are beginning to disappear as new generations are born. So too are differences in the birth rate. Thus the age and sex structures of black and white British people are gradually becoming more similar to one another.

It has become increasingly clear that the black population suffers disproportionately in every significant index of deprivation. Getting work, losing work, living conditions, educational and professional opportunities – black people do less well than whites. The early reformers thought that the reason was the colour bar – discrimination. So they outlawed it in a series of increasingly tougher race relations acts.

Discrimination undoubtedly still exists in spite of these legal protections. But the way that it works has been shown to be more complicated than was originally supposed. Discrimination wasn't just a case of a 'no blacks' notice, for example. It might be just as effective to use indirect means. A language test or a policy of never advertising vacancies could deny blacks an equal chance, for example. The 1976 Act made 'indirect discrimination' unlawful but it didn't stop such practices.

In the past decade, far more white attention has been focused on the other issues that lie behind the unequal deal that blacks get. The law is now seen as having more limited force. Instead the question of *racial disadvantage* is now receiving far greater prominence. It was the subject of a government 'Think Tank' report in 1972-3, of a sustained series of studies by the independent research institute Political and Economic Planning (PEP) and its successor, the Policy Studies Institute (PSI) and, most recently, by the Home Affairs select committee, whose inquiries were carried out in the months leading up to the riots and rush-released on 20 July because of the riots.

'Racial disadvantage' is a term thought up by experts. It is a term deployed by policy analysts and policy makers without consultation with the people they deem to suffer from it. It shares this with many other items and conditions which are grindingly familiar from the literature on race but which – like 'ethnic minority group' and so many more – have blossomed without any sort of community sanction. Having made this protest against bureaucratically imposed language, it remains the case that it must be used until a better popular vocabulary has emerged, but it is used without joy.

All that racial disadvantage means is that black people are not equal with whites in their opportunities and rewards in society. Compare blacks with whites in terms of jobs, housing, education, access to services, and the evidence shows what Home Affairs select committee called a 'complete fabric of social and economic disadvantage'. The possible relevance of this disadvantage to the riots is that it may bear so heavily upon blacks in the cities (where most of them live) that they may feel driven to violent action. So what is the true extent of racial disadvantage in Britain and how far can it be seen as a direct cause of the riots?

There is an immediate problem in answering the first part of the question. If racial disadvantage actually exists, it can be measured. But to measure it, you have to have accurate information. Yet some of the most basic information is unavailable because it has not been collected. As the select committee complained: 'It is impossible to discover the simple factual truth about some of the most significant and apparently straightforward matters.'[9] In some cases, no questions have been asked. Central government failed to include an 'ethnic question' in the 1981 census and many local authorities have made no attempt to monitor race in their areas. In some cases, the wrong questions have been asked. In the 1971 census, for instance, questions were asked about the place where parents and grandparents were born. These questions were helpful in a limited way but they failed to identify blacks and whites as such, since there were blacks whose relatives were born in this country and whites whose relatives were not. The longer that the black population has lived in Britain, the less relevance this question can have. Many reasons for the failure to collect racial data have been put forward. The most generous explanation is that black communities are afraid that the data will be used against them, above all in some form of expulsion or repatriation programme. A more cynical explanation is that government (and this applies with particular force to local government) is colour blind and either does not realize or does not wish to know about the racial dimension of its responsibilities. In 1982, after Scarman, monitoring social data is becoming more politically acceptable, for if it is accepted that racial disadvantage exists, and that it should be eradicated, it makes little sense to refuse to collect racial data, if only for the purpose of monitoring whether the policies are having the desired effect. If no information is collected, how will anyone ever know?

However, the absence of the best information is not the same as no information at all. Enough work has been done to make certain patterns of disadvantage quite clear. Moreover, some of the issues are quite clear on only impressionistic evidence.

Employment

Black people have 'worse' jobs than whites and earn less. This, said the select committee in 1981, is 'the most important immediate cause that limits their chances in life'.

The 1976 PEP study, *The Facts of Racial Disadvantage*, found that there were big differences between the jobs that are done by white and black people. Only 8 per cent of West Indian men were in non-manual jobs – compared with 40 per cent of white men. Among men of Asian descent, 8 per cent of Pakistanis were in non-manual jobs, compared with higher proportions for Indian and Afro-Asian men (20 and 30 per cent respectively). But even those Asians who were successful in getting non-manual jobs found it hard to get the best posts at managerial level and above. Looking at the jobs league from the other end, the reverse pattern emerged. While 18 per cent of whites worked in the semi-skilled or unskilled manual labouring sector, the proportions among blacks were much greater – 26 per cent of Afro-Asians, 32 per cent of

West Indians, 36 per cent of Indians and 58 per cent of Pakistanis. Meanwhile at every level in the jobs league, blacks work more on shift work than whites; overall 31 per cent of black workers are on shifts, compared with 15 per cent of whites. There could be a connection between the low-skilled jobs in which West Indian men are disproportionately represented and the fact that a significantly higher proportion of West Indian women (74 per cent) are workers than in the population as a whole (43 per cent). So those who are quick to criticize the lack of parental control among West Indians need to take account of the work patterns of those parents.

To get a better job, get an education. That's how white workers in Britain have approached low status in the twentieth century, or so they like to think. Unfortunately, blacks have already tried this route – and found it no real answer. The PEP study provided glaring proof. In its survey, 79 per cent of whites with degree standard qualifications were in professional or managerial jobs – among blacks with the same qualifications it was only 31 per cent. It found that almost a quarter of blacks with degree standard qualifications were in manual jobs – with 3 per cent of them even in unskilled manual jobs.

In other words, the original pattern of black jobs, unskilled and semi-skilled, is still being reproduced, generations after the big influx of immigration. This is true of West Indians, who are concentrated in manufacturing and service jobs, like transport and building. It is also true of Asians, when compared with whites. In Bradford, for example, a town of between ten and twenty per cent black population, mostly Pakistanis, most still work in the lower reaches of the declining textile industry. Homeworking, often with very low wages, is also widespread among Asian and Cypriot women. But the pattern is not general in all trades. There are several major sectors of industry – not just grades within industry – where black workers are rarely employed. These sectors include mining, printing, shipbuilding, fishing and the energy industries, as well as more white-collar jobs. On the other hand, although black labour accounts for only about six per cent of the total workforce nationally, there are sectors where it forms a very sizeable element of the labour force. For instance, in night-time textile work in Lancashire and Yorkshire or in the National Health Service.

Inequality strikes even harder in the distribution of labour of any kind. Black people suffer higher rates of unemployment than whites and have done so consistently for the past decade or more. The 1971 census showed that unemployment among ethnic minority men in general was slightly higher than among the male population as a whole – 6.8 per cent compared with 4.9 per cent. But that general figure masked unemployment rates among particular groups that were much higher altogether. In the 15–20 age group the rate was already 20 per cent for West Indian men compared with 9 per cent for whites. There were also high rates among young West Indian women and among Pakistani and Bangladeshi women. As male unemployment rose through the 1970s, the rate for male blacks rose faster. Partly, this is because blacks are concentrated in the most vulnerable sectors of the economy. However, even within particular skill and age groups, blacks have been shown by researchers to be more likely to lose their jobs than whites. Although this is an area where the lack of proper monitoring provides maddeningly incomplete results, it is clear that blacks have been losing jobs faster than whites. Both the Home Affairs select committee and the Scarman Report accepted this as a fact. Local studies bear it out and evidence to the select committee made clear that it is widely believed to be the case even in areas where full research has not been carried out. In areas such as Brixton and Liverpool 8, unemployment among young blacks far exceeds national levels. In Brixton, Scarman found that an estimated 55 per cent of black males under nineteen were registered jobless – while the actual level is undoubtedly higher due to non-registration. Similar claims of between 50 and 60 per cent black jobless were made on Merseyside during the visit of the select committee in October 1980. Even if they were an overestimate at the time – as government officials claimed – the rapid rise in unemployment in the year before the Toxteth riots means that the rate was of that order. In Moss Side, the Hytner inquiry concluded that unemployment among young blacks could be as high as 70 per cent and 'among all under nineteen years it certainly appears to exceed 60 per cent'.[10]

There are strong indications that these extremely high levels of young black joblessness became entrenched in 1981. In the first place, the general level of unemployment maintained its very high level. More specifically, the demands of the labour market are moving away from unqualified labour (this is so whether or not unemployment remains at its 1981–2 levels). However, the Rampton report on West Indian children in schools, published in June 1981, found that they were more likely than white or Asian children to acquire poor or average exam qualifications. It found that 97 per cent of West Indians (compared with 82 per cent of Asians and 84 per cent of others) left school with less than five CSEs or O levels and that most of the 97 per cent did much worse than this. They are therefore at a further disadvantage in the competition for jobs.

The Home Affairs select committee pointed to a further problem. Recent studies of samples of school leavers and YOP trainees showed that in some cases West Indian school leavers were significantly better qualified than whites. The whites were nonetheless more likely to be employed. Qualified or not, it seems, West Indians stand to lose. This caused the select committee to draw some bleak conclusions: 'Taken together these developments may cause many young West Indians to reject with some bitterness the way of thinking and way of life both of the mainstream society and of their parents, and to find that this leaves them with nowhere to go.'[11]

Housing

To Lord Scarman the connection between housing and the riots was evident. Anyone who walks down Railton Road or Mayall Road will see, he reported, that the environment is in decay and that the housing situation is very serious. In the Housing Action Area covering those two streets, only twenty-two houses were officially regarded as in satisfactory repair in 1977. Despite a declining population, the borough of Lambeth is still 20,000 dwellings short of the target of a separate home for every household. The council waiting list numbered 18,000 households, and almost twice as many homeless families in the borough were black as white.

Many studies of racial disadvantage have emphasized the importance of housing in reflecting and determining the pattern of race relations. In the 1960s an official study of housing in London pointed to the problems faced by blacks in getting local authority housing. At the back of the queue, they were faced with either buying expensive property in poor condition or living as furnished tenants in equally low standard lodgings. Since then, patterns have changed. This reflects changes in the law (outlawing discrimination, for example, and squeezing the rented sector) as well as such factors as the passage of time which opens up access to council housing. Broadly, the present tenure pattern shows that while Asians are more likely than whites or West Indians to be owner-occupiers, West Indians are now more likely than the other groups to live in council housing and very few West Indians own their own houses.

Over the past decade a number of studies of race and council housing have shown that blacks get inferior places to live. In 1975, the Runnymede Trust showed that blacks were generally under-represented in council housing and that black tenants of the GLC were far more likely to be given prewar flats while whites were more likely to get the newer estates, comprised of houses and terraces. This accusation spurred the GLC to set up its own survey. To its consternation, this survey confirmed the Runnymede findings. Of its non-white tenants, 91 per cent lived in inner London, compared with 63 per cent of its white tenants. Just over half of non-whites lived in interwar flats; just under a quarter of whites lived in them. Some 4 per cent of non-whites lived in 'cottage' accommodation, but among whites the proportion was more than 25 per cent.

The GLC's response was that these discrepancies were not being caused by discrimination. The reason was that the housing allocation procedures were working in favour of whites. For example, the homeless (among whom blacks were over-represented) were more likely to accept anything they were offered, because of their urgent need. So they would congregate in the more available/less desirable housing. Nor did the process end there. Once an estate began to fill with blacks, the housing authorities began to assume that whites would refuse offers to live there. So they didn't even bother to offer these homes to whites. The GLC survey showed that it was a myth that blacks or whites choose to congregate in particular areas — only about half of each colour were allocated to the area of their choice.

Other local studies have found similar evidence of the way the administrative processes that are not intentionally discriminatory work in effect to the disadvantage of blacks (and of other important groups too). A survey in Islington in 1977 found that the 'points system' in council housing allocation was working against blacks. A similar pattern has been established in Bedford. Liverpool provides another good example of the colour-blind approach. The city council told the select committee in October 1980 that, although it kept no ethnic records of its tenants, it had adopted 'a range of policies and systems which are designed to deal with housing need, irrespective of the race, colour or creed of the persons concerned, and to do so in the fairest way'. Fine, wholly unoriginal words. However, a survey by the Merseyside Area Profile Group found the same sort of imbalance in the standard of council housing available for blacks and whites as Runnymede and the GLC had found in London. The difficulties confronting blacks were compounded by the local authority's tendency to place 'problem' families and individuals in these difficult-to-let properties. These Merseyside critics pointed to the misuse of discretion by housing managers to reinforce the disadvantage of blacks.

However, it would be misleading to suppose that proper ethnic monitoring would, in itself, have protected black tenants from these problems. The most recent study of racial disadvantage in housing has been based in Nottingham, which has carried out ethnic monitoring in its housing records since as long ago as 1968. The research officer of the local community relations council therefore examined local housing allocation between 1975 and 1978. He found that West Indians were more likely than other groups to have to get their council housing through the low priority waiting list system, that they were half as likely as whites to get transfers once they were in the system, that they were least likely to obtain houses and twice as likely as whites to be allocated to flats complexes. The biggest contrast of all was that West Indians were two and a half times more likely to be allocated to the most unpopular 'deck-access' maisonettes. Even if they were allocated to houses, blacks in general were likely to be given older, inner-city properties, while the majority of whites moved to houses outside the centre, needing less rehabilitation.[12]

Council housing, although proportionately more important for West Indians, is not the only housing issue in which black people face disadvantage. As noted above, Asians tend to be owner occupiers in greater proportion than either West Indians or whites. They have, however, tended to acquire small properties in areas where house prices are low. This has caused two problems. First, it bars them from access to council housing and, second, it has frequently meant that large Asian families are crowded into unsuitably small properties. Although some councils have tried to respond to the needs of Asian families, the mass of public and private housing units are undersized for large families. Finally, although race relations legislation has done much to outlaw discrimination against blacks in the private sector, indirectly discriminatory practices by estate agents, building societies and letting agencies have been shown still to exist and some direct discrimination has been uncovered by CRE investigations. In Birmingham, for example, Asian inner-city house buyers in the mid 1970s were disproportionately dependent upon bank loans at the highest interest rates (whites tended to prefer building society or local authority loans), leaving little finance available for rehabilitation of the old properties they were likely to buy. Research in Leeds has also suggested inadvertent discrimination against Asian buyers by building societies which are reluctant to lend in parts of the city preferred by Asians. In the private rented sector discrimination still occurs. A recent survey of bed and breakfast hotels in London showed that at least one in ten refused to take black tenants.

Next to jobs, housing is undoubtedly the most important problem facing any member of society. For most people, housing is the major item of expenditure while employment is largely a problem of income. So it is not surprising that discrimination or disadvantage in housing should be seen as particularly important. In so far as a general sense of inequality of opportunity, and of indignation against that inequality, was a cause of the riots, inequality in housing must be seen as very important too. A more specific connection is harder to support. As with job problems, the riot map is not coincident with specific housing problems. Some riots took place in areas of old, poor quality housing (Brixton, for instance), others in areas where greater rehabilitative efforts had been made (such as Bristol), others still in massively redeveloped areas (Moss Side). The riots in Leeds took place in a part of the city which contains many tree-lined streets. In general, the riot areas displayed such a combination of housing and planning factors that few generalizations can safely be made. As with some areas of highest unemployment, many of the country's worst housed areas saw little rioting. Above all, though, there is little evidence that the rioters who were mainly young had suffered direct experience of the difficulties of obtaining good council housing or a mortgage. This is not to say that there was no rubbing-off effect on the young of such difficulties as experienced by their parents and communities. Still less is it to say that housing problems have been overestimated; if anything, the reverse is true, certainly in analyses like the Hytner Report on Moss Side. Nevertheless, if riots are caused by the direct experience of those who rioted, inadequate housing cannot be accepted as a prime cause of what happened in Britain in 1981.

Education and services

On that basis, education would seem to be a far more relevant experience. As the Home Affairs select committee put it:

Disadvantage in education and employment are the two most crucial facets of racial disadvantage. They are closely connected. Without a decent education and the qualifications which such education alone can provide, a school leaver is unlikely to find the sort of job to which he aspires, or indeed any job. Conversely, pupils who learn from older friends of the degree of difficulty encountered in finding employment may well be discouraged from striving to achieve at school. In other words, there is no point in getting ethnic minority education right if we do not at the same time sort out racial disadvantage in employment and vice versa.[13]

This problem is easier to state than to answer − or so it would seem, judging by comparison of the enormous amount of study and discussion of ethnic minority education with the lack of progress. Nor should it be overlooked that there are many children in the schools who are not black and whose education nevertheless has not been 'got right'. Nor should the successes of black pupils be overlooked because they fail to fit a particular theory.

Measuring educational achievement in terms of exam success is controversial, but it is an important measure if for no other reason than that industry, the professions and higher education all use it as a principal criterion for selection. Concern about the 'under-achievement' of black pupils has a long history. In 1963, for instance, West Indian children in the London borough of Brent were found to be doing worse at reading, spelling and arithmetic. Since then, a number of other studies (mainly in London) pointed to West Indian under-achievement. A select committee report in 1977 called for a special study of the problem. In 1979, the Labour government set up a committee of inquiry under Anthony Rampton, chairman of Freeman's Mail Order, one of south London's largest employers, and an officer of the local community relations council in Lambeth. The inquiry was not, however, confined to the education of West Indians; it was asked to look at all ethnic minority education.

In June 1981, Rampton produced his interim report, dealing with West Indian children. A further study of Asian children is under way at the time of writing, chaired by Lord Swann, who replaced Rampton as head of the inquiry amid accusations that Rampton had been too 'pro-black' (though others claimed he was inefficient). Research commissioned by Rampton firmly re-emphasized the facts of under-achievement. As mentioned earlier, only 3 per cent of West Indians obtained higher O level grades or grade 1 CSEs, compared with 18 per cent of Asians and 16 per cent of all other school leavers. Similar under-achievement was revealed by research on CSE and GCE English and maths results. And, at A level GCE, only 2 per cent of West Indians gained passes, compared with 13 per cent of Asians and 12 per cent of other leavers. This picture is not unchallenged, though. One researcher, Geoffrey Driver, found some West Indians aged between twelve and sixteen doing better than their white counterparts and West Indian girls doing better than West Indian boys. The basis for his findings has been much criticized, by Rampton among others.

It needs to be emphasized, too, that other ethnic groups are under-achieving. The Inner London Education Authority has produced evidence that the worst problems, worse than West Indians, are faced by Turkish pupils. Nonetheless, there is clearly a special problem facing West Indians. The reasons for this under-achievement are many. The most common allegation by West Indians themselves is that racism is the cause. The relative success of Asians, however, means that this claim cannot be accepted without qualification. Rampton therefore concluded that while racism alone cannot explain the under-achievement of West Indians, it does play a major part in it. The most common way it works, he argued, was in the stereotyping of West Indian children as problematic, difficult or slow. By treating them in this racist way, the stereotyping becomes a self-fulfilling prophecy. Other reasons have also been suggested. Lack of contact between parents and schools was widespread in Brixton, found Scarman. Many West Indian parents blame lack of discipline in the schools. The select committee found that Jamaican schools maintained 'a degree of discipline . . . which had by and large disappeared from British education'. Parents' expectations of such regimes in British schools have been disappointed, which has led some to send their children to special community evening schools. Among radicals, criticism of the curriculum is strong. West Indian pupils, they argue, are alienated by being taught white culture, especially in history and the arts. Whether that criticism explains adequately the under-achievement in maths, though, must be doubtful. The select committee report placed more emphasis on the inadequacies of teacher training and the lack of black teachers. 'The presence on the staff of multi-racial schools of ethnic minority teachers is worth a mass of lessons in African or Asian history,' it concluded.[14]

Among the most potent fears of West Indian parents is

the belief that their children are too readily removed from mainstream schooling. For the reasons of mutual teacher–pupil low expectation already mentioned, West Indian children are said to be unfairly and disproportionately assessed as requiring special education and are frequently placed in schools for the educationally subnormal and in special disruptive units. Some hard evidence to support this claim does exist, but is now a decade old.

As with so many other aspects of racial disadvantage, the facts are not fully available, because of the failure to keep ethnic records. In the case of referrals to disruptive units, the limited evidence available to Rampton did not bear out the claims. However, the belief that this discrimination is practised is widespread and, as Scarman commented in another context, the belief is as important as the fact.

However, there are still two further areas of education service which could have a special effect in giving West Indians a stigma. The first is school careers advice. Ethnic minority school leavers are disproportionately dependent on careers advisers, and charges have been made that school leavers with high job ambitions are discouraged by careers advisers who attempt to steer them towards lower status job openings – even when these are less available due to recession. Again the evidence is contradictory, though Rampton accepted that the pernicious stereotyping of West Indian children produced cases of unintentional racism of this kind.

A particular problem caused by inadequate careers advice affects youngsters who aspire to an apprenticeship in a skilled manual trade (and research indicates that more young blacks have this aspiration than other young people). Recruitment to apprenticeships is generally limited to sixteen-year-olds so proper careers advice in the fifth form is vital. Without it, parental encouragement to stay on at school as a means of improving qualifications may be counter-productive. Blacks are specially dependent on such advice because whites have other assets in getting apprenticeships, such as family connections, which help them to get openings by word of mouth rather than open competition.

The second area is further education. It follows from school under-achievement that further education can be of disproportionate value to West Indians. This is not an ideal position but the facts show that few local authorities have put much thought or effort into providing this extra support. The select committee found evidence of lack of attention to providing special help for blacks in further education from such riot areas as Liverpool, Manchester and Bristol.

Evidence of the stereotyping of black youth by other agencies of local and central government confirms the picture. Social workers, probation officers and other public officials who deal with black individuals are trained in ways which give them little specialist knowledge of particular black needs. The Commission for Racial Equality's campaign on youth in multi-racial society has pointed the finger at many of these failings and at the lack of a coordinated approach which can reach out to support black youth rather than to drag them into self-reproducing dependency on a range of state institutions ranging from fostering through to prison. In 1978, the CRE and the Association of Directors of Social Services produced a survey which found that more than a third of social service departments provided no organized training of staff on the needs of black clients and fourteen had no black staff. They concluded that response to black needs was 'patchy, piecemeal and lacking in strategy'. Similar criticisms have been made of professional neglect of the ethnic minority dimension of work in the probation service.

As the select committee pointed out, the black unemployment and black under-achievement problems are mutually reinforcing and interdependent. To that extent, it is obviously difficult to isolate those factors to do with education which may create the disadvantage which may lead to the alienation which may lead to the riots.

Anyone who reads the literature on race and education is bound to be struck by the tiny amount of progress that has come from a mountain of reports and discussion. But even to the extent that grievances against such failures can be isolated, it is not clear that they had any particularly decisive or direct effect on the riots. Nor are all the educational problems of the inner cities only felt by blacks. If there is a connection with the riots it seems more likely to be the failure to get a job rather than the failure of the schools that is more important. But is even this true?

This is one aspect of the findings of two social psychologists, George Gaskell and Patten Smith. During the winter of 1979–80 they interviewed 240 black and white young Londoners between the ages of sixteen and twenty-five. Of the unemployed blacks and blacks in self-help groups in the survey, over half had no qualifications. Their aspirations were very conventional and straightforward: material possessions, a pleasant job, marriage, a happy family life. The jobs they would most like to do were in the skilled manual category. They blamed a mixture of factors: lack of will-power, lack of qualifications, being black, lack of jobs and not being clever enough.

Had they been 'alienated from white society', suggest Gaskell and Smith, they would surely have put more blame on external factors. Moreover the blacks in this survey held positive attitudes towards going to college, towards Jobcentres, careers offices and benefit offices, towards the school system and further education, towards the media and towards other British people. They were critical of the way these agencies worked in practice but, the authors said, 'The important thing is that we did not hear the type of global rejection which you might expect from the alienated – phrases like 'They are run by whites'.'[15]

What this research argued was not that there was not deprivation. On the contrary, it was of a high level. Nor did it argue that the young black Londoners felt no despair or hopelessness. Once more, the contrary was the case, and young blacks (even those with jobs) felt it more strongly than young whites. What it *did* show was that 'To describe these young men as alienated or estranged doesn't help you grasp the problem. The indiscriminate use of such popularized sociological concepts goes against an understanding of the social processes involved.' These young blacks, the survey suggested, viewed society positively and wished to succeed in it, but they felt they stood little chance of success. Perhaps the real key to understanding the links between young blacks and the riots came when Gaskell and Smith asked their respondents what stood between them and success. The spontaneous unbidden response of between 20 and 28 per cent of the deprived blacks was 'trouble with the law'.

6 The uprising:
The riots of July 1981

A much larger force than was sent to Bristol would be of no avail against a more general and well organized insurrection, aided and counternanced by other places in the same state.

Francis Place, 1832

During the early summer of 1981 the nation's attention was focused on Lord Scarman's inquiry into April's Brixton riots. It was a piece of live theatre with all the ingredients of good drama: a story of conflict on the streets the extent of which no one had experienced in their lifetimes, interpreted by lawyers, policemen, blacks and the odd vicar and journalist. Over the proceedings, which were played out in Lambeth town hall, presided the gaunt and lanky judge, Baron Scarman of Quatt in the county of Salop, the veteran troubleshooter of the British state. The instant empathy he established with the black community, particularly the Rastafarians of whom he seemed to make a special study, his tough talking at the police and his frequent witticisms made him something of an overnight hero in Brixton – or so many wanted to feel. The public sighed with relief. The violence was over, and out of the ashes some good, or at any rate some answers, might grow. The inquiry was cathartic. It was also good fun.

All that was shattered over the weekend of 3–5 July, almost three months after April's riots, when rioters took to the streets again, first in Southall, west London, and then in Toxteth, Liverpool. The violence turned out to be much worse than it had been in Brixton and led to rioting in many other parts of the country, in cities and even villages in eighteen areas, which lasted for more than ten days. Night after night the nation's television screens were illuminated with scenes of blazing buildings as police with riot shields confronted angry crowds. Petrol bombs were met with CS gas; there was an orgy of looting, and for a while it seemed that a sort of civil war had broken out. In mid July the violence vanished as quickly as it had come, only to blaze again in Liverpool at the end of the month for three days before the royal wedding. This spate of rioting led to the first and only death: David Moore was a victim of increasingly 'positive policing' and was killed in a hit-and-run incident after he had been knocked down by a police Land Rover. Two police officers were later charged with manslaughter. The marriage of Prince Charles to Lady Diana Spencer seemed to mark the end of the 'short, hot summer' as Britain settled into a rosy glow of patriotism and romance. But underneath, the divisions remained. If anything, July's rioting had added to the confusion about the causes of the violence; in some areas it left a legacy of even greater bitterness between police and community; and it gave a cruel irony to Lord Scarman's proceedings in Lambeth town hall. On the last day of phase one of his inquiry into the events of April's riots, violence returned to the streets of Brixton with more stone-throwing, petrol-bombing and looting.

Although this outbreak of rioting happened in the space of a few frenetic weeks and seemed to involve most parts of England, there were important differences in the circumstances which sparked off the violence in the different areas as well as in the people who took part. In Southall the cause was clearly racial, beginning as a fight between Asians and white skinheads; in Toxteth where, like Brixton, police–community relations were in a state of crisis, whites as well as blacks appeared to participate, and a small incident set off a great riot. The common form of the disorders quickly became pitched battles between youth and the police, but they overwhelmingly broke out in multi-racial inner-city areas where black people share the poverty of whites – only much more acutely.

Southall

The first explosion came in Southall, a suburb in the west of London containing 30,000 Asians, traditionally considered to be a relatively law-abiding community. Asian youth had, however, been growing increasingly militant (see Chapter 3) over the years as a result of such events as the death of Gurdip Singh Chaggar at the hands of white youths in 1976 and the violent confrontation with police in 1979 when Blair Peach was killed. Their fear of the National Front and of white skinheads was very real, because Asians had physically suffered at their hands. On 3 July a bunch of 300 skinheads was bussed into the area from London's East End for an 'Oi' concert at the Hamborough Tavern. Four of them entered a shop and began to abuse the woman shopkeeper. They smashed a window and advanced along Southall's main street, The Broadway, breaking more windows as they went. Asian youth reacted strongly. Hundreds gathered suddenly around the pub containing the skinheads and the police tried to intervene by forming a cordon around the Hamborough Tavern. The Asians were incensed at the idea that the police might be protecting the skinheads, and serious violence broke out. Molotov cocktails were thrown, the pub was set alight, police riot shields appeared and a major battle ensued. Perhaps because the police were stuck in the middle of two warring sides, they took the brunt of the stone-throwing. Sixty-one policemen were injured but there were even more civilian casualties, perhaps as many as seventy. That night twenty-one arrests were made.

The next day an Asian youth in Southall was heard to shout at the police, 'Brixton was nothing.' The remark was revealing and suggested that the Southall riot became as much a battle with the police as with the skinheads. To that extent it resembled what was to happen elsewhere. But unlike the other major riot-hit areas, Southall was not an inner-city area with high crime levels. Its Asian community is relatively deprived, compared with its white neighbours, and faces racial discrimination and higher unemployment, but at levels nowhere near as high as black Liverpudlians.

Liverpool

Liverpool 8, or Toxteth as it is also known, is another matter. There decades of neglect of the well-established black community had fuelled decades of racial disadvantage to create a throughly deprived community. The House of Commons committee investigating these conditions, whose report was written before the riots, commented:

Racial disadvantage in Liverpool is in a sense the most disturbing case of racial disadvantage in the United Kingdom, because there can be no question of cultural problems of newness of language, and it offers a grim warning to all of Britain's cities that racial disadvantage cannot be expected to disappear by natural causes.

Conditions in Liverpool 8, which houses most of the city's 30,000 blacks, were well documented. The Think Tank had produced a report on it shortly before the rioting, which remains unpublished, in which it warned of the danger of increasing social tension, and there had been many surveys previously. Unemployment among the Afro-Caribbean population, about half of whom are 'black British', is estimated as high as sixty per cent. Many of these people had lived in the area for generations, the descendants of African seamen and local white women, yet their prospects appeared worse than those of blacks in other cities who had arrived in Britain much more recently. The Liverpool Black Organization has said: 'The chances of finding a job in Liverpool if you are black, a school leaver, and live in Liverpool 8, are practically nil.'

Black Liverpudlians under-achieve in the education system and play very little part in established city life: there are few black teachers, only two black school governors, and only 169 blacks working for the city council which employs 22,000 people, the largest employer in Liverpool.[1] Few blacks are to be seen driving buses or shopping in the city centre. Moreover the local authority had, until the riots, pursued a passive colour-blind policy whereby it said it did not discriminate but had done nothing positive to help blacks to train or to apply for jobs. It had not even declared itself an 'equal opportunity employer'. White people shared in the poverty of the area as well; they were part of the seriously deteriorating relationship between the police and the Toxteth community, but it was black–police relations which were particularly critical. 'If this relationship between the police and the black community is not rectified, then the future can only present us with even more problems and more Bristols,' the Liverpool Black Organization warned before the violence.

On the same night as Southall erupted, Toxteth experienced the spark which was to set it alight. A black youth was chased by police and fell off his motorbike when they caught him. He was pulled away from the police by a gathering crowd of forty black youths and spirited off in the same way as Bailey had been in Brixton. Two hours of fighting followed that night after which both the police and young Liverpudlians were prepared for more. There is some indication that what followed was premeditated.[2] On Saturday 4 July an anonymous telephone caller reported a stolen car in Toxteth. Three officers went to investigate and were promptly showered with stones and bottles. Within minutes a crowd of 150 black and white youths took over Upper Parliament Street, the area's main artery. Cars were overturned and set on fire, shops burned and others looted. Police, lined up behind riot shields, faced groups of masked men hurling missiles and petrol bombs. At one point a masked gang, armed with pickaxe handles, attacked a BBC television team, capturing and destroying a £12,000 camera. Violence raged throughout the night, ending at 7 a.m. on Sunday after the police staged a baton charge.

The real crescendo came on Sunday night when the 800 policemen were totally overwhelmed by hundreds of black and white youths and resorted to the use of CS gas, the first time it has been used against rioters on mainland Britain. The police admitted during the night that the rioting was out of control and called in reinforcements from Lancashire, Cheshire and Greater Manchester. Rioters commandeered milk floats, a stolen fire engine and a cement mixer and drove them straight into police lines. They were armed with every conceivable weapon, including lengths of scaffolding which they thrust at the riot shields like medieval knights. One policeman was speared in the head by a spiked six-foot railing. As a blanket of smoke rose into the sky, the rioters pressed forward yelling 'stone the bastards' and parading their trophies – police helmets and riot shields. At one point they managed to seize a fire hose which the police had been using on them and turn it on the officers. Faced with this attack, the police had no alternative but to retreat, leaving behind them a no-go area open to a crowd of jubilant looters. 'Police have abandoned parts of Liverpool to a mob,' said David Alton, the local Liberal MP. 'Scenes like this can never have been seen in a British city under the rule of law this century.'

The looting was almost as devastating. Children as young as four and five joined in and were egged on by their parents. 'They brought shopping carts to ship it all out,' said one eye witness. 'Refrigerators, dryers, you name it. I even saw one lady hold up a piece of carpet and ask if anyone knew whether it was 6 ft by 4 ft.' As the rioting continued and the fires threatened to engulf the Princes Park Geriatric Hospital, a temporary truce was called to evacuate the hospital of its ninety-six patients. They were bundled into taxis or ambulances while the crowd held fire. During this lull Kenneth Oxford, Merseyside's chief constable, was able to reach for the CS gas.

He said that by 1 a.m. the police had been subjected to three hours of attack of unprecedented scale and ferocity. 'The single offensive tactic we possessed, the baton charge, proved increasingly ineffective,' he said in his report on the violence. 'Our principal strategy, of containing the rioters by forming lines of police officers behind riot shields, resulted in increasing numbers of police casualties.' On this one night 282 officers were injured, 229 of whom needed hospital treatment and 46 had to be kept in hospital.

The chief constable said he was worried that the rioters might try to attack the city centre, a suggestion which is vigorously rejected by the Liverpool 8 defence committee, who say the crowds were dispersing. So at 2.15 a.m. he gave the historic order that tear gas should be used, in the full knowledge that this breached Home Office guidelines which restricted use of the gas against armed and besieged criminals only. The gas had the desired effect – it scattered the crowds – but in the process caused injury, some serious, to five men. This only came to light twelve days later in a *New Statesman* report which revealed that the fifty-nine small gas projectiles fired should never have been used to control crowds. They were designed to flush out dangerous or armed men by piercing doors or windows, and the instructions that came with them said they should not be fired at people because they could cause serious injury. (The manufacturers describe them as lethal cartridges). At least two people were seriously injured in Toxteth and required operations in hospital; one man was hit twice – once in the chest, 'gouging an egg-sized hole', and once in the back.

The following day the Home Secretary supported the police action, saying they had been right to use the gas and had no alternative. When the *New Statesman* revelations appeared it was assumed that William Whitelaw had not known that the safety warning had been breached. It later transpired that he did, though he made no reference to it.

Merseyside's chief constable, Kenneth Oxford, set up

his own inquiry into the use of the gas, in which he defended the decision to use CS as 'a correct use of the minimum force which was necessary and available'. He said he was fully aware that the cartridges should not be used again against rioters. In this instance they had been fired by highly trained marksmen and had not been aimed directly at the rioters but against hard flat surfaces and cars which were being driven at police lines, he said. 'The information available to me indicates that the injuries which occurred were likely to have been caused by ricochets or erratic flight following impact.' Mr Oxford's report made no mention of the manufacturers' warnings on the CS gas canisters. Labour members of the local police authority were thoroughly dissatisfied. The Home Secretary, however, reiterated his support for the decision to use the gas, which he said was necessary and justified.

The violence continued on Monday 6 July, although it did not reach the ferocious intensity of Sunday because the police, in a massive show of strength, quelled it more quickly. A frightened Liverpool city council asked for troops to be placed on standby (a request which was turned down) and traders began to count the cost of the worst violence this century. Perhaps the most celebrated building to be destroyed was the Liverpool Racquet Club, described by one local as a 'private club for the rich – solicitors and bankers'. It was an obvious target for class resentment and was burnt to a cinder.

As in Brixton the hunt was on immediately for outside political activists who, it was suggested, had orchestrated the violence. Without them it was felt such rioting would not have taken place. There were reports of cockney and Scottish voices being heard in the crowd of rioters, and such suspicions were further raised when leaflets by the Labour Party Young Socialists, defending those arrested and calling for the dropping of all charges, were distributed on the Monday. Labour MPs in the House of Commons disassociated themselves from them. Evidence of outside agitation was thin but it was alleged that the rioting was organized by a group of young men masked in balaclava helmets, IRA style. The police talked afterwards of guerrilla tactics having been used by motorcycle gangs who lured the police into housing estates where they were attacked by stone-throwing mobs of mainly black youths. According to the police's figures, a total of 781 policemen were injured during the rioting, and there were 1070 recorded crimes and 705 arrests.

Manchester

As the police licked their wounds, and condemned the 'hooligans' and their parents for not keeping them indoors at night, more street violence broke out on Tuesday night in a similar district, Moss Side in Manchester. There was fighting in London too, in a relatively salubrious northern suburb, Wood Green, which has in common with Moss Side a large modern shopping centre. The Wood Green disorder, created by a crowd of three to four hundred youths who went on a looting and smashing spree, was dismissed immediately as an attempt to imitate the rioting elsewhere. Moss Side was more serious and led to five nights of rioting.

As an inner-city area containing a sizeable West Indian population, whose youth suffer from high unemployment and social stress, Moss Side was expected to riot once other urban areas had gone up in flames, or so the Hytner Report thought. The report of the inquiry into Manchester's disturbances, chaired by Benet Hytner QC, concluded:

In our view the cause of the disturbances was that it was expected, by reason of beliefs based in the main on myth, that trouble was inevitable in Moss Side, and that there were sections of the Moss Side population who were ready and willing to fulfil these expectations.

This phenomenon came to be termed 'copycat rioting', which is not to suggest that similar underlying conditions creating a disposition towards violent protest did not exist in these areas, but simply that the rioting elsewhere was the spark.

A preliminary critique of the Hytner Report, *The Hytner Myths*, is scathing about this analysis. It says that black people took to the streets because they suffered the same

> brutal realities at the hands of the police as the blacks of Brixton and Toxteth. If there was a 'chain reaction' it was one which inspired courage: people who might not otherwise have openly protested were inspired to do so by the example of others . . .
> The factor of importance is not the existence of a black population per se, but the fact that wherever a black population lives certain police attitudes and styles are likely to follow.

At 2.30 a.m. on the night of Tuesday (7–8 July) after Moss Side's Nile Club closed a crowd of mainly black men spilled out on to the street. A brick was thrown at a shop window and the trouble spread as other shops were attacked with petrol bombs. The Hytner Report suggested that the violence stemmed from white people taunting young blacks about how they were slower than blacks in Brixton and Toxteth because they had not yet rioted. It concluded that this incident was therefore not planned. The rioting was put down in about an hour but returned during the next day – Wednesday – this time with much greater force. The police had decided to adopt a 'low profile', a move suggested by community leaders who met with senior officers that day, but violence was expected and the shopping centre closed in mid-afternoon. During the day crowds gathered on the grassy mound between Princess Road and Quinney Crescent. Four of these people, later arrested by police, came from Cardiff, Liverpool, Glossop and London. (The outsiders were therefore a small minority and there was no evidence of planning by any organization as the police had suggested.) Violence did not break out until after 10 p.m. when youths began to smash up shops. Then the crowd, which had grown to more than 1000, attacked the police station, overturning cars and causing considerable damage. Serious disorder was curbed by 4 a.m.

Manchester police, who had been badly mauled in the Toxteth rioting where they had gone to help out their colleagues at the weekend, were not prepared to tolerate this level of violence. Their chief constable, James Anderton, immediately decided to reverse his 'low profile' policy and to seize the initiative. He talked about the previous night's rioting as 'close to anarchy' and guerrilla warfare and said the storming of the police station was 'an astonishing and well-executed attack' aided by spotters and CB radios. There was to be no more soft policing because community leaders could not control the community. Instead the rioters would be dispersed in lightning sweeps by high-speed, mobile police units, a tactic employed with success in Ulster. This is exactly what happened on Thursday 9 July, the third night of rioting, when fifty-four vans swept through Moss Side charging at crowds with their back doors hanging open. Inside were small bands of officers dressed in new protective crash helmets who were able to make arrests and break up the crowds. The new tactics were successful but they left behind fearful memories in Moss Side.

The Hytner Report concluded:

We found a great deal of evidence, much of which came from apparently reliable and respectable people, white and black, that many of the policemen in Moss Side in vehicles on July 9 were actively spoiling for trouble with young blacks. There was evidence of police vans touring the area with officers leaning out of the back shouting racial insults at black youths and taunting them to come and fight.

Eleven community workers said later in a letter to the *Guardian* that the police were 'uniformed hooligans beating their trancheons against their vehicles, and chanting slogans such as "Nigger, nigger, nigger – oi, oi, oi!" '[3] Serious allegations were made to *The Times* about black youths, including a youth club leader, being beaten up by the police. A local white GP said he had seen injuries to civilians which he never expected to see in England; and Dipak Nandy, a race relations expert who now lives in

Manchester, called the violence on Thursday a police riot of the kind he had witnessed in Chicago in 1968.

There was more rioting in Manchester on the Friday night as stone-throwing youths attacked Moss Side police station for the second time. They were repulsed by a large force of officers in riot helmets. The violence finally ceased on 11 July. After five days of rioting twenty-seven policemen were injured, hundreds fewer than in Liverpool, 22 police cars damaged and £5000 of damage was done to Moss Side police station. There were 241 arrests, almost half of which were under the Public Order Act; the majority of those arrested were white, unemployed and aged between seventeen and twenty-four. Forty-eight were aged under seventeen.

The rioting spreads

By the time Moss Side was peaceful, violence had broken out all over the country and the Home Secretary was considering the use of water cannon. He announced that the government would bring in a new law to require parents to pay the fines of children under seventeen. During the week of the Moss Side eruption the violence spread to other parts of Greater Manchester (leading to a grand total of 475 arrests in that police authority) and there was rioting in areas of Liverpool outside Toxteth. By the end of the week London was affected, and rioting broke out again in Brixton, on the last day of phase one of Lord Scarman's inquiry; it also broke out in at least half a dozen other parts of the metropolis as crowds of youths smashed shop windows, looted and overturned cars. Woolwich, Lewisham, Stoke Newington, Balham and Fulham were affected.

On Friday 10 July, one of the worst days of widespread rioting, trouble was reported in nine towns apart from London – Reading, Ellesmere Port, Nottingham, Sheffield, Wolverhampton, Hull, Preston, Slough and in Handsworth, the multi-racial area of Birmingham which observers were predicting would be next on the list despite (or perhaps because of) its impressive community policing experiment. This widespread violence led to shopkeepers boarding up whole areas of London and other cities in anticipation of further disturbance over the weekend. In many cases their fears were justified. Urban communities had begun to live under siege with rumour spreading like wildfire and the police quite unable to counter the hysteria. Much of the violence on Friday night was of a relatively small scale but petrol bombs were thrown in Brixton and in Dalston, east London. By 1 a.m. the Metropolitan police had made 231 arrests and there were more than forty injuries to officers, including a fractured skull and a broken leg.

It was not only Brixton which erupted again on 10 July. Southall was also ablaze with stone-throwing crowds preventing a fire engine reaching burning cars. The police described the behaviour of Asian and black youths there as 'mindless unprovoked hooliganism'. In Brixton rioting raged for seven hours and was sparked off by the arrest of Lloyd Coxsone, a Rastafarian and well-known local black businessman, who had been trying to cool tension between young blacks and police in the area. He had approached policemen who were arresting a man and pulling his hair. According to Mr Coxsone the police promptly set upon him. 'They dragged me into a shop and hit me with a truncheon,' he explained. 'I had handcuffs on and they beat me up. When other policemen came they dragged me into a van by my feet and hit me with a truncheon.' After Mr Coxsone was released that night he went out among the rioters and succeeded in quelling some of the violence. The police thanked him. The same day the Home Secretary announced a one-month ban on public processions in London because of a large march planned by the Anti-Nazi League to mark the funeral of the Khan family who were burnt to death in east London in a racialist attack. It was felt that serious violence would have erupted otherwise and there was also concern about two National Front marches scheduled for 10 July. That day the *New Standard*'s front page splashed with a story of how Special Branch police officers were searching for four masked men who had been spotted at the riots in Southall, Toxteth and Moss Side. The Metropolitan police press office said it knew nothing about that and, as far as it was concerned, the allegation was untrue.

Against this backdrop, disturbances continued to break out in English towns and cities all over the weekend. Violence flared again in most of the cities which had seen trouble on the Friday night but it also spread, notably to four cities in Yorkshire, Bradford, Halifax, Huddersfield and Leeds, and to normally quieter spots such as Cirencester in Gloucestershire, where a firebomb was thrown at a police car, and Knaresborough in Yorkshire. Police and politicians seemed to be agreed that the new wave of violence was sheer hooliganism and that the search for underlying causes should be called off. (There had been similar 'copycat' violence in Finsbury Park and two other areas of London on Easter Monday after the main Brixton riots which led to 100 arrests and 101 casualties. Again there was a tendency to see these events as sheer hooliganism.) It also became clear on the weekend of 10–12 July that many of the rioters were thoroughly enjoying themselves. Many young people described the riots as 'daft' or a 'laugh'. A mining apprentice in Yorkshire told the *Sunday Times*:

Rioting's just like gang-fighting really. You've got one set of lads chucking bricks at another set of lads who're wearing a daft uniform and they're chucking bricks back at you. But with all this unemployment it had to come, hadn't it? It gave them a reason so they went and kicked hell out of the coppers.[4]

On Saturday night disturbances broke out in Lancashire with more than 500 youths in Blackburn breaking shop windows and with disorder in Preston, Blackpool and Fleetwood. As a result at least 147 people were charged. In the Midlands rioting continued over the weekend. On Saturday there was more violence in Handsworth, Birmingham, and order was restored only after police in riot gear had staged baton charges. In Wolverhampton petrol bombs were thrown by multi-racial gangs and a total of 200 people were arrested in these two cities. There was trouble in Leicester where rioters were said to be using CB radios and youngsters on bicycles to coordinate attacks on the police. There were also disturbances on Saturday night at Southampton, Portsmouth, Luton, Derby, Nottingham and Sheffield. In Yorkshire, Leeds saw the worst violence after pitched battles between youths and helmeted policemen which began shortly after 2.30 a.m. on Sunday morning. The disturbances were concentrated in the Chapeltown area and lasted for five hours, with cars being overturned and set on fire, petrol bombs thrown and shop windows smashed.

The violence did not stop on the Sunday. There was more trouble in Leicester, Huddersfield and in Battersea Park, London, where a crowd of roller skaters attacked and injured three policemen. The most serious violence occurred in Leicester where police behind riot shields met large gangs of rioters wielding petrol bombs. Acid was also thrown and there were thirty arrests. Other towns suffering from the weekend rioting included High Wycombe, Birkenhead, Aldershot and Gloucester. Margaret Thatcher, the Prime Minister, was so concerned about the rash of rioting that she spent eight hours through Saturday night with the Metropolitan police, visiting Brixton police station and talking to senior officers at Scotland Yard. She was reported to have consulted the Home Secretary several times over the weekend and to have briefed him on the conclusions she had reached after her session with the police.

Newspaper reports on Monday 13 July gave some indication of ministerial thinking. Reading between the lines it looked very much as though Thatcher was pushing for tough new measures to bring the rioters to justice quickly (specially convened magistrates' courts were in fact sitting at the weekend), revive the Riot Act in some way and limit the right to trial by jury. It looked as though she was dragging a reluctant William Whitelaw behind her. It was clear that ministers regarded the first round of rioting – in Brixton and Toxteth – as real riots and the subsequent spread as pure hooliganism requiring short, sharp action. Whitelaw commented: 'It is criminal hooliganism from many people who have no motives other than simple greed. The causes of that are just the same as the causes of crime and there is a good deal of copycat activity.' The *Daily Telegraph* reported that the Queen was very worried and had called for a report.

Thatcher also made a lightning visit to Liverpool in which she promised strong support for the police and more riot equipment if necessary. The government reaction appeared increasingly hard-nosed. Mr Whitelaw said he was making army camps available for people arrested during the riots because of overcrowding in the prisons, and that the police could have armoured vehicles if they wanted them. And Monday saw another night of rioting.

The Times decided in a leader that the arguments in favour of a modified and circumscribed return of the Riot Act were persuasive. Senior police officers went to Ulster to learn how to quell violent street riots, and while they were there Mrs Thatcher said that all chief constables could use water cannon, CS gas and rubber bullets if they wanted to. Mr Whitelaw echoed this later. The army gave the police a demonstration of how to use water cannon.

Just as it looked at though there might be a lull in the violence – in fact there was one peaceful night on Tuesday 14 July – rioting returned to the streets of Brixton, after a police raid on eleven houses in Railton Road, the front-line. A total of 176 officers were used in the raid, with 391 standing by, and the police said they were acting on a tip-off from a normally reliable source that petrol bombs were being stored in the houses. Armed with warrants for bomb-making equipment and illegal drinking the police smashed into the houses. According to the inhabitants, who later showed journalists around their damaged homes, the police wantonly smashed windows, lavatories, television sets and furniture with axes and crowbars. No bombs were found, although some days later the police had the compensation of finding a crate of bottles, with evidence that they were being prepared as bombs, on nearby waste ground. Local inhabitants were furious and it was also understood that Whitelaw was very angry with the police. The raid had led to about £5000 of damage, which was met by the police, and to another night of rioting. Afterwards five people were charged with possession of cannabis and one with obstruction. The police action was seen as a revenge for the April riots by the black community, particularly because it was directed at the little pocket of houses which forms the heart of the front-line. Much of Railton Road's criminal element lives here. It is where the illegal drinking, gambling and drug dealing takes place and where the police say stolen goods are disposed of.

An immediate inquiry was set up by the Metropolitan police commissioner. Three and a half months later it reported that damage was caused by officers in gaining entry to and searching the houses but that 'most' of this was 'unavoidable'. This suggests that some of it could have been avoided. The report added that the raid was fully justified, given that it took place at a time of civil disorder. It did not address itself to whether the raid was justified in view of the rioting it caused. Formal complaints were made against police officers in connection with two of the houses and the papers were referred to the Director of Public Prosecutions, but he decided not to take action.

The renewed rioting in Brixton on 15 July marked the end of the most serious riots of the short hot summer. The following day the House of Commons had its long-awaited debate on the disorders during which the Home Secretary produced a much more measured performance than might have been expected from the previous week's repressive noises. The preoccupation with maintaining law and order and with attributing the violence to criminality was modified. For a start, Michael Heseltine, the Environment Secretary, was appointed to head a task force to look at the causes of and possible solutions to the rioting in Merseyside. The Home Secretary thereby showed that the government recognized the relevance of social and economic factors, and he said as much. He also made clear that he had won the battle in the Conservative Party over the introduction of repressive emergency legislation to control rioters. He said he would not be hurrying through a new Riot Act to make it an offence for people to be out on the streets after they had been told to disperse by the police. This idea would be examined, in consultation with the Lord Chancellor, the Attorney General and the Lord Advocate. There were already wide-ranging powers in common law to deal with these circumstances, he added. What the enigmatic Mr Whitelaw was saying apparently was that he might or might not introduce a new Riot Act some time in the future after proper reflection. The speech had something for everyone.

By making the right noises at the right time Mr Whitelaw did something to salvage the government's rather battered reputation. His remarks earlier in the week that chief constables could use water cannon, CS gas and rubber bullets if they wished were interpreted as not as hard-nosed as some people thought. They were a sop to rebellious Tory backbenchers, but the Home Secretary knew perfectly well that most chief constables remained reluctant to use this hardware. His determination that detained rioters should be sent to army camps pleased Conservative backbenchers because they thought it represented a new get-tough policy. It did not. The camps had to be used because the prisons were full. Instead of falling victim to almost two weeks of virtual civil war, therefore, the Thatcher government emerged severely bruised but not beaten. The appointment of Heseltine as minister for Merseyside was derided at the time but it did indicate that the Cabinet was worried about butter as well as guns. Heseltine, a rather unlikely saviour of Toxteth, managed to convey that he cared about Liverpool and so also did Prince Charles who expressed a wish to help Toxteth financially and later visited the area shaking hands and embracing people. Whitelaw and Thatcher had not achieved this in their visits to the city. The Home Secretary had not even got out of his car.

Last of the riots

While Michael Heseltine was in Liverpool, rioting erupted again, lasting from 26 to 28 July, and there was also a night of trouble in Keswick in the Lake District between 1000 'mods' and the police. The three vicious nights of rioting in Toxteth were blamed on continual police harassment of the black community by the Liverpool 8 Defence Committee, set up after the riots. After the final night of rioting, when a young man was killed and another seriously injured, Margaret Simey, who chaired Merseyside's police committee, said in a celebrated statement that conditions in the area were so bad that people ought to riot. 'I would regard people as apathetic if they didn't riot,' she said, adding that the police were out of control.

Police and rioters were in effect at war, with the rioters paying off scores which had accumulated for years and the police getting their own back for having been so humiliated earlier in the month. Howard Parker, a Liverpool University lecturer and expert on police–adolescent relations, said: 'In the earlier riots in Toxteth the police got hammered. They were seen to get hammered. Last week they were instinctively out for revenge.' It was hard luck for people who got caught in the crossfire between the two groups. Injuries were serious and some well-documented cases emerged of deliberate police violence towards innocent people. But the rioters were as vicious. They poured boiling water over police officers and dropped a television set on them from a block of high-rise flats. A total of thirty-two police officers were treated in hospital as a result of these riots and one suffered a fractured skull. A taxi-driver, Albert Fitzpatrick, suffered near-fatal injuries after he had been set on by five men who appeared from behind a barricade in Upper Parliament Street, Toxteth, on 27 July. After being beaten up in his cab, he drove away, swerved and hit a tree. He had to undergo an emergency brain operation and was left semi-paralysed and epileptic.

Merseyside police had borrowed the hot-pursuit tactics used to such effect by James Anderton's force in Moss Side. Police Land Rovers were deployed to charge at groups of rioters, scatter them and arrest troublemakers. Chief constable Kenneth Oxford justified the switch in the following way: 'To put it crudely the people have spat in my face. It is the only way that I can protect them from themselves.' Police in Toxteth went about their task with enthusiasm. It was to have fatal consequences. Two youths were rammed by Land Rovers: Paul Conroy, aged eighteen, suffered a broken back after the vehicle mounted the pavement and crushed him against a brick pillar. He was dragged off to a police van and, as he was bundled inside, an officer was heard to shout, 'Make way for the nignog, boys.'[5] (The youth was white.) When he regained consciousness he said that officers beat him up. After Conroy's injuries became known, the chief constable said: 'They can see the vehicles coming and they know what will happen if they get in the way.'

David Moore, aged twenty-three, and disabled from a childhood accident, was not able to get out of the way. On the night of 28 July he was struck by a police van which was pursuing a group of rioters, and his death attracted considerable publicity. Two Merseyside police officers were charged with manslaughter but acquitted after a short trial in April 1982. The driver of the van was found not guilty by a unanimous verdict of the jury and his companion was acquitted at the direction of the judge. The judge told the jury that conviction required proof of a very high degree of negligence going beyond carelessness and dangerous driving. At the time, however, the death contributed to tension between police and community in Liverpool.

There were repeated calls for the removal of Kenneth Oxford, Merseyside's chief constable, including one from the *Economist*, and police behaviour came under increasing attack, particularly from the Labour-controlled police committee and from black spokesmen. The events of late July fuelled the great debate which had begun to rage nationally about the role of the police and the breakdown in relations between the police and the multi-racial communities of Britain's inner cities.

The cost – and the punishment

Police authorities throughout the country were faced with a massive bill under the Riot Damages Act. A total of eleven authorities were confronted with claims amounting to more than £17m for damage to buildings and their contents in July. That sum does not include the cost of damage to police vehicles and equipment or the damage to cars belonging to members of the police. As in Bristol, after the 1980 riot, these claims were met very slowly because of the steps that had to be taken to ensure that they were not being duplicated, that they fell within the scope of the Act and that they were not inflated. People are compensated for the value of what they have lost, not for its replacement, and no account is taken of loss of trade. If Bristol is anything to go by, few of the sums claimed will be paid out in full. The damage in Liverpool was much worse than anywhere else – about seven hundred claims were made amounting to £11m, compared with a £1m bill in Manchester. The government estimated that in total the damage caused by July's rioting was probably nearer £45m and offered to help the worst-hit authorities such as Liverpool with meeting the bill.

Meanwhile the 3000 and more people arrested as a result of the rioting in July and in Brixton in April were being processed through the courts. Many were dealt with quickly in the special magistrates' courts convened for the purpose in the first few days of media and political hysteria following the height of the disturbances over the weekend of 10 to 12 July. On Monday 13 July there were loud calls for rioters to be brought to book fast, with the *New Standard* commenting: 'The looters and petrol bombers should find themselves before a magistrate within days, if not hours – and facing exemplary sentences.' In many cases this is what happened. As a result riot defendants were remanded in custody for relatively trivial charges with implied threats that if they pleaded guilty their cases would be tried much more quickly. It was clear that short cuts were being taken and that some magistrates saw their job as helping the police rather than administering justice. Much of this abuse has been well documented in the *Legal Action Group Bulletin* which concluded in an editorial in its August issue that normal judicial principles and standards were being disregarded:

Overheated press statements, many of them generated by members of the Government who should know better, demanding quick justice, riot courts, new riot laws, heavy deterrent sentences and prison camps are inimical to the cool and orderly dispensation of justice.

The *LAG Bulletin* said that some magistrates had refused guilty pleas and that the police had refused to proceed with cases and objected to bail. Prosecutors privately admitted that they were ready to proceed in cases but had been instructed not to. The implication is that this was to muscle defendants to plead guilty. At the same time there were newspaper reports of heavy prison sentences on people charged with offences for the first time. An unemployed eighteen-year-old from Islington was jailed for thirty days for stealing a video recorder from the back of a van, and a three-month sentence was imposed on a painter and decorator from Tottenham for stealing a pair of trousers from a shop in Brixton Road. Another eighteen-year-old youth received three months gaol after he admitted stealing three shirts. It is difficult to escape the conclusion that the rioters were treated differently from normal defendants. At the same time magistrates were being put under a great deal of political pressure and suddenly had an enormous number of defendants to deal with. They reacted predictably.

After the first few weeks of rough justice and quick sentencing the number of riot cases being heard in the courts slowed right down so that no very clear national picture had emerged of sentencing patterns at the time of writing. Ten days after the July disorders more than two hundred people had been dealt with for their part in them. The police used summary charges, particularly 'threatening words and behaviour', rather than charges which would enable defendants to elect trial by jury. The exception was Liverpool where many people were charged with theft. The police had apparently learnt the lesson of Bristol, and riot charges were not brought. It was quickly clear that magistrates were not reluctant to use their maximum sentencing powers of six months' imprisonment and that much of the evidence was based on police identification alone. Of 220 cases analysed by *The Times*[6] there were sixty immediate prison sentences, and fifty youths, aged sixteen to nineteen, had been sent to detention centres for up to six months. The rest were given suspended sentences or fines ranging from £10 to £500, or were bound over to keep the peace.

Some examples give an idea of what was happening. In Leeds a 38-year-old shop assistant was imprisoned for fifty-six days (after having spent seven days in custody) for threatening behaviour. In Chester, gaol sentences of eight and four years were imposed on two men in their early twenties for unlawful assembly and for possession of a fire bomb. Judge Robin David was quoted as saying:

I am very distressed at the way the media dealt with the riots in Toxteth. One sees the media spending all its time interviewing people justifying the disturbances but no time interviewing people who have been absolutely terrified.

There were special problems in certain courts. In Nottingham, where more than one hundred people were arrested, three solicitors drew up a report in which they said they were not allowed to see their clients before they appeared in court and that custodial sentences were imposed without legal representation or social inquiry reports. The report went to Nottingham county council which announced that it would give legal aid to those in gaol who wished to appeal against imprisonment. The *LAG Bulletin* explained that on 13 July about eighty-five defendants in custody appeared before the justices.[7] Three extra benches had been appointed to deal with them and all consisted of magistrates known for their firm views. Before the defendants were brought in a police inspector made a speech in court urging heavy sentences. None of the defendants saw a duty solicitor before their court appearance; they were put in the dock in quick succession and most pleaded guilty. According to LAG the chairman of the bench would announce that the court was considering a custodial sentence and asked whether the defendant wanted an adjournment:

There was no attempt to explain in plain language what this meant and most decided to be dealt with on the spot – perhaps influenced by an announcement from the chairman that 'This bench and not only this bench, the whole bench, will only be prepared to consider bail in exceptional circumstances.'

Many defendants had already spent fifty hours in police custody.

The report added that most had no previous convictions but that the usual inquiries were not carried out before sentencing, such as whether the defendant had a family, job or money. When local solicitors saw what was happening they protested and, after a while, were allowed to represent the defendants, but only after they had gone into the dock and made their plea. Nottingham's chief clerk to the justices protested about this report in the *LAG Bulletin*, saying that it failed to recognize the great burden of responsibility on the magistrates 'to do justice to all manner of people', including people who were terrorized by the rioting. George Yandell said that of the 106 defendants appearing in court after the weekend's rioting, 69 were represented by solicitors. Of eighteen appeals to the crown court against the sentences, none had been successful.

Similar abuse was evident in Bradford but there was an extra political element in that city because twelve youths were charged with very serious offences indeed: conspiracy to cause explosions, conspiracy to cause grievous bodily harm and charges under the 1883 Explosive Substances Act which requires the fiat of the Attorney General. The way in which these young men have been treated has caused concern to lawyers, but it is a reflection of the way in which suspected rioters were treated generally in that city. A now famous case, which led to a landmark decision, concerned Tarlochan Gata-Aura who pleaded guilty to using threatening behaviour after he was arrested on 11 July because he realized that otherwise he would be remanded in custody. His solicitor told him that his chances of bail were negligible if he pleaded not guilty, as he wanted to, and that all those pleading guilty were being fined and released. Gata-Aura pleaded guilty and was released. But he later appealed against his conviction on the grounds that he had pleaded guilty under duress, and at Bradford crown court he won his case.

Gata-Aura explained that when he was originally arrested he had been refused permission to see a solicitor. He was put into a cell with ten others and during the next 24 hours ten more prisoners arrived. They had to take it in turns to sleep on benches and the floor. Two days later he was interviewed and charged with threatening behaviour with intent to provoke a breach of the peace. He did not understand this and was denied permission to see a solicitor. On the Monday he was allowed to see a lawyer and told him he wanted to plead not guilty.

But as they were talking a goaler opened the door to say that all guilty pleas were being dealt with that day and that not guilty pleas would be remanded in custody. The solicitor confirmed this so Gata-Aura decided to plead guilty but asked the solicitor to explain the reasons for this to the court. He did not do so.

At the time of writing the case of the 'Bradford Twelve' had not yet come to trial, though it had been committed to the crown court. The case had already come to be seen as a political trial and was a *cause célèbre* in the North, particularly because the defendants were held in custody for long periods. The youths belonged to the United Black Youth League, which had campaigned for Anwar Ditta, a British-born Asian, to be reunited with her children. The twelve were arrested after the police discovered a cache of 100 petrol bombs after the Bradford rioting. Despite the fact that they all pleaded not guilty, they were refused bail on a blanket basis. Eventually they were granted bail, but only after a long struggle by their lawyers and after some of them had been in custody for several months. Their solicitors objected to the length of time the case was taking to be committed, about the conditions that were laid down when they were given bail and about the prosecution grounds for objecting to bail. One eighteen-year-old with no previous convictions had to produce a surety of £20,000 whereas others had to produce only £1000. A condition of bail was that they were not allowed to take part in demonstrations or processions, which led some observers to comment that the magistrates were more worried about the defendants embarrassing the authorities than absconding. Prosecution counsel had objected to bail on the grounds that anti-police leaflets were being handed out by other people outside the court.

As time went by there were numbers of acquittals. Of the forty-five cases of people charged as a result of the April riots in Brixton with threatening behaviour who pleaded not guilty, twenty-two were either dismissed, found not guilty or no evidence was offered. A white nurse who lives in Brixton and was charged with throwing bricks at police was cleared after it was discovered that wrong information had been given about her maliciously to the police. Gloucester crown court were relatively lenient on a gang of petrol bombers. The organizer, a 'self-confessed anarchist', pleaded guilty and was sent to borstal but a second was ordered to do community service and to pay a fine, a third was cleared and the others paid fines of £200 each. In Liverpool a man who said he was bullied by the police into making a false confession was cleared of seven charges after he had been held in custody for six months. His defence counsel said: 'Mr O'Donoghue had no injuries when he was arrested but the next day, when he appeared in court, he had a black eye, the left side of his face was swollen and he had bruises on his leg and thigh.' The defendant was found innocent of arson, possessing offensive weapons and making an affray.

Preliminary statistics of court cases in Merseyside, where more than five hundred people were arrested as a result of the disturbances, show that the great majority of defendants were white (108 out of 125). This contrasts with Brixton where 302 out of 449 people – 67 per cent – charged in connection with both the April and July riots were black. In both places the majority of defendants were unemployed; in Brixton as many as two thirds. This may provide a rough and ready guide to who was rioting. But in Brixton it was alleged that the police set out to arrest young blacks. The majority arrested in Brixton for threatening behaviour, the most common charge, were juveniles, aged between fourteen and sixteen. This contrasts with a national age for the rioters of between twenty and twenty-two. A second analysis of riot cases in *The Times* in November 1981 drew up an identikit picture of the average person to appear in the courts: he or she was young, unemployed and living close to the rioting. It found little evidence of outside involvement in the riots.

But during sentencing, judges and magistrates made clear how seriously they regarded the offences of threatening behaviour, theft, assault, affray, carrying an offensive weapon and criminal damage with which the rioters were charged. The sentences meted out were to be seen as deterrents – short, sharp shocks to ensure that young people did not riot again. Time will tell.

7 'There must be causes for them': Explanations of the riots

The process of trying to give a satisfactory explanation for the riots began before the dust had cleared. But the experience of the riots was a shattering one and the process was full of uncertainties. British society stumbled and groped through the debris of its cities and its assumptions in a search for explanations that would do justice to the seriousness of what had taken place. The uncertainties were by no means dishonourable.

The explanatory confusion was at times almost poignant. When the leader of Greater Manchester county council was asked, in the autumn, for his views of the Hytner Report on the Moss Side riots, he replied: 'I think that most reasonable people would assume that the riots were irrational. But there must be causes for them.'[1]

Immediate responses

In July itself, any immediate attempt to explain why the riots of 1981 were taking place ran up against political barriers. There were those, notably the Prime Minister, who seemed to equate explanation with excusal and who thus dug in against trying to identify the causes behind the riots. Speaking to the nation in a party political broadcast on 8 July (the Wednesday after Toxteth) Margaret Thatcher emphasized her priority: 'Nothing can justify, nothing can excuse and no one can condone the appalling violence.' *The Times* commented that 'She failed to raise the tone of her remarks to the level of events. Not for the first time she was unable to strike the right note when a broad sense of social understanding was required.'[2]

A week later, with the riots beginning to die down, Thatcher's general tone remained strict. The message was strongly reminiscent of years of official comment on Northern Ireland. For now, she said, the riots are a law and order issue. 'Until law and order and public confidence have been restored,' she told the Commons, 'we cannot set about improving the economic or social conditions of this country.'[3]

This was itself an interpretation of the riots. Although, on her visit to Liverpool on 13 July, the Prime Minister seemed to accept that mistrust between the police and the community had been a factor, she continued publicly to explain the riots more in terms of criminality, lack of discipline and greed than in terms of deprivation or unemployment. She agreed, she told Parliament, with the *Daily Mirror* which had labelled the riots 'a spree of naked greed' – though the newspaper was quick to retort that it had emphasized many other causes too.

Answering MPs' questions on 9 July, Thatcher observed: 'In the area where violence and rioting had occurred, a good deal of it has been carried out by children of school age, some them between nine and sixteen. That was nothing whatever to do with the dole queue.' A week later she attacked the influence of liberal social legislation in the 1960s: 'Mr Jenkins' saying that a permissive society is a civilized society is something that most of us would totally reject.' This was, however, the week in which the former Labour Home Secretary was fighting the first parliamentary by-election, at Warrington, for the newly formed Social Democratic Party, so her attack had a party political flavour. But another of her comments the same day emphasized the deep-seatedness of her views when she said: 'A large part of the problem that we are having now has come from a weakening of authority in many respects of life over many, many years. This has got to be corrected.'

The Prime Minister was not alone. Others also placed

the blame for the riots on what they saw as a weakening of social and personal discipline. One SDP member of Parliament, James Wellbeloved, considered them 'the penalty for a decade or more of undermining and subverting respect for decent authority'. Several Conservatives took the same view. Ray Whitney, pointing to the violence in his High Wycombe constituency, dismissed any socio-economic explanations: 'It was sheer vandalism and criminality. It was a breakdown of the discipline of society and those are the problems we have to tackle.'[4] Another Conservative, Sir Hugh Fraser, dug out one of his party's favourite explanations – the absence of national service. Some Labour MPs took a similar view. Lambeth MP John Fraser told Parliament he saw many reasons for the riots, including the breakdown of the family.

Though some blamed John McEnroe for setting a bad example during the Wimbledon tennis championships, many thought that schools were to blame. The general secretary of the engineering union, Sir John Boyd, said that moral decay and lower educational standards were the reasons for the riots. A number of West Indian parents voiced similar fears in evidence to the Hytner inquiry into the Moss Side riots, and the inquiry itself seemed to agree. Conservative MP Ian Lloyd blamed 'some of the seditious sociological clap-trap that is passed on in our schools as education'. This found an echo from government education ministers. The Secretary of State, Mark Carlisle, felt that the riots should make people 'think again about moral education'. His colleague Lady Young called on parents to support schools in teaching 'moral values'. While the junior education minister, Rhodes Boyson, a former headmaster himself, told a journalist: 'If we destroy the authority of the headmaster and his staff, society will reap dragons' teeth in the form of juvenile revolt.'

Of those who looked for disciplinary explanations, no group was more insistent that the police, who frequently saw the attacks on them as symptomatic of a wider anti-authoritarianism. 'I have no doubt that we are the readily identifiable symbols of authority and discipline which is anathema to these people', said Merseyside's chief constable, Kenneth Oxford.[5] The embattled Mr Oxford tried repeatedly to shift the spotlight off the police themselves. 'Parents have a responsibility to discipline and control the movement and behaviour of their children', he said on 5 July. Two days later, he said at a press conference: 'There are many people postulating views as to causes but let us not look for short-term palliatives, let's go back to basic civilized discipline.'

Such views were not confined to the police in the public eye. Letters by ordinary officers in the widely read weekly *Police Review* showed similar sentiments. Eric Roberts, from the Greater Manchester force, suggested after Brixton that 'a big part of the downward trend is the deterioration of discipline'. A London sergeant, Alan Pitcher, saw the riots as 'anti-establishment, anti-legislation and above all anti-police', while another Manchester constable wrote that the problem 'was spawned with the inception and subsequent development of the welfare state which coincided with the decline, particularly in the last decade, of the traditional agencies of political and cultural socialization – the home, the school, workplace and church.'[6]

In general, and particularly while the riots were going on, the police were extremely reluctant to concede that there was substance in the extensive criticism of policing methods and policy. They tended to look for explanations which were consistent with the maintenance of their existing attitudes and practices. The Police Federation, representing rank and file officers in England and Wales, saw the Brixton riots as proof not of police failures but police success. 'If there was smouldering resentment against the police amongst black youths in Brixton that weekend,' said an editorial in the federation's magazine, 'it was caused by the very success of the police measures against crime.'[7]

The federation's chairman, James Jardine, resented

the search for causes. 'It seems that in the view of some people any behaviour, no matter how criminal, can be excused if it takes place in a deprived area and the criminal elements happen to be mainly black,' he told his annual conference in May. The federation's parliamentary spokesman, Eldon Griffiths, took a similar view in July. 'There is another factor – criminality,' he told the Commons. And these views reflected those of ordinary officers writing to *Police Review*. 'I fully accept that deprivation, inner-city decay and various other equally colourful phrases are relevant,' wrote Sergeant Alan Barron from London; 'but let us not forget that violence and damage perpetrated in the majority of cases is pure and wanton with no racial or political connotation.' And one anonymous Merseyside officer went even further: 'There are a lot of theories about what caused the riots. Some say it's unemployment, some say bad housing, some say it's because of the police, and some say it's political. Has anyone thought it could have been old-fashioned wickedness?'[8]

Some chief constables supported the emphasis on criminality. After the riots in Leicester, the local chief constable, Alan Goodson, was anxious to deny a racial content. He blamed gangs bent on criminal hooliganism: 'They were hell bent on damaging windows and in some cases, stealing and that is what they were intent upon. In no sense was it a race riot.' Goodson's near neighbour, the chief constable of Nottinghamshire, Charles McLachlan, offered a similar explanation for his own local problems: 'This wasn't racial, it was pure hooliganism.'

Outsiders and copycats

The 'pure hooliganism' doctrine was gratefully taken up by many to explain the later phases of the rioting in many cities, and the outbreaks of rioting in several smaller towns. Police were prominent among those who suggested that the riots were the work of outsiders, conspirators or agitators. We have already noted that such theories have been floated throughout history to help explain riots. 'The conspiracy theories of urban violence have rarely been substantiated,' writes the sociologist P. Lupsha, 'yet they are common to every period and culture,'[9] In 1981 such theories formed part of the daily bread of the press and many opinion formers. Some were crude, others were more modest, setting the role of organizers alongside other factors. But the common theme was disbelief that communities could be capable of such acts as riots by themselves. The *Police Review* journalist Brian Hilliard responded to Brixton with a set of wide-ranging swipes at various 'external' factors:

The Brixton riots are a success story. A success for the anonymous writers who painted 'Bristol Yesterday, Brixton Tomorrow' on walls well before the violent weekend. A success for the Lambeth working party who produced a report on police/community relationships that mixed unconfirmed exaggeration with obvious lies in 100 pages of amateur research three months before the riots. A success for the Sunday journalists who made routine reference to police harassment without getting nearer the truth than Hampstead Garden Suburb. The riots are a success for the conference speakers who referred to Brixton as the worst station in the country without speaking to any of the officers there. A success for the manufacturers of petrol bombs and the street leaders who sprang into concerted action on Saturday afternoon.[10]

The search for reds under the beds went on all summer. While the *Daily Mail* warned of masked motorcyclists, and Special Branch officers searched for the four men behind the riots, Ronald Butt, writing in *The Times*, blamed 'the wide range of race relations bodies' ranging from 'the most reputable who nevertheless constantly harp on disadvantage of the immigrants' to 'much less reputable local bodies which peddle black hatred for white society'. Butt's blame of 'mischief-makers and do-gooders' was taken up by the Police Federation in its evidence to Scarman. The problem was 'well-educated activists' who are 'getting young blacks to believe they are victims of police oppression'.[11]

A Liverpool 'law and order' campaigner, Charles Oxley, told the *Mail*: 'I am convinced that the whole thing was politically motivated.' Chief Constable James Anderton of Greater Manchester said the same thing about Moss Side. A number of MPs made more specific claims. Handsworth MP Sheila Wright told Parliament that the violence in Birmingham had been 'planned and orchestrated'. Another member, William Shelton, explained that 'the great conspiracy theory – a man in the East End planning the riots and pulling strings' – was nonsense, but that nevertheless outsiders were at work. He blamed the Labour Party Young Socialists, GLC leader Ken Livingstone and, above all, the Workers' Revolutionary Party:

I wonder to what extent it is pure coincidence that the first of their youth training centres happens to be in Brixton. A second, I believe was in Toxteth – certainly it was in Liverpool – a third in Manchester and another in Nottingham. Moreover, I understand that it is planned to extend them to 25 in all. Its 1981 manifesto refers to the struggle for workers' revolutionary government. I wonder to what extent it is a pure coincidence.

Several other conspirators were picked out by the press. *The Times* revealed that in Moss Side members of the Revolutionary Communist Tendency were 'present during the riot'. Several newspapers fastened on the role of a member of the Militant Tendency in the Labour Party, Clare Doyle, who worked in Brixton and addressed a meeting in Toxteth. The SDP's Shirley Williams revealed, to the sound, some felt, of grinding axes, that Militant were 'training units' in riot areas.[12] Ray Whitney revealed the role of 'Miss Anita Lloyd and her provocateurs' in High Wycombe. Nor were all the alleged conspirators left-wingers, though interestingly none was ever black. A right-winger was found too – Edith Glastra of Birmingham, described by the *Daily Mirror* as 'the 50-year-old housewife who has been dubbed Evil Edith'.

Another factor blamed by many was the media. Some police complained that politically biased reporting helped to foment trouble – the *New Statesman* being a favourite target. But the main influence ascribed to the media was simply that it gave people ideas. Inevitably, the veteran campaigner Mary Whitehouse was quick to make this point. In a telegram to the BBC and ITN on 11 July she claimed: 'Massive television coverage of acts of vandalism and violence is contributing to the spread of riots; it creates excitement, teaches techniques and encourages imitation.' This view seems to have been widely accepted. Both the BBC and ITN acknowledged in response to Whitehouse that television was to some extent responsible for encouraging 'copycat' rioting. C. H. Rolph, writing in *Police Review*, concurred: 'Who in his right senses can deny that the lady is right?' Labour's front bench spokesman on home affairs, Roy Hattersley, agreed too. 'Some of last week's violence,' he said on 16 July, 'was the result of mindless imitation of what had been seen on television.' Some months after the riots, the former Labour MP Eric Moonman published the results of his own inquiries with young people in Toxteth and London. 'The influence of television in their responses to the situation could not be doubted', he concluded. 'TV made it look easy, they knew what kind of things to do.' Moonman gave special emphasis to the effect of television coverage of the Northern Ireland crisis – 'that long running saga of social breakdown in Britain which nightly fills the television screens with violent defiance of authority, street fighting and neighbourhood strife'.

Few attempts to deny this argument have been made, though one correspondent to the London *New Standard* claimed that the local grapevine was a much greater encouragement. On the face of it, this is strange, since opponents of Mary Whitehouse had previously gone to great lengths to deny her claims that life can imitate television and the cinema. An article in *The Times* by Peter Watson, published after the riots, attempted a more precise version of this explanation.[13] Watson argued that the kind of people who can become rioters or football hooligans are the same kind of people who are most affected by what they see on the television. Both, said Watson, will be working class, adolescent and of impressionable age and they receive least parental counter-argument to real life violence seen on television. In January 1982, however, a research survey commissioned by the British Film Institute claimed that there was no evidence of rioters being affected by the coverage of the riots or of their being encouraged by the presence of cameras (where the opposite was true). The researcher claimed: 'These youngsters spend their time on the streets. They were influenced by rumours of something going on, passed on by others. Most of them do not even watch the television news.'[14]

The racial dimension

In spite of the observably high level of black involvement in many of the riots – including all those which received most publicity – public figures were very reluctant to pontificate on the racial aspects of the causes of the riots. It was as if there was no publicly acceptable framework for discussing the racial dimension. There were, however, two exceptions.

On the one hand, there was widespread acceptance that what happened in Southall had a distinct racial character. The local MP, Sydney Bidwell, made his view clear immediately. 'These events arose from provocative action by skinheads, some of them members of the neo-fascist racist organisations,' he said in Parliament on 6 July. This explanation was rarely disputed. The double social and political unacceptability of people who were both skinheads and organized made it clear to many outside west London that there was a racist threat to the Asian community of Southall. Home Secretary Whitelaw accepted this view in his speech in the major parliamentary debate on the riots on 16 July. Thus explanations of the riots tended to put Southall into a separate category.

The second exception was of a different kind. Enoch Powell was the only major white public figure or opinion former to claim that the cause of the riots was racial. Powell's response to Brixton was to tell the government that 'they have seen nothing yet'. In July, interviewed on BBC radio by John Timpson, he said: 'We have had deprivation, unemployment and all the rest for generations and people have not turned out to wreck their own cities and to attack the police.' Powell told the interviewer that the battle may 'correspond with the incidence of something else' – the high concentration of the New Commonwealth ethnic population, 'as we must officially call them'. In Parliament the following week, he went further. There were 'two over-arching facts', said Powell: a high proportion of the young population in some cities was black and this population will double or treble in the next generation. The result, he feared, would be civil war.

Powell's arguments were widely rejected by other members of Parliament. Opinion surveys, however, indicated that they, or something like them, were shared by perhaps a quarter of the white population (though not, as in Powell's own case, to the apparent exclusion of all other causes). Other critics who emphasized race did so rather more obliquely. Right-wing columnist Peregrine Worsthorne regarded Brixton as 'the iceberg tip of a crisis of ethnic criminality which is not Britain's fault – except in the sense that her rulers quite unnecessarily imputed it – but the fault of the ethnic community itself, from whom the cure must come, as has the disease'.[15] Some police spokesmen made similar points, though again their language was different from Powell's very idiosyncratic and delphic use of English. The police used terms like Jim Jardine's 'people who in many cases have nothing but contempt for the *ordinary* values of our society'. Or they drew revealing distinctions as in the Police Federation magazine's editorial on Brixton. This said that as well as 'disaffected underprivileged black youths', the population of Brixton consisted of 'thousands of *ordinary* citizens' (our italics in both cases).[16] The implication was clearly that 'ordinary' people and values are white people and values and that therefore the problem is a black problem.

This reluctance of most whites to discuss racial causes of the riots broke down on some limited and specific issues. As we have seen, Southall was one issue. So was discussion of the influence, if any, of the government's Nationality Bill. This Bill was proceeding through the parliamentary process throughout all phases of the 1981 riots. It had begun its progress before Brixton and ended it only in November 1981. The Joint Council for the Welfare of Immigrants argued in its annual report that the bill had had the undeniable effect of weakening the black community's sense of security (not just that of the Asian community) and that this should be seen as a factor in provoking the riots. A similar point was made in evidence to Scarman by the West Indian Standing Conference.

The deprivationist argument

The relative absence of racial analysis in the debate over causes contrasted starkly with the vociferousness of those who attributed the riots to social and economic causes. Margaret Thatcher, as we saw, fought hard to oppose the view that unemployment and deprivation lay behind the outbreaks. In part, this was for obvious partisan reasons. Her political opponents were lambasting her government over the rate of unemployment, therefore for her to have conceded that it was a cause of riots would have been to hand a political weapon to her enemies.

The size of the deprivationist school, however, went far beyond the Labour Party, whose membership was ebbing away in the summer of 1981. But Labour was at its core. The party leader, Michael Foot, and his front bench home affairs spokesman, Roy Hattersley, to an even greater degree, argued consistently that unemployment and social deprivation were the deep causes of the riots. In April, Hattersley responded to the announcement of the Scarman inquiry and its terms of reference by saying that 'the inquiry must go further than policing procedures', and stressed employment and housing. The following day, Foot followed up in similar terms, arguing that 'unemployment is a primary cause of such difficulties'.

If anything, the deprivationist lobby grew more clamorous during and after the July riots. On 7 July, Foot argued once again that the Scarman terms of reference should be extended to 'the deeper causes of deprivation'. Other Labour MPs, even or especially those with large black populations in their constituencies, backed their leader strongly. Moss Side's MP, George Morton, stated: 'The basic cause of the problems is unemployment.' Joan Lestor, representing Slough, agreed: 'The causes of the riots are the economic situation, the deprivation and the lack of hope that that brings.' She continued: 'It would . . . be a great pity if . . . we were to allow ourselves to sink back into platitudes and explanations that it is all a matter of race or of the National Front, the Young Socialists, or any other group of people.' Perhaps the most mechanistic claim came from the Liverpool Labour MP Eric Heffer, who said: 'There must surely be a correlation between what happened and the fact that there is 40 per cent unemployment.'

By virtue of his position on the front bench, it was Hattersley who argued the deprivationist case most often and at greatest length. He accepted that in different places the violence was triggered for different reasons, but he saw them all taking place in 'decaying central areas of old cities where there is intolerably high unemployment, unacceptably low levels of social services and abysmally inadequate housing'. This was the cause of despair and 'even the skinheads who invaded Southall last Saturday are part of the pattern of disadvantage and deprivation'.

Hattersley seemed to ascribe everything to socioeconomic causes. Racial attacks, he said, were related to the whole question of urban deprivation and the product of that deprivation: 'The causes of such incidents are social and economic ... Until the social and economic circumstances are changed, such incidents are likely to continue.' To some extent, of course, Hattersley's insistence was directly related to Thatcher's denial. The more the Prime Minister dismissed deprivationist explanations, the more Labour would advocate them. But there can be no doubt about how emphatically Hattersley stuck to his thesis. He argued it harder than ever in the debate of 16 July, even though Conservatives such as Whitelaw (and Thatcher too, to a limited extent) had begun to concede that deprivation had at least some relevance to the riots. In that debate, Hattersley said: 'I repeat that I do not believe that the principal cause of last week's riots was the conduct of the police. It was the conditions of deprivation and despair in the decaying areas of our old cities.'

This was, for the most part, the Labour line on the 1981 riots. It was not just people like Hattersley on the right of the party who held it. As we have seen, left-wingers like Lestor and Heffer were equally strong deprivationists.

Deprivationism was not Labour's exclusive property, however. Former Conservative prime minister Edward Heath told a conference on 1 July: 'If you have a half a million young people hanging around on the streets all day you will have a massive increase in juvenile crime. Of course you will get racial tension when you have young blacks with less chance of getting jobs.' That was before the riots resumed. Once they had done so, the then Secretary of State for Employment, James Prior, was quite explicit too. 'Undoubtedly the present high level of unemployment is a fruitful breeding round for the sort of thing we are seeing,' he said in a speech in Cheshire on 10 July. 'We must recognize that to have such numbers out of work leads to a disaffected people.'[17]

Those who emphasized unemployment and deprivation included press, trade unions and the churches. An early supporter of the thesis was a Liverpool historian,

Philip Waller, who wrote a feature article in *The Times* on the Tuesday following Toxteth entitled 'Liverpool: Why the Clue to Violence is Economic not Racial'. He argued that the racial element in the riots was a 'chance consequence of the economic conditions'. Even Rudy Narayan, the black lawyer, argued that unemployment was important. He saw the Toxteth riot as 'a product of the frustration and the bitterness of people who cannot find jobs and people who see certain people prosper but they can't even get a job in the street'.[18]

The deprivationist theory was flexible and tenacious enough to counter-attack against government spokesmen's attempts to shift the argument on to other causes. When William Whitelaw argued that the participation of young people of school age in several riots showed that unemployment could not be the central cause, he was attacked by a distinguished specialist on racial disadvantage. Nicholas Deakin, professor of social administration at Birmingham University, responded: 'It is not clear why he and other Conservatives do not appreciate that unemployment affects families in ways often more cruel than individuals.'[19] This view was supported by a London psychoanalyst, Dr Moses Lanfer, who argued that the unemployment of a father disrupted family life and discipline so that riots may also be expressing the despair and violence of the father via the sons. The deprivationist thesis contained several elements, but unemployment was the one that was most consistently emphasized. Nor is this surprising. Rising unemployment through 1981 was a central political issue, constantly in the public mind. It is hardly astonishing that an issue widely regarded as the country's principal problem should be so readily connected to such disturbing events. Unemployment provided a ready framework of explanation.

This was less true of other aspects of the explanation. There were few people in 1981 to argue that high unemployment was acceptable. But the question of spending on the inner cities and social services was more disputed. The Conservative government was committed to reducing public expenditure and was conducting a fierce campaign against local authorities in the urban areas to enforce lower spending. The Brixton riots took place in the London borough, Lambeth, which at that time was the focus for this argument. And, with Labour making big local election gains in May in many of the inner-city authorities, the issue became even more politically divisive in the summer of 1981. There was less unanimity on the public spending issue than on the need to reduce unemployment. Voters who supported Labour could not even be counted on to support increases in spending that entailed higher rates – as a referendum in Coventry in the autumn indicated. As a result, inner-city deprivation had a party political aura which made it – far more than unemployment – an issue for Labour to press and for Conservatives to resist. There seems to have been a feeling that to put the emphasis on inner-city spending would be to take sides in a 'politicians' battle' – a battle between Michael Heseltine on the one hand and Ted Knight, Ken Livingstone and the Labour metropolitan authorities on the other.

Thus, although inner-city issues were frequently bracketed with unemployment in the deprivation thesis, they were normally seen as secondary and there were fewer attempts to establish a distinct causal link between these issues and the outbreak of riots.

There were attempts, nonetheless. Brixton's MP, John Tilley, told Scarman in evidence that, although joblessness was the biggest factor, the fact that people spent a lot of time on the streets because of over-crowding in the home and lack of recreational facilities was a major cause of his local riots. A Labour activist blamed the Moss Side riots on planning errors. And C. H. Rolph in *Police Review* agreed:

Do you notice how every fresh outbreak of street voilence, including all the arson, criminal damage, teamwork robbery and assault on police, is explained according to the predilections of the explainer? Too many police, not enough police, racial hatred, hatred of racial hatred, unemployment, lack of ethical education, the decline of religious faith, indifferent parents. Among all these attributions, I don't see why I shouldn't advance my own pet contributory cause of the current social disorders. I put a lot of blame on the planners, the busybodying administrators of the Town and Country Planning Acts.

Planning blight is ruining countless lives and we should be asking ourselves what kind of youth we expect to emerge from what we hopelessly call our 'inner city areas'. Some of the causes of mob violence may *seem* immovable but planning blight isn't one of them.[20]

Opinion polls

Opinion polls seemed to bear out the view that most people didn't rate these issues too high as causes of the riots – whatever their views about them in other contexts.

A fortnight after Brixton, a MORI poll was conducted in London for the *New Standard*.[21] The pollsters asked: 'What do you think were the main causes of the recent riots in Brixton?' There were some important contrasts between the answers of black and Asian respondents and the answers of the sample as a whole. But there were also some important similarities. Overall, 40 per cent of the sample mentioned unemployment – easily the most popular cause. Then, in order, the respondents mentioned: blacks' behaviour (22 per cent), racialism (18 per cent), bad housing (15 per cent), police behaviour (13 per cent), education (5 per cent), too many police (3 per cent) and too few police (2 per cent).

Black and Asian respondents also made unemployment the main factor – half of them (49 per cent) mentioned this cause. But 33 per cent of them then mentioned police behaviour, followed by racialism (17 per cent) bad housing (12 per cent), blacks' behaviour (11 per cent), too many police (7 per cent) and education (1 per cent). So this poll showed that while all respondents put unemployment first, blacks were even more likely to blame unemployment and far more likely to blame police behaviour. On the other hand, they were less likely than whites to blame housing, education and racialism and much less likely to blame blacks' behaviour.

The MORI/*New Standard* poll was partly confirmed in an Audience Selection survey for Capital Radio at approximately the same time. People were asked: 'What was the main reason for Brixton?' Here again, 37 per cent of blacks blamed police behaviour, compared with 13 per cent of whites. Young people (aged between thirteen and twenty-four) of all colours were even more concerned about this cause, blamed by 52 per cent of blacks and 21 per cent of whites. High unemployment was blamed by 29 per cent of blacks and 24 per cent of whites. But on this issue, young people did not respond uniformly. Fewer young blacks (25 per cent) blamed unemployment while more young whites (31 per cent) did so. Whites were more likely to blame racial problems than blacks. Almost one in five whites (19 per cent of all ages and 18 per cent of the young people) mentioned this cause, compared with 6 per cent of all blacks and only 3 per cent of young blacks. When it came to living conditions – the nearest approximation in this poll to urban deprivation – 7 per cent of all blacks and 10 per cent of all whites gave this answer. Among young people there was a slight twist to the results, with living conditions blamed by 11 per cent of young blacks and 7 per cent of young whites. So the Capital Radio poll again showed that blacks – and in particular young blacks – were much more likely than whites to blame police behaviour, while whites were more likely to blame living conditions and racial problems.

The Capital poll also asked whether the riots were planned or spontaneous. Here, the contrast between blacks' view and whites' views was very dramatic. Almost five times as many blacks (68 per cent against 14 per cent) said they were spontaneous as said they were planned and organized. Whites, though, thought the opposite, by almost two to one (57 per cent to 32 per cent). But the 13–24-year-olds had slightly different views. More young blacks (76 per cent of them) as well as young whites (42 per cent) said that the riots were spontaneous, while 21 per cent of young blacks and 53 per cent of young whites thought they were planned and organized.

These results should be compared with a national poll conducted by MORI for *The Times* at the end of August, after the summer riots. The pollsters asked respondents to give the main causes of the riots, and 62 per cent highlighted unemployment – over twice as many as mentioned any other cause. Next came 'racial tension/blacks' (26 per cent) followed by police behaviour (17 per cent), and 'agitators/militants' (12 per cent). Only 8 per cent mentioned 'bad housing/urban decay'. Other causes – mentioned by 7 per cent or less of the poll – included government policies, breakdown of parental authority, media coverage and hot weather. Connected MORI polls among young people in Croydon and Newcastle both gave pride of place to unemployment – 64 per cent in Croydon and 61 per cent in Newcastle – which in both places far outdistanced any other answer.

The final relevant poll was an ORC survey published in the *Guardian* just after Scarman reported, although the survey was taken between mid August and mid September. Here too unemployment was the most common cause, supplied by 48 per cent (and 58 per cent of those aged between eighteen and twenty-four). 'Boredom among youth' got support from a quarter of all age groups and 'race/race prejudice' from one in ten respondents. This poll yet again showed different perceptions between the age groups: almost three times as many 18–24-year-olds as over-45s blamed the police; twice as many suggested frustration or feelings of injustice. Age differences showed up the other way round, too: twice as many over-45s as 18–24-year-olds blamed 'immigrants' and outside agitators, while three times as many blamed lack of parental control. In some ways the most telling answers of all came when the pollsters asked; 'Where did your sympathies mainly lie – with the police and the authorities or with the young people who were protesting and rioting?' Only among those aged between sixteen and twenty was support greater for the latter, 38 per cent as against 34 per cent who supported the police. This contrasted very sharply with the views of all other age groups: 18–24s favoured the police by 52 to 16 per cent (the rest supported neither side or didn't know), 25–44s favoured police by 59 to 19 per cent, while over-45s favoured police by 70 to 12 per cent. It suggests that, whatever other factors were involved, the riots were a revolt of the young, supported by the young.

So, to summarise the polls, they showed that most people in Britain blamed the riots on unemployment while only a small percentage blamed inner-city deprivation. Between a fifth and a quarter of the population, mainly white, blamed blacks or racial tension. Among blacks, however, at least a third (and more among young blacks) blamed police behaviour, a cause that was much less likely to be supported by whites (although between 10 and 20 per cent did so). Far more blacks than whites believed the riots were spontaneous.

What everyone said

The polls confirm what Lord Scarman also confirmed, that in black communities the police were seen as a central cause of the riots. In this view, the police were not merely to blame for particular incidents which triggered the riots, nor were they even the visible representatives of a society or a state or a government that was denying people jobs or houses. They were seen as the actual source of the pent-up grievances.

The formal expression of this view was widespread. The West Indian Standing Conference told Scarman that the cause of the Brixton riots was 'a deep wedge of fear' between blacks and police. Local groups in Lambeth agreed. 'Racist and provocative policing' was the cause, said the Lambeth Council for Community Relations. 'Continuous heavy handling' by police was blamed by local youth groups. These views were echoed all over the country by local groups. The Liverpool 8 Defence Committee blamed police abuse and aggression and claimed that 'Everyone on the streets had a personal grudge against the police.'[22] The root cause, the committee said, was 'the methods used by the police' and 'harassment by the police of the black community'. Toxteth's MP, Richard Crawshaw, didn't go quite that far, but he too blamed police: 'These events came about because, rightly or wrongly, there is a genuine belief, not only in the black community, that in that area the enforcement of law and order is not even-handed.' And another Merseyside MP, Robert Kilroy-Silk, took the view that if high unemployment was the cause, riots would have broken out elsewhere in the area, where it was worse than in Toxteth. His view was that 'there may be something seriously wrong with the relationship of the police with this community'.

Views were no different in Moss Side. No inquiry into the riots was needed, the Moss Side Defence Committee claimed, because everyone in the area already well knew the causes: 'indiscriminate meetings, raids, frame-ups and harassment laced with racist abuse, which the police have been dishing out in this community'. The committee saw the riots as 'a legitimate protest by those who suffer from real, readily identifiable and desperate injustices. Of these, the most important is the intimidating form of policing which has been directed against Moss Side people, especially black youths, for many years.' Unemployment was not so important as 'the treatment of Moss Side as a dangerous alien colony, full of actual or potential criminals, which demanded forceful and repressive policing'.

Similar opinion formed a large part of the evidence submitted to the Scarman inquiry, particularly by local groups from Brixton. Scarman's terms of reference obviously encouraged this, but witnesses' persistent attention to the police cannot be explained simply by their strict adherence to the constraints imposed by the Police Act. After all, a number of witnesses – like the

Commission for Racial Equality – were able to raise all kinds of social and economic issues if they wished to. The concentration on the police was a matter of choice not compulsion and the subject dominated the oral evidence in the second phase of the inquiry in September.

The search for causes of the riots focused increasingly on policing questions during the autumn. All other causes were forced to the sidelines for a while. The public debate centred on policing methods, recruitment, training, the complaints system and accountability. Police chiefs were worried by this development. Their response was to begin making behind-the-scenes compromises and changes, in the expectation that Scarman's report would – as it did – concentrate on detailed policing issues. The chief constables also tried to shift the argument away from policing and law and order, a major change of tactics from their own immediate responses to the riots. Police evidence to Scarman now began to highlight other issues. Sir David McNee said in his written submission that the causes of the Brixton riots were many and 'not all arose from the problems of policing Brixton'. Lancashire's chief constable, Albert Laugharne, warned: 'A simple bashing of police will not do as a solution for Bristol, Brixton and Toxteth.'[23]

When Scarman was published, at the end of November, police again tried to broaden the debate. McNee responded to the report: 'As to the underlying causes, I note that aspects of the environment, such as shortage of housing, lack of leisure facilities and unemployment, are recognized as contributing to the conditions which produce disorder.' Jim Jardine commented that 'Scarman recognizes that we have been picking up the blame for other people's dirty work.' Barry Pain, president of ACPO, argued that government and the local authorities now had the responsibility to remove 'the breeding ground of discontent in inner-city areas', and added: 'I do not accept that the police service was the cause of the riots.' The police, who had been so dismissive of deprivationist explanations in July, were by November happy to emphasize them in order to take some of the weight off their own shoulders.

What of the rioters themselves? What did they say caused them to riot? Unfortunately, few successful attempts were made to catch their voices. Newspaper reports of Brixton contain few direct quotes from the rioters. However the message that the police were seen as the main cause gets through. ' "It's not a race riot", we were constantly told along a blazing Coldharbour Lane,' reported the *Observer*. ' "It's more of a police–community thing." ' Other anonymous voices agreed: 'It's not against the white community, it's against the police.' 'This was the black man's Christmas.' A petrol bomber told the Indian journalist, Sashthi Brata: 'They don't want to know till we do something. Got to tell them we're here.' A black man was asked what he thought of McNee's claim that outsiders were responsible. 'Tell him to go back to Scotland,' he replied. 'Him don't know about London.' A Greek Cypriot woman pointed at the destruction: 'Put this down to everyone who lives in Brixton.'[24]

Journalists need 'good quotes'. It is impossible to say how much testimony is still buried in their notebooks, or was never recorded – all discarded as lacking the necessary journalistic value. This was not necessarily the fault of the journalists. The riots were violent and dangerous. Rioters were not going to stop to give interviews. Many were abusive and even violent to attempts to question them. But the loss to anyone trying to answer the question 'Why did it happen?' is obvious. And no amount of subsequent surveys or questioning can recapture the actual thinking of the participants at the moment when they rioted.

The same problem applies to the July riots. A young Moss Side black told a reporter: 'Everybody says "Look what they have done" but nobody asks why.' A group of teenagers in Wood Green gave their views: 'police provocation', 'the police keep pushing us around', 'things are so expensive', 'it's that Mrs Thatcher'. 'It's not deprived. Look at those houses,' said a young Moss Sider, while another added: 'What else could we do? We are unemployed.' In Leeds a seventeen-year-old black man told the local paper: 'Nobody is organizing us. We have all seen the riots on television in Liverpool and London and it seemed good fun.' Another said: 'Most people will blame it on the fact that nearly everybody round here is out of work and that could be right. It is certainly one of the causes, if not the only one.' A few – but only a small number – of the rioters who were charged in courts gave some explanation. 'It was the thing to do. You're the ones to get,' said Mark Carey, sentenced to six weeks in prison for assaulting a police officer in Brixton. Anthony Vickers told Manchester crown court that he threw a petrol bomb 'to make a name for myself'; he got three years' imprisonment.[25]

The Hytner Report

Inquiries into the riots and their causes therefore faced many difficulties. On top of the conflicting interpretations, there was little direct evidence – except from the police side – from those who took part. The story and the analysis had to come from those who had observed. The rioters themselves were anxious to remain anonymous and were suspicious of the motives of the inquiries. Moreover, by the time their hearings got under way, views had now been formed.

The Hytner inquiry into Moss Side reported in October. It found that the cause of the rioting was that it was expected. Beliefs which were mainly based on myth led people to assume that trouble was inevitable in Moss Side. There were plenty of people ready to fulfil those assumptions. The report said:

They were a mixed group, and included a criminal element, those who sought an opportunity to express their frustration and desperation due to existing or impending unemployment, and those who wished to vent against the police hostility coupled with their deeply held belief that whatever the police did to them there was no effective redress for their grievances.

To this mix of motivations were added particular factors affecting blacks. They were 'alienated from their parents' and they were bitter against white society because they had experienced 'insults and discrimination' in many fields. Once the rioting started, Hytner concluded, others joined in because they were caught up in the excitement of events. A few aimed 'to stir the pot' from political motives. Some sections of the white community – they were mainly older – took advantage of the rioting to loot:

Their motivation may well have been greed though in the case of some it is only fair to record that their moral values – which held firm among the older West Indians and all Asians – were undoubtedly to some extent eroded by financial pressures brought on by the widespread unemployment in the area.

Hytner dismissed the notion that black people were more disposed to riot than were whites as 'patently absurd'. He also rejected the view that the riots were directly linked to unemployment. That link mattered, he said, but it became important with young people, not with older generations: 'There is every difference between rendering a man unemployed in middle age and leaving youngsters without a job or the hope of a job when they finish their schooling.' The older man has 'a stake in society (his family, his house etc.)', whereas the young have not. Hytner concluded:

We believe as a result of our enquiries, that the raw material for rioting is made when young people are left, rightly or wrongly, with the impression that they have nothing to gain from established society, particularly where they have hitherto not yet gained any stake in it. Where this grievance is underlined by disappointed hopes, a belief that they are and will continue to be discriminated against and that they are continually surrounded not only by the affluence of others, but also advertising pressures to engage in material acquisition, their resistance to lawless conduct will be that much weaker; the situation will deteriorate further if habits born of enforced idleness bring them into conflict with the police.[26]

The Hytner Report was bitterly criticized for evading

what the Moss Side Defence Committee saw as the central, indeed the only, issue: policing methods. It was deeply biased and distorted, they claimed. Their objections were put together in a document entitled *Hytner Myths*. The conclusion on the policing of Moss Side and the links between this policing and the riots must be that the final word has not been said. The evidence on the scale of the problem is genuinely conflicting, as the Home Office study of the policing of Moss Side makes clear. Although the Home Office researchers were not attempting to examine the causes of the riots, they did offer some thoughts. They felt that rumour and hearsay were probably important within the West Indian community because of its strong group consciousness. Thus, a hostile incident could become widely known and might also be exaggerated in the telling. But age was important, too. There was a basic hostility to police among a minority of all ages, but particularly among the young, and this was clearly a big enough platform to sustain outbreaks of unsuccessful rioting.[27]

The Scarman Report

The resonance of Hytner's conclusions was minimal when compared with those of the Scarman inquiry. Scarman was published on 25 November in a deluge of national publicity.[28] It received saturation coverage in all the media. Of the national dailies, only the *Sun* didn't make it the main front-page story. The report – desperately overpriced at £8 for 154 pages of text (it contains an excellent map, however) – became a rare bestseller for Her Majesty's Stationery Office. It is unlikely, though, to match the sales of HMSO's all-time most successful publication, the Denning Report on the Profumo scandal. The British prefer sex to violence.

Scarman's conclusions ranged from the details of what actually caused the Brixton riots to a wider analysis of contemporary policing problems (in which he placed great emphasis on the inadequacy of police training in racial awareness), possible changes in the law on such matters as the police complaints procedure, and social policy. Although he saw these issues as bearing on the general problem of the Brixton riots, Scarman did not examine them because they were 'causes' of the riots. He concluded that the riots could not be understood 'unless they are seen in the context of . . . complex political, social and economic factors', notably the acute deprivations of blacks. 'Their experience leads them to believe that their opportunities are less and their risks are greater,' said the report. 'Young black people feel neither socially nor economically secure.' But, he continued, matters are even worse. Political insecurity is also a factor. It is caused by low levels of black representation and by the liberty with which those who are hostile to blacks are able to march and demonstrate. So blacks are forced on to the street, where they make their protests, and some of them live off crime. This brings them face to face with the police. The clash is 'ready-mixed'. Nonetheless, Scarman was very careful to avoid concluding that there is some inexorable process at work here, leading inescapably to riot. In an important passage he states:

None of these factors can perhaps usefully be described as a *cause* of the disorders, either in Brixton or elsewhere. Indeed, there are, undoubtedly, parts of the country which are equally deprived where disorder did not occur. But taken together, they provide a set of social conditions which create a predisposition towards violent protest.[29]

The report rejected the argument that the cause of the Brixton riots was simply the history of policing in Brixton. It also rejected the view that the riots were simply a protest in which a violent attack on the police formed the one opportunity of protesting against frustration and deprivation. But Scarman's report was primarily about policing and he was compelled to conclude that 'a significant cause' was a loss of local confidence in the police in which the young, especially the black young, were suspicious of everything the police did. This had its background in the policing issues which are discussed in other parts of this book. The violence arose, said Scarman, from 'the spontaneous reaction of the crowds to what they believed to be police harassment'. The riots were neither planned nor premeditated. When they did erupt they attracted others:

And there can be no doubt that the rioters, both the young blacks whose spontaneous reaction against the police started it off and the supporters whom they attracted from Brixton and elsewhere, found a ferocious delight in arson, criminal damage to property, and in violent attacks upon the police, the fire brigade, and the ambulance service.

Scarman's central verdict on the Brixton riots was this: 'The riots were essentially an outburst of anger and resentment by young black people against the police.'[30]

The Scarman Report was greeted with a wave of adulation. William Whitelaw said that he welcomed, accepted and endorsed the main themes. Roy Hattersley offered his 'deep thanks'. Sir David McNee called the report fair and thorough. ACPO called it 'an objective study'. The Police Federation described it as 'a historic document which demands and deserves the immediate attention of all sections of the nation'. The CRE's David Lane dubbed it 'a brilliant analysis'. Press reaction was equally enthusiastic. The *Sunday Times* called it 'a masterly document . . . lucid and compelling . . . even-handed'. The *Observer* regarded it as 'an historic act of affirmation'. The *Daily Mirror* saw the report as 'one of the great social documents of our time'. Where there were doubts they centred on whether the report might not be too radical and in favour of blacks.

The *Daily Mail* thought that it was telling the police to turn a blind eye to black crime and dismissed the call for positive discrimination. Other doubters felt that the official response would blunt the recommendations. Scarman had created a watershed in policing policy, said the *Guardian*; but it may be 'merely a watershed in a history of neglect'. And *New Society* argued: 'If Scarman has created optimistic expectations, it is against a back-cloth of deepening pessimism. The price of failure now could be much higher than the price already paid for the past failures.'

Out on the street, for those who cared to ask, the response was also cautious, to put it mildly. *Race Today*'s Darcus Howe called it 'way off beam', though he carefully avoided saying the report was a whitewash. Lambeth council leader Ted Knight announced himself 'bitterly disappointed'. The Brixton Defence Campaign said that the report had confirmed its worst fears:

Scarman has legitimized the action that the police took in April, and anybody who does that obviously can't have any feelings for what has been happening on the streets around here for years. It won't surprise the kids on the street: this is what they expected.

Some doubt was cast on this claim by a poll taken in Brixton on the weekend after the report was published. This showed heavy support, especially among blacks, for the immediate implementation of specific recommendations in it. Only one in ten people said that none of its proposals should be carried out. Whether they expected them to be, however, is another matter.

But these reactions centred on what Scarman proposed, rather than on his analysis of the riots. On this there was an ominous silence. It was as if there was now An Official Answer and thought was no longer necessary. At Westminster, Scarman was now, as the *Guardian*'s Michael White put it, 'the lord they love to laud'. The Parliamentary debate on Scarman was a low-key affair, with little of the visionary language which had greeted the report itself. The report was being assimilated in every sense. As Britain froze into the harshest winter for two decades, the urgency of Scarman seemed to be replaced by bureaucratic torpor and the scarcely discernible sound of official fudging.

8 Beginning of the end or end of the beginning? The riots and policing

What they [the police] need is support and not criticism.

Margaret Thatcher

I'm not against the police; I'm just afraid of them.

Alfred Hitchcock

It was not surprising that the debate about the riots should rage around such issues as the inner cities and unemployment. These questions underpinned everyday life in the riot areas. Moreover, as we have seen, they were well-worn, familiar territory for argument, comfortable old armchairs of discussion. What was less familiar and less comfortable was the way to tackle discussion of the police. The riots placed policing in the centre of public debate for probably the first time in twentieth-century Britain. Whether it now remains there is hard to foresee. But the events of 1981 forced a wide discussion of several new issues.

Public opinion polls have traditionally shown a high degree of support for the police. An ORC poll in *The Times* in September 1980, for example, found that a mere 3 per cent of people rated the police as 'bad' – compared with 71 per cent who rated them good and 26 reasonable. The poll showed only two issues which gave British people a sense of pride compared with other countries – 54 per cent thought the British were more tolerant and polite, and 83 per cent thought we had a better police force. A Gallup survey the previous year reported that three quarters of the population felt no unease about the police at all and that only 5 per cent had been made uneasy about the police as a result of the death of Blair Peach. There are important qualifications to note, though. On particular issues, notably corruption, people were less confident: a MORI/*Sunday Times* poll in February 1980 found only three out of ten who disagreed that there were now more corrupt police than there used to be. Many practising lawyers will confirm that in areas such as London this view is reflected in an increasing scepticism of juries towards police evidence. Polls have also found that only a third of people are satisfied with the police complaints system. The other qualifying comment is geographical: in certain areas, the police's reputation was far worse than others. Nearly four fifths of the people interviewed in a Brixton survey in April 1980 had little or no confidence in the police and two out of three thought blacks were worse treated than whites. Compare that with only one in ten who thought the same in a survey taken in north-west England at the same period.[1]

Nevertheless, there have been good grounds for the frequent police claim that they enjoy a very high degree of public confidence. The riots seem to have weakened that confidence. One swallow doesn't make a summer, nor does one poll mark a break in the mould. Yet an *Observer*/NOP poll in October 1981 indicated some important slippage in the police's standing.[2] One in four people reported that their confidence in the police had decreased, compared with only one in eight whose confidence in police, compared with 83 per cent who had 'great respect' in a 1962 poll. Among 18–24-years-olds only 27 per cent had great confidence. On the other hand, only 11 per cent had little or no confidence, although this figure almost doubled among the young and among those who had had 'unfriendly contact' with the police. So the poll did not show a revolution in public thinking, or a collapse of confidence. It did, however, show some significant erosion in traditional views. Most important of all, the poll suggested that policing was beginning to lose its status as an issue 'above politics'.

People seemed to be starting to take sides, not so much on the police as such as on a host of different policing issues as revealed in the detailed parts of the poll. Policing was being brought in from the cold and it was the summer of riots that had forced the change.

The debate about policing was focused on the Scarman inquiry. Any initial doubts that the inquiry would be too narrow to bring out the major issues were eventually dispelled. The recurrence of rioting in July ensured what was already becoming clear, that Scarman would not only have to deal with events in Brixton but with much broader issues of national policing policy. In turn, the riots and the inquiry stimulated a series of local developments, some of which were already simmering before the riots brought them to the boil.

Accountability

The riots provided fresh fuel for a challenge to the existing system of formal police accountability to the community which had been developing since the mid 1970s. The challenge took a different form in London than elsewhere because the formal arrangements in the capital are quite different from those in other parts of Britain. The reasons for the challenge and the issues involved are, however, broadly similar.

In spite of increasing levels of coordination, Britain still has a devolved police system. In the nineteenth century, Parliament passed legislation requiring local boroughs and counties outside London to recruit their own forces. In the boroughs, the police were controlled by local council watch committees composed of elected members only (not all adults had the vote of course). In the counties, control was less representative: from 1888 onwards, the police were run by committees comprised half and half of local councillors and local magistrates. In Scotland, urban police forces were controlled by commissioners, some elected by ratepayers and others appointed by magistrates and councils. Rural Scottish forces were run from 1889 by joint committees of county councillors and government-appointed commissioners. During the first half of the twentieth century, coinciding with the extension of the right to vote to all adults, the powers of these local committees were gradually whittled away. Control began to fall increasingly into the hands of chief constables, while the local authorities ceased in several cases to be more than paymasters – and half-paymasters at that, since central government, as now, provided fifty per cent of the funds for all forces. Gradual reduction in the numbers of police forces also reduced the degree of local control.

A series of conflicts between the local committees and chief constables after 1945 led to a rethink. In 1960 the government set up a royal commission on the police which led in turn to the passing of the Police Act 1964 (covering England and Wales) and the Police (Scotland) Act 1967, which form the legal basis for the present system of police accountability. The royal commission, in a famous phrase, argued that the problem of police accountability was, in effect, the problem of controlling chief constables. While it endorsed the principle of local police forces, the commission argued that the 'general policies in regard to law enforcement' should be 'free from the conventional processes of democratic control and influence'. The 1964 Act established a new model for all 'police authorities' in England and Wales, comprising one third local magistrates and two thirds local councillors. The police authority's task was to be 'the maintenance of an adequate and efficient police force'; in effect this means providing the police with the tools for the job, the power to appoint the most senior officers and to call for the dismissal of the chief constable (subject to the approval of the Home Office in both cases). Direction and control of forces remained in the chief constable's hands. This is the existing system in England and Wales. However, since 1964 the number of police forces has been dramatically reduced as a result of Home Office directions and the reform of local government in 1972.

Between 1966 and 1981, the number of forces outside London fell from 115 to 41, nine of which are combined over more than one local authority area (for example, Thames Valley police covers Buckinghamshire, Oxfordshire and Berkshire). In Scotland, the role of the police authority is identical but six of the eight forces are responsible to the full local regional council while the two combined forces are responsible to joint committees of the relevant councils. Thus in Scotland magistrates play no part in police authorities.

Conflicts under this system have arisen over two main issues: attempts by the police authorities to control aspects of the policing of an area, and to a lesser extent attacks by police authorities upon the public statements of chief constables. The ambitiousness of attempts at control has varied greatly. In South Yorkshire a row developed over the police's refusal to detail an officer to supervise a busy pedestrian crossing. In West Mercia, police authority members clashed with the chief constable over their wish for him to introduce 'community policing' (see below), a far broader issue. Meanwhile in Merseyside there was conflict in 1979 over the chief constable's refusal to give the authority full details of the police inquiry into the death of Jimmy Kelly. Chief Constable Oxford was reported to have told some members: 'Keep out of my force's business.' Both South Yorkshire and Merseyside set up working parties to examine their relationship with the local police. It was against this background that Jack Straw MP unsuccessfully tried to have the law amended in November 1979 to give police authorities five new powers: the right to decide general policing policies; the right to obtain more information from chief constables; greater powers of appointment; a role in supervising local complaints against the police, and closer liaison between the police authority and the national police inspectorate.

Although Straw's Bill failed, it was an important sign that the old system was failing to give satisfaction. It provoked bitter police hostility at all levels on the grounds that it implied partisan control of policing. Calls for a further reorganization of police on a regional level to escape local authority control were made by chief constables. The government firmly opposed any change in the law, although Home Secretary William Whitelaw recognized that there was scope for more effective police authority practice. In a lecture in September 1980 he conceded:

I think it has become increasingly desirable that police authorities should see themselves not just as providers of resources but as a means whereby the Chief Constable can give an account of his policing policy to the democratically elected representatives of the community and, in turn, they can express to him the views of the community on these policies . . . Developments on these lines would, I believe, do much to ensure that police forces adapt sensitively to meet the need of the communities they serve.[3]

Two developments unconnected with the riots took the argument further. First, as a result of the big improvements in police pay (basic pay rose 55.8 per cent between may 1979 and August 1982), police forces were now able to recruit up to their permitted maximum strength. At the same time, however, even law and order budgets were having to be trimmed as part of the Conservatives' attempt to hold down public spending. The result was that in 1980 a number of police forces suddenly found themselves overbudgeted. Cuts had to be made. Thus police authorities and chief constables found themselves willy-nilly faced with the need to choose between priorities. In 1981 it happened again and the problem seems unlikely to disappear. So far the effect has been felt on such issues as cadet recruitment (now all but abolished in many forces), delays to costly building projects, civilization of certain administrative tasks, and tighter controls on vehicle use (a frequently overlooked reason why forces are now keen to have police back on the beat). Training too was being seen at one point as a likely casualty; in the wake of Scarman's considerable attention to the subject that is now less attractive. It may only be by pay restraint that the Home Office will be able, in the mid 1980s, to get several chief constables off the hook in these budget disputes. Otherwise, the police may find that capital-intensive projects in the computerization and armaments fields may come under attack not just from those members of police authorities who dislike them but from those who simply cannot see a better way to balance the books.

The second major development of 1981 affecting the police accountability argument was Labour's successes in the local elections in May. This came as a nasty shock to some chief constables. A number of police authorities were now filled with critics of policing policies; the chairmanship of several important authorities changed hands and, even where there was no overall change, the nomination of more Labour councillors to police authorities stirred up previously tranquil waters. In Thames Valley, for instance, it meant that the introduction of a new crime intelligence computer system suddenly became a divisive issue at the quarterly meeting of the authority. The privacy and security aspects of the plan were questioned and members challenged whether the £1.5m expenditure was a good way of using ratepayers' money. 'This authority isn't what it used to be,' one veteran member complained. 'Then we were all pals together. Now it's a power struggle.'[4] Another series of disputes took place in West Yorkshire following the May election. Authority members criticized police handling of the Yorkshire Ripper murders and called for more facts about the police investigation into the allegations against the chief constable, Ronald Gregory, and other senior officers. In October 1981 the police authority voted against Gregory's recommendation that they should pay a special award to the two officers who arrested Peter Sutcliffe, who had been convicted of the murders.

These clashes were dwarfed by disputes arising out of the riots themselves. In Greater Manchester, Chief Constable James Anderton became involved in a big row with members of the police authority over the handling of the

Moss Side riots, in particular over allegations that the local divisional commander had refused to cooperate with local community representatives in defusing the tension. Anderton's characteristically colourful response was that 'I would not crucify any of my officers in public to please or placate any disgruntled people ... We hear a lot nowadays about the much heralded concept of "democratic community policing" and the need for more involvement by local representatives in the management of police affairs. Well, if this was a practical example then all I can say is – God help us!'[5] In September, Anderton clashed with the authority again over his refusal to give formal evidence to the Hytner inquiry. He was overruled when he attempted to read a report on the riots to the authority meeting. Anderton complained that he was being gagged and later told the *Daily Express* that he feared that he could be sacked if a Labour government were returned. After a special authority meeting later the same month, he claimed that his differences with some Labour members were irreconcilable, though they did not amount to a rift. At the end of September the *Observer* revealed that the Greater Manchester police had acquired two modified submachine guns without informing the police authority. The Labour chairman of the authority, Councillor Peter Kelly, first learned of the purchase of the guns from the press but he declared himself satisfied with Anderton's subsequent explanation that the weapons had been adjusted to single-shot use. The county council leader, Councillor Bernard Clarke, was not so happy. He complained that the police had misled the council. By the end of the year, it seemed as if relations had begun to calm down. Anderton reacted favourably to the Hytner Report (as well he might) and told the police authority in December 1981 that his force planned to monitor 'every crime or report of damage or social misbehaviour, whether or not a complaint is made'.[6] Any emerging patterns would be considered and additional policing resources deployed. Complaints from blacks of discrimination would be dealt with immediately and special steps would be taken to allay blacks' fears. But Anderton clashed with the authority again in January 1982 over his handling of the riots; whether relations between parts of the Moss Side community and the outspoken chief constable will ever be very good seems unlikely. With James Anderton, nothing is certain.

In Merseyside, the election of a Labour majority on the county council also brought a change in the police authority. Here, as discussed earlier, Margaret Simey took over the leadership of the authority with a reputation as a stern critic of the police going back many years. Labour campaigned in the May 1981 Merseyside elections on the basis of what is almost certainly the most detailed local commitment to police reform that had hitherto been put before any British electorate. Their manifesto called for police to be 'firmly under democratic control' and questioned the need for increased police spending. The authority needed more powers, along the lines of the Straw Bill, but a more vigorous use of its existing powers was also needed. The manifesto contained detailed proposals on complaints, stop and search, traffic, drink, public order, open spaces, computers, training and race. These proposals were a direct threat to the chief constable, Kenneth Oxford, whose belief in secrecy has already been noted and whom a Conservative former chairman of the county council once described as 'arrogant – he talks of *his* police force. It isn't. It's ours. Everyone's.' To which Oxford retorted: 'If I'm arrogant then the spice of arrogance is a necessary constituent of command.'[7]

Early in 1981 private moves were made by local councillors to have Oxford sacked. The attempt was averted by William Whitelaw. The riots revived the 'Oxford must go' campaign, but again Whitelaw managed to defuse it. Margaret Simey never supported these calls. Her strategy was simply to force the police to take the police authority seriously through applying tough political pressure. In Simey's words, 'A police authority is not a police admiration society.' In September, the authority voted that Oxford had acted improperly by spending £53,000 on riot gear during July. To show their displeasure, the authority banned him from buying any more. 'What we are arguing about is who has the right to spend the money,' said Simey. 'For too long we have left the running of the police authority to the professionals while the people have been left out of the decision making. The authority ought to be more political.' The move infuriated the Police Federation. In November, the federation chairman, James Jardine, said:

I have words, which I had better not use, for a police authority member who tried to pillory a chief constable for having the effrontery to buy protective equipment . . . All that our members in Liverpool have had from their own authority has been criticism and, in some cases, downright abuse and distortion.

Two months after the riots, the authority snubbed Oxford again by refusing to do more than 'receive' his report on the Toxteth riots. Instead the authority pushed ahead with its own inquiry by an eighteen-member working party, which produced an interim report in October. This pressure forced Oxford to produce new plans for policing parts of Toxteth, which went into effect in January 1982, with a local team beat system in Upper Parliament Street. Although they got backing from the police authority, the new moves were introduced without prior consultation. With fighting between police and youths continuing in Toxteth into the winter, the situation remained volatile.

The other major developments in the campaign for police accountability were centred in London. Although Britain has no national police, it does have a state police. The Metropolitan force was established by Parliament in 1829 and is answerable directly to the Home Secretary. Then as now (though for different reasons) central government felt that the policing of the capital should not be under the control of Londoners. Even so, Londoners pay for the Met. Boroughs are precepted for about forty-two per cent of the Met's income, which totalled £434m in 1979–80.

Although there is regular informal consultation between London boroughs, the Greater London Council and the Met, there is no other formal relationship between them. Campaigns for police accountability have therefore focused on establishing some sort of statutory local control over the country's largest and most important police force. The stimulus for these campaigns was a combination of locally based frustration against the kind of policing methods described earlier in the book and a resurgence of interest among the left in the London Labour Party in policing. In March 1980, a conference in the Mary Ward Centre, Bloomsbury, established a Campaign for a Democratic Police Force. The following month, frustration boiled over in Lewisham at the refusal of Scotland Yard to press for a ban on a National Front march. Lewisham council threatened to withold its precept from the Met for the following year unless it received assurances of better policing and greater accountability. In the event, Lewisham paid up but the refusal caused a stir. The *Daily Telegraph* called it a 'Boston tea party'. The *Guardian* thought it an unnecessarily sensational deed, while the *Evening Standard* said: 'Such an arbitrary and petulent step undermines the whole process of consultation and trust on which the government of a borough must be based.' Margaret Thatcher condemned attacks on the Met in a classic short sharp remark: 'What they need is support and not criticism.' It was ironic that at precisely the same time and without press coverage or Prime Ministerial indignation, a Conservative local authority was threatening to do exactly the same thing as Lewisham. Epsom and Ewell is one of a number of areas of Surrey, Essex and Hertfordshire which, although not part of Greater London, are part of the Metropolitan police district. One reason why Epsom and Ewell set up a working party to examine ways of saving itself its annual £600,000 contribution to Scotland Yard was the high cost of policing marches. The chairman of the local finance committee commented: 'There is considerable dissatisfaction with the level of control over policing in our area, probably similar to that felt in Lewisham. The difference is that Lewisham do not have the same choice. Their decision was to withold payment. Ours would be to move out into Surrey.'

The hostile press reaction to Lewisham's move was as nothing compared with the furore which greeted the election in May 1981 of a Labour administration of the GLC pledged to creating a local police authority with powers equivalent to those envisaged in the Straw Bill. The manifesto also proposed the disbanding of the SPG, the Special Branch and the Illegal Immigration Intelligence Unit and that all police officers would have the right to join a trade union. Very little research had gone into these proposals and still less attempt had been made to explain them to the electorate. This helps to explain why a *New Standard*/MORI poll taken in May 1981 found only seventeen per cent of Londoners, including identical proportions of blacks and whites, and only one in four Labour voters, supporting GLC control of the police. Labour's plans were subjected to a bitter press campaign against 'Marxist lawlessness' and 'police bashing'. An article in the fanatically anti-Labour *New Standard* (London's only evening newspaper) headlined 'How the Left Aim to Handcuff the Police' declared that the GLC was 'openly at war with the police who are seeking to suppress violence in this city'.

Had it been made, the criticism that Labour had not fully thought through a policing policy for London would have been hard to answer. As it was, though, the riots and the Scarman inquiry succeeded in generating a vital degree of extra credibility for what the GLC was trying to do. What it is trying should not be underestimated. Under the chairmanship of a young black councillor, Paul Boateng, the GLC set up a police committee with a support staff headed by Martin Ennals, former secretary-general of Amnesty International, to advise and research on policing London. This means that, paradoxically, a local authority with no powers over the police became in 1981 the first local authority in Britain with administrative staff working full-time on policing. Whatever the future of the GLC's moves it is inconceivable that this is not the shape of things to come – professional local government policing departments similar to those which deal with other services.

These changes both reflected and stimulated local accountability movements in London boroughs. In September 1981, Tower Hamlets set up the first full-time local monitoring project at borough level, financed by the GLC. It runs a 24-hour phone advice service for local people with police problems and compiles evidence on local policing issues. Local monitoring projects in other boroughs have followed. The Newham monitoring project began collecting details on racial violence in 1980. A Lambeth project was launched in December 1981, building on the work of that borough's inquiry on policing which had reported in January 1981. An accountability campaign for Camden started up in December. Similar moves were under way in at least five other boroughs at the beginning of 1982. The GLC hopes to give them financial backing.

Scarman recognized that Scotland Yard was not locally accountable. In characteristic language, he observed:

The opportunity to ignore local (but not national) opinion exists in the Metropolitan Police: and he would be a bold man (bolder than I) who would affirm that the existence of an opportunity does not breed the temptation to make use of it, especially when it is convenient or saves trouble.[8]

However, the report ducked the question of the creation of a local police authority. Scarman's prescription for London (and for other police forces) was to set up statutory local liaison arrangements involving police, local councils and 'other community respresentatives'. These committees would have 'real powers' including a supervisory role in police complaints, a right to inspect police cells and a right to discuss operational policing policies.

In London, he also advocated the setting up of an advisory board at force level, but the main thrust of his proposals for consultation in the capital was at borough level.

Even this modest plan was unacceptable to police chiefs. The Association of Chief Police Officers, the chief constables' pressure group, opposed statutory liaison, partly because it mistrusted who those 'other community representatives' might be. The police preferred voluntary meetings. In December 1981 William Whitelaw caved in to the police objections and announced there would be no statutory liaison as recommended by Scarman. Whitelaw promised an endless vista of good intentions and in January 1982 he chaired an attempt to resurrect a liaison scheme for Lambeth. But it was a salutory reminder of just how strongly senior police oppose any extension of formal accountability and, equally, of just how close their thinking is to that of the Home Office, which as London's police authority has a vested interest in resisting any encroachment upon its powers.

Police complaints

The riots and the Scarman inquiry helped to challenge police autonomy in another area, that of complaints against the police. It was not so much that the riots directly exposed faults in the complaints system. What happened was that, by weakening police credibility, the riots gave fresh impetus to demands for change in a system which had been under attack for much of the 1970s. Faced with unprecedented levels of public doubt about current policing policies, defence of the *status quo* became increasingly untenable. At times in the autumn of 1981, it almost seemed as though all other aspects of the debate about the riots had been abandoned in favour of a concentration on the complaints problem.

Effective police complaints procedures enjoying public confidence are important because the powers of the police to control the liberty of the individual are so far-reaching. More than any other profession, police need to be straight and need to be seen to be straight. The Police Act of 1964 confirmed long-standing practice by enshrining the right of the police to investigate themselves. Challenge to this power arose in the late 1960s as the extent of corruption, particularly within the Metropolitan CID, was gradually unearthed. Among the Met's detectives, writes Robert Mark, corruption was 'routine'.[9] But the complaints system also came under attack over abuse of police powers in such cases as the assaults by Leeds police on a Nigerian vagrant, David Oluwale. By 1972, the *Sunday Times* specialist on race and police, Derek Humphry, could already write that 'to continue to argue the case for reform of the system whereby members of the public may lay complaints against policemen is to risk boring the reader'.[10]

Although police accepted the need for change they resisted particular proposals with tenacity. 1971 brought a Home Office working party on complaints. No major change followed. In 1972, a select committee identified the complaints system as the main contentious issue between police and black people. The Home Office set up a review which did not see light of day until early 1974. This review led to the most recent change, the Police Act 1976. The Act introduced an 'independent element' into the procedure – the Police Complaints Board, with powers of review. However, under the present system, all complaints are first recorded and then investigated by the police themselves. The completed investigation is then reviewed by the deputy chief constable. If a possible criminal offence of any kind is involved, the file goes to the Director of Public Prosecutions and the case may then come to court. If the DPP decides against prosecution or if no criminal offence was involved in the first place, the deputy chief then decides whether to bring disciplinary charges. If he decides against, the file then goes to the Police Complaints Board. Then, and only then, does the independent element come into play. The board can ask for extra details and has the ultimate power to order a disciplinary charge. If a charge is brought and admitted by the accused officer, the police alone decide the punishment. If the charge is denied, the board gets a report before the hearing and can again ask for more details. It can also order the case to be heard by a tribunal including two board members. Normally, however, cases are heard by the chief constable alone and he too makes the final decision about any punishment.

The figures imply that this system does not work. Between forty and fifty per cent of the complaints are withdrawn. This could be because they are vexatious. That is the police view. A more likely explanation is that complainants are discouraged from pressing ahead, either because they have little faith in the outcome or because they are put under pressure to withdraw. About one per cent of surviving complaints end in a successful disciplinary hearing, though eight per cent lead to an officer being warned or reprimanded. That leaves a lot of dissatisfied customers. On the face of things, the much-vaunted Police Complaints Board has been a rubber stamp for police actions. Between the Act coming into force in June 1977 and the end of 1980, the board reviewed 39,497 police investigations. It disagreed with the police's conclusions in a mere sixty-five cases – less than one in every 500. It never used its power to call for a case to be heard by a tribunal. It adds up to a system that lacks credibility.

It shouldn't be automatically assumed that police always get away with bad practice, or even lawbreaking. An Oxford police constable, for instance, was gaoled for nine months in November 1981 for punching a prisoner and hitting him in the groin. An Essex constable got two months for assaulting a motorist, also in November 1981. And victims do sometimes get redress through the civil courts. A Stoke Newington West Indian was awarded £3270 in July 1980 for false imprisonment, assault by police and malicious prosecution. A Bury St Edmunds woman won £12,000 damages against the Met in February 1981 for wrongful arrest and detention. In the same month, an Islington woman won £300 for assault against the Met. And in November 1981 a Lincoln man won £2500 damages against South Yorkshire police for being beaten up in a police car. So those who claim that there is no redress are wrong. But these few successes pale into insignificance when compared with the difficulties in bringing successful cases on corruption, and with the ineffectiveness of the complaints system in providing a proper level of recompense.

Many lawyers will confirm that the complaints system doesn't work and some now advise clients not to bother trying. Some of the most telling evidence to Hytner on this point was from local solicitors. A Manchester lawyer, Philip Jones, told the inquiry that not one of the fifty or so complaints he had handled in the past decade had been successful. In a case arising from the Southall disturbances of 1979, a volunteer manning a first-aid post was knocked unconscious by a police truncheon in front of two witnesses. Two and a half years later, he was informed by the DPP that there was insufficient evidence to bring a prosecution. His solicitor commented that it was as good a case against the police as he had ever dealt with. It got no further than the others had done before. 'The system is hopeless,' he said.

The Police Complaints Board itself recognized that all was not well. In July 1980, it published a review of its first three years' work. This recommended that complaints arising from serious injuries should be investigated by a special squad of police officers on secondment under the direction of someone with judicial experience. The Home Office's response was yet another working party, composed almost entirely of police or its own officials, which reported in March 1981. In view of its composition it was not surprising that the working party rejected the idea of a special squad, while conceding that investigation of serious cases might be supervised by either the DPP or the board's chairman. In the summer of 1981, the Home Office set up yet another internal working party to try to reconcile these proposals.

Meanwhile the riots had begun and, with Scarman appointed, it rapidly became clear that he too would have to consider the complaints system. An unpublished Home Office report, leaked to *The Times*, suggesting that some investigations were more concerned with discrediting the complainant than with investigating the complaint, only added to the discredit of the system. The pressure for changes grew stronger. In September the Labour Party conference voted by a massive majority to scrap the 'highly inadequate' system in favour of an independent procedure. In October, a Labour MP, Alf Dubs, tried to bring in a parliamentary Bill to set up a police ombudsman's office. Members of other parties were rejecting the existing system too. Shirley Williams of the Social Democrats told a police audience that the procedure is 'not confidence inspiring' and added that an independent investigating authority should replace it. And David Steel told the Liberal assembly: 'We must demand that police action be made open to an independent complaints body. The present system has proved itself wholly inadequate.' Steel's comments, in which he also bitterly attacked the police raids on Brixton in July, were part of his keynote speech to his party conference and were a good example of how the riots forced policing issues on to the centre of the political stage in the autumn of 1981.

The police are pretty conservative. They stick to tried and tested procedures and don't like them to be changed. So in the police world, the about-turns of several police leaders on complaints in late 1981 were unprecedented. In October, three chief constables separately broke rank with ACPO to propose indepedent complaints schemes. All three, James Anderton, Peter Imbert of Thames Valley, and Albert Laugharne of Lancashire, were influential, relatively young chief constables. Their proposals differed in various ways but all agreed that the case for the police abandoning their monopoly of complaints investigation no longer stood up. Anderton's reasoning was particularly interesting. 'A future government might set up a system with no police involvement,' he feared, so reform now might prevent an undesirable wholesale switch to complete independence. The chief constables were soon joined by an even more improbable advocate of change. By mid October, there were very strong signs that Scarman was going to come out in favour of a reform. So, in early November, the Police Federation announced that it had 'come round to the view that the task of investigating complaints should be handed over lock, stock and barrel to a new independent investigating body'. In return, the federation wanted officers to have the full protection of suspects' rights, legal representation and a right of appeal to a crown court. The reaction to this change of heart was very favourable. Newspapers which had previously bitterly attacked anyone who ever criticized the police about anything fell over themselves to support the federation. The *Daily Express* suddenly discovered that the existing procedure was 'not only unfair to complainants but also undermines police authority,' while the *Sun* announced: 'We hope that Home Secretary Willie Whitelaw will speedily set up a fully independent body so that justice is not merely done, but is seen to be done.'

Scarman duly reported in favour of a change. 'My own view,' he said, 'is that if public confidence in the complaints procedure is to be achieved any solution falling short of a system of independent investigation available for all complaints (other than the frivolous) which are not withdrawn is unlikely to be successful.'[11] He backed the introduction of a conciliation process in the handling of minor complaints, aimed at an informal handling of cases where people were really more interested in getting an apology than in pursuing an officer through the disciplinary process or the courts. He also called for the expansion of the police disciplinary code to make racially prejudiced or discriminatory behaviour a specific offence, for which the normal penalty would be dismissal from the force.

If anyone thought that the issue was now settled, then they were forgetting their recent history. Scarman gave the Home Office a let-out on complaints. Maybe he wrote up his views on complaints in haste to see the report published, but in this section of the report Scarman preferred to offer various alternatives, and not to commit himself unequivocally to one particular solution. As a result, when Parliament debated the report, William Whitelaw was content to announce that the Home Affairs select committee would conduct yet another inquiry – the eighth by a governmental or parliamentary committee in thirteen years – to provide 'a sound basis on which I can put forward detailed proposals'. Whitelaw announced that consultations would begin with the police on Scarman's proposed new disciplinary offence, but he ruled out the possibility of automatic dismissal for it. This was an odd response, since Scarman (in paragraph 5.42 of the report) had specifically rejected such a sanction, preferring to say that dismissal should be the 'normal' penalty. It soon became clear however that the police were opposed to the new offence in any event.

The charge which is most frequently made against the police complaints system is that the police should not be their own investigators. It is a common theme in many of the critical comments quoted. It was the stated reason why the chief constables and the federation changed their views. Scarman put it in a nutshell: 'By and large, people do not trust the police to investigate the police.'[12] And Norman Fowler, now Secretary of State at the DHSS, wrote in 1978; 'it is the most common criticism of any police complaints procedure and it is also the most difficult to answer.'[13]

The various schemes put forward by Alf Dubs, Shirley Williams and the rest (even by the Police Complaints Board itself) have obvious advantages though they differ greatly in detail and in effect. They are all to varying degrees more independent and therefore more likely to win public confidence. It follows that they are all more likely to encourage people to submit complaints that ought to be made and to persist with them once they have been submitted. There is however an extremely serious practical objection to them all. Though they may have greater credibility, would they actually lead to more successful complaints? This is surely the real objection to the existing procedures. What aggrieved citizens, their representatives and supporters want is certainly open and fair justice. But their basic desires are that their complaints should be upheld, that the offenders should be punished and they themselves should be compensated. They also want the police to act properly in the future. The question of who investigates the complaint is an important one, but it is surely less important than getting justice.

This raises several important questions about the debate on policing. The police, for all their changes of tactics on complaints, have never accepted publicly that the complaints system doesn't work in an investigative or judicial sense. Their prime concerns, and their reasons for changing their views, are public relations needs. Those who have criticized the police on the lack of independence of the complaints system (and on other issues too, let it be stressed) have all too often taken a very similar position, concerned more at the poor reputation of the process and at the effect this can have on the police's reputation generally than at the effects of what they are advocating.

International experience seems to support the pre-Scarman police view that fully independent investigation will not necessarily lead to more successful complaints. To say this is not to endorse the police's reasons for holding this view. But, for example, the 1976 Marin commission of inquiry into complaints against the Canadian police concluded that the investigation stage should remain in police hands because of 'certain stubborn realities that could not be ignored'.[14] These included the experience of the American civilian review boards which flourished briefly in the 1960s. In many instances these boards met with a brick wall of police non-cooperation, while in other cases investigators who were unfamiliar with police were easily sidetracked.

If this is correct – and it is only fair to point out that it is disputed – then the considerable and relatively successful pressures for changes in this aspect of policing may have been confused by a red herring. Outright independence of the police complaints procedure may ultimately create as many problems as it currently appears to solve. Police who are the subject of complaints are in a very strong position to frustrate investigations unless there is some independent corroborating evidence. Obviously there are ways of reducing that advantage, such as tape recording of interrogations. Completely independent handling would however do nothing to reduce it and if the Police Federation's safeguards were introduced at the same time, they would considerably strengthen it. The whole episode illustrates the lack of practical radical thought which characterizes certain aspects of the critics' proposals on policing. It is one thing to see that the present system is unacceptable, but quite another to know how to build an alternative.

Policing methods

This inequality between diagnosis and prescription has come to a head on the complaints question. It is also a feature of the debate on the third and last theme of this chapter: policing methods. It almost seems superfluous to describe again at length the ways in which the British police have become a more aggressive controlling force over the past two decades. Several important books and pamphlets have mapped this process and there is now an established school of journalism which concerns itself with these issues in detail.[15]

In brief, there are three main aspects of this development – centralization, violence and snooping. *Centralization* has been marked by a reduction in the number of local forces, of which one important feature is the existence of combined forces covering more than one local government area. There has also been an increase in the regionalization of policing, not as part of greater devolution, as in other services, but as a shift towards larger units. Training, major crime operations, criminal intelligence, technical support services, inspection and emergency planning are among the policing functions which are now organized at a regional level. Some chief constables, such as Anderton and Laugharne, have argued for the whole force to be regionalized. Other aspects of policing are organized on a national basis: command training, scientific and technical research, criminal records and car licensing in the Police National Computer, drugs and immigration intelligence, major mutual support, public order operations and so on. Policing budgets and a range of practical guidelines – as well as senior appointments – are determined nationally by the Home Office and Whitehall. Chief constables are organized at national level through the Association of Chief Police Officers, while the other national police representative bodies and the associations of local authorities also participate in a range of national coordinating functions. The Metropolitan Police also perform a number of national policing duties – such as diplomatic protection – while, by virtue of their size, they effectively control specialist units like the Special Branch.

Police *violence* has been marked by growing accusations of maltreatment of individual suspects during public disorder and in the police station. Three street deaths (Kevin Gately, Blair Peach and David Moore) and an increase in deaths in custody from eight in 1970 to thirty-two in 1979 have been blamed on police. Innumerable charges of police brutality (some of them proved) have also been made. Police now carry guns at least eight times more often than they did in 1970, approximately 12,000 police are trained to shoot and many forces have created specialist firearms units. A more extensive range of weapons is now in police hands, ranging from revolvers to rifles and shotguns. All forces are equipped with CS gas and plastic bullets, while armoured vehicles, helicopters and water cannon are being acquired. Specially trained squads on the SPG model now exist in most forces, while all forces train their police in riot control duties and maintain police support units which can be deployed anywhere in the country on crowd control. Crowd control police now dress in military-style protective helmets and clothing and regularly carry riot shields.

Accusations of *snooping* centre on the generalized gossip known as criminal intelligence which is maintained for everyday use by the force collator system. Sophisticated eavesdropping techniques can be used: telephone tapping, bugging, letter-opening, closed circuit television. Plainclothes photographers, agents provocateurs and spies have been employed. Computers are in widespread use without any form of externally enforced data protection. Thames Valley has computerized criminal intelligence, 'the police notebook'. The Police National Computer contains details on up to four million people and nineteen million vehicle and driver registrations. Police radio communications have been revolutionized. Particular attention has been paid to the Special Branch – Britain's political surveillance police – and to the drugs and immigration intelligence-gathering operations, all of whose records are computerized too. The links between the Special Branch and the Security Service (MI5) have been exposed. Jury-vetting and the Prevention of Terrorism Act have shown the misuse of political intelligence gathering. Statements bracketing terrorists, socialists, demonstrators and the like have been made by senior officers, stirring fears that police are as much concerned with repressing dissent as with catching burglars.

These preoccupations derived further credibility from the course of events in 1981. As we noted earlier, the official response to Bristol had been to investigate better ways of providing police mutual aid for crowd control. The immediate response to Brixton was to order new types of helmets and to improve protective clothing and shields. And the official reactions to the July riots, especially the rhetorical reactions, encouraged the police to stock up with better riot control hardware and suggested the reintroduction of the Riot Act. Add to this the widespread belief that the report of the Royal Commission on Criminal Procedure, published in January 1981, heralded an increase in arbitrary police powers and it is not difficult to see why the debate around Scarman was seen by many as a smokescreen, behind which the police had already taken the key decisions to go for a more militaristic approach.

All of these issues have combined to dominate new left thinking on the police and they were already clearly reflected in the London Labour manifesto of 1981, mentioned earlier in this chapter. Professor Stuart Hall, for instance, in his 1979 lecture, *Drifting into a Law and Order Society*, and more recently in an article in *New Socialist*, has argued that they are evidence of what he calls a 'drift into a heavily policed authoritarian democracy'.

Why have these things occurred? Though there are some who would deny that certain of these developments have happened at all, nobody now argues that none of it is true. The argument has become a little bit more sophisticated. One approach is to say, usually accompanied by references to 'the finest police force in the world' and the public opinion polls mentioned earlier, that these complaints are being made by 'anti-police' critics who are all but agents of Moscow anyway.

Peter Hain has pointed out that the publication of a book he had edited containing detailed criticism on the complaints system and the Prevention of Terrorism Act, was greeted by the Police Federation with a review headed 'It's that Hain again!' Police paranoia was even admitted by one free spirit in the force. Inspector Graham Marsden of Nottinghamshire wrote in a letter to *The Times* in early 1980: 'We seem to be approaching a position wherein no one can speak about the police, except in the most glowing terms, without being accused of lese-majesty. Even caring friends are alleged to be part of an orchestrated campaign to defame a blameless service.'

Another common response is to stress that all these aspects of policing are highly marginal to 'everyday policing', which consists of catching criminals and helping old ladies across the road. James Jardine of the Police Federation, for example, addressed his annual conference in 1980 in these terms:

There have been times in the past year when some of us were beginning to wonder what kind of service we belonged to. To hear some politicians, and some commentators, you might think that the police service is full of men who combine all the worst qualities of humanity. Such men, it seems, are brutal bullies who go about the streets terrorizing innocent young people. Or else they are sadists who beat helpless prisoners to death in dark and secret dungeons. Or they are members of special squads who, in the words of one Member of Parliament, roam around with firearms, smoke grenades, CS gas and even submachine guns. They are racialist bigots. They are anti-trade union. Or they are corrupt and plant false evidence against innocent people. They use the 'sus' laws to victimize the young coloured population. Of course, when it is put like that, the picture is an absurd distortion of the truth.

This is a widely held view, and there can be no doubt that many police are both baffled and hurt by the accusations. Nevertheless, the most common rebuttal of the critics' arguments takes another form. It says that the police are purely passive participants in the law and order process, simply responding to developments over which they have no control. They are forced, it is argued, to pick up the pieces. If there is more violence, they say, then they must have more weapons. If there is more crime, they must have more powers. Crime and disorder are seen as 'problems' which exist quite outside the sphere of policing, which their own methods do not stimulate and to which the police can offer only a response. However, the argument is frequently made in very general terms in order to justify any particular response. All policing choices thus acquire a spurious inevitability, which is protected by the professional autonomy of the force. This argument was used repeatedly during the 1981 riots as a sanction for any and every policing decision, and as an underlying justification for all the new hardware which was being demanded.

The inadequacy of this approach was challenged in the

mid 1970s from within the police. The challenge was largely associated with one man, the chief constable of Devon and Cornwall. John Alderson's view was that reactive policing arising from this passive responsiveness was becoming self-reinforcing. The police were becoming too dependent on high technology and demands for further powers and were simply losing contact with reality. In 1978 he said:

The concept of the constable as a citizen in uniform appointed to keep the peace is the keystone of a unique and valuable concept of policing. But social pressures tend more and more to seduce police thinking and public awareness away from this towards a quasi-military reactive concept . . . The modern generation of officers are beginning to see themselves as mobile responders to incidents. Technology is seductive. The car, the radio and the computer dominate the police scene. The era of preventive police is phasing out in favour of a responsive or reactive police.[16]

The story of the Devon and Cornwall 'community policing' alternative has been frequently told. Starting in a suburb of Exeter and gradually extending to other parts of the force area, Alderson attempted to emphasize the social work aspect of policing. By harnessing youth workers, community groups, social services and the police into a collective unit under police leadership, the Devon and Cornwall force aimed at a preventive approach to local juvenile crime through direct intervention in local social policy (youth projects, voluntary schemes, planning and transport decisions) and a more visible local beat patrol system. This approach was widely publicized and won considerable national support among liberal politicians and newspapers. Alderson himself was quick to exploit every opportunity to put his message across. He gave special attention to press relations, gave frequent interviews and lectures and wrote a book expounding his philosophy (books by serving chief constables are almost unknown). Alderson became the thinking person's copper.

There is little doubt that Alderson's initiatives were highly unpopular with his fellow chief constables. They found themselves under pressure to emulate his community policing, their own areas persistently compared unfavourably with the Devon and Cornwall promised land. When they called for massive increases in police powers, Alderson warned that a violent backlash might be the result. When they called for more spending on police to fight crime, Alderson claimed that such a policy would be 'almost completely misplaced'. When they mobilized thousands of police to protect National Front election meetings, Alderson quietly opened a local hall early, allowing anti-NF protesters to fill it, thus forcing the meeting to be abandoned.

These contrasts became even more pronounced in the summer of 1981. As the tear gas settled over Toxteth and chief constables queued up for more canisters and fresh weaponry from a government that appeared eager to supply their every need, Alderson denounced their approach. He flatly turned down the offer of plastic bullets, launchers and CS gas. Using the equipment would have fatal consequences, he said. This remarkable defiance, though, was as nothing compared with the effect within the police of Alderson's submission of evidence to Scarman. In a carefully timed press statement, he captured the front page of almost every daily paper with his criticisms of government and police alike:

Some seem hell-bent on sacrificing a police style which is the envy of the world just because of a few hours' madness on the streets. A hundred and fifty years of British police heritage down the drain ... The official response in the aftermath of the rioting falls far short of the stimulus needed to achieve a worth-while solution. The Home Office have come up with dehumanizing equipment such as plastic bullets and CS gas; greater police powers and the prospect of a detention camp on Salisbury Plain. Meanwhile many police leaders seem unable to grasp the need for radical change. Once we start tooling up to declare war on the public, the policemen become the unwitting victims of violence – they fill the hospital beds. If we are to save

237

ourselves from incessant conflict we must start talking hearts and minds, not CS gas and plastic bullets. We should be seeking to preserve our great tradition of policing-with-the-people and declare our abhorrence of the alternative now on offer.

Not for nothing did one newspaper review this episode under the headline 'How Alderson Mugged the Yard'.

Alderson's evidence to Scarman was not all that revolutionary, for all that it called for local community police councils and an initiative on community policing, police training and attitudes. As Scarman himself observed, Alderson's evidence seemed to be essentially a restatement of the traditional theory of British policing. What was revolutionary was that Alderson's submission broke the unwritten rules of non-intervention in another force's sphere of influence. He was breaking rank, going against the culture, going against ACPO. And not just against any old force but against the Met, the largest, most important, least self-critical, most corrupt, most criticized, least accountable police force in the land. The reaction was indignant. Chief constables were furious and the Police Federation's main speechwriter, Tony Judge (a Labour GLC councillor), wrote that his submission 'appeared to contradict the mainstream of the Metropolitan police submissions and lined up Alderson with the various groups who saw the riots as the culmination of a generation of police failure. In this, he is deemed to have spat upon the cloth, and he is unlikely to be forgiven.'

Nor was he. As Alderson himself wrote a few months later, his remarks caused considerable offence to chief constables: 'It is still regarded as something akin to disloyalty to be seen to disagree in public on policy and philosophical matters.'[17] By late 1981, Alderson no longer cared so much whom he was offending. In December he attacked the Home Secretary for refusing to press ahead with Scarman's proposal for statutory local liaison. Whitelaw had mugged the Scarman Report, he now said. The following month, he ordered that the

Devon and Cornwall Special Branch files should be weeded out to get rid of unnecessary information on anti-nuclear activists, opponents of bloodsports and members of the anti-apartheid movement, among others. The move was an implicit rejection of one of the most cherished aspects of reactive policing methods. Early in 1982, Alderson announced that he would retire in April of that year so that he could speak more freely on policing, and it was widely expected that he would then stand for Parliament on behalf of the Liberal Party.

Alderson's continued criticisms and his resignation help to put in perspective the defensive claims which other police forces made in response to his policing experiments. Although some police chiefs, notably those of the Met, chose to attack him on the grounds that community policing was acceptable for country cousins but not for the macho world of the inner city, others responded more cleverly. They simply absorbed the criticism by blandly assuring a somewhat sceptical public that Alderson was only making a fuss about something they were all doing anyway. 'I've been employing community policing for years,' Barry Pain of Kent announced. 'The difference between me and John Alderson is that I don't go around shouting it from the roof tops.' If that was generally true, it seems strange that Alderson should feel so strongly that the police were still going down the wrong road that he resigned. And strange too, if all the police were so strongly committed to community policing, that Superintendent David Webb who had pioneered community policing in Handsworth, should also resign at the end of 1981, saying that his colleagues paid only lip service to the idea.

There probably isn't a chief constable in Britain who does not now extol the virtues of putting more officers back on the beat. This was already true before the riots, and had been given practical effect in many areas ranging from Strathclyde to Dorset, from Humberside to South Wales and even including the Royal Ulster Constabulary and the Met. 'Bobbies on the beat' appeals to all kinds of nostalgic sentiments about the supposed nature of policing in some simpler golden age. And it is very common to confuse an increase in foot patrols, a decline in car patrols, a few police lectures in civic responsibility to local schools and more residential police, with community policing in the Alderson manner.

The fact that community policing means such different things to different police forces is one reason why it is dangerous to regard it as a panacea. In some forces the term is applied to community contact, liaison or relations branches which have a purely specialist task of making links with local people. Their job is essentially to give the police a good name. They themselves are sometimes derided by their colleagues who meanwhile get on with the job of 'real policing'. In other forces, community policing can mean that resident constables are deployed, more or less full-time (though how much more and how much less is an important variable) in a particular locality, normally a housing estate. Their job involves chatting up local residents and making themselves available, but these officers still have a fairly traditional policing function, keeping tabs on the locals on behalf of the force at large and pulling them in if there is any trouble. In yet other areas, community policing may simply mean that officers walk or cycle from the local police station where once they glided around in cars. The Devon and Cornwall version, with its emphasis on concerted local initiatives, devolved decision making and its greater involvement of the force as a whole, is quite different again. All that glisters is not community policing.

Since the riots, moves of various kinds have gone on apace. The question that seems to be asked all too rarely is: is this the policing that the community actually wants? It didn't appear that way to estate residents in Stoke Newington, north London, in 1981 when their 'community home beat officer', PC Walker, tried to arrest a teenager for swearing at him, failed to catch him and summoned thirty local support police who ended up in the boy's parents' flat arresting five people, four of whom were subsequently acquitted of assault and obstruction. One witness told the court: 'Nobody likes the police. They keep pulling us up for no reason. Especially PC Walker. Nobody likes him. He talks to you bad.' Does anyone seriously believe that more police on the streets of Brixton are going to give the local people more confidence when the police are unwilling to discuss operations with community leaders other than those of whom they approve? In those circumstances, bobbies on the beat sound suspiciously like Swamp 81.

The comedian Alexei Sayle has an appropriate line. Round his way, he says, they've now got community policing. You're walking along the street, a police van pulls up, a squad of coppers leap out, pin you to the ground and tell you the time. So is the answer simply to import Aldersonian policing methods into London and the other cities? There are many objections to the Devon and Cornwall approach. First and foremost, no community policing is going to win hearts and minds unless it is policing which is controlled by the community. All the various projects which cluster under the community policing banner – even Alderson's – are open to the very serious objection that they are police led, that they are policing done *to* the community and that they are not policing chosen by the community. This does not mean that the objection applies with equal weight to all cases. It has much greater force on Merseyside, say, than in the west country. Although Alderson argues that public definition of policing methods will produce 'democratic policing of the highest order'[18] (a concept of which he seems to approve), in practice his experiments have been initiated and coordinated by police. This danger has been pointed out by left-wing critics and, importantly, by some police too. Superintendent Colin Moore has written, on the basis of his experience leading the Exeter scheme: 'The policeman's leadership qualities, recognized by many in the community, must be subdued so that they are seen in terms of "service" rather than as a new velvet glove on the old iron hand: a more insidious form of social control. There are real dangers here.'[19]

The second vital criticism of all community policing projects is that they are seen by the police as complementary rather than contradictory to reactive policing. It is all very well sending officers back on the beat to win local confidence. But that work can be negated, and becomes suspect, if the old forms of policing are going merrily on in the background. One saturation operation can undo years, literally, of other work and discourage trust in the police's motives for initiating the change. For all the reintroduction of various forms of community policing there has been almost no dismantling of reactive policing. In some places it is still being reinforced. Alderson's rejection of Special Branch record-keeping practice is a very rare – and a very recent – exception. Devon and Cornwall still keeps its police support units, for example, and at its headquarters in Exeter it has one of the most important police firearms training centres in the country. In the cities, the problem is even more acute, above all in London. The ostentatious dismantling of reactive policing is now probably a precondition to progress on the community policing front in these areas. The police have so far failed to face up to the fact that what they may give to the public with the left hand they still take away with the right. Whether a force like the Met, dominated by the big-spending department mentality, will ever be prepared to eat humble pie publicly is open to doubt.

With these major reservations, though, there is no reason in principle why community policing along the Devon and Cornwall lines would not work on the grand scale in the cities. The claim that what works in Devon won't work in Deptford is a mere assertion on the Met's part, unsupported by any serious evidence, an assertion that is characteristic of a force dominated by the big budget, public order, anti-accountability approach. But even if it were possible to compel these forces to change, and even if it were possible to dragoon officers steeped in a wholly different policing culture to accept the new approach, there would still be enormous stumbling blocks in terms of recruitment, training, racial awareness, crime work and public order practice. Putting it simply, even if the entire police force decided today to change to the Alderson approach, it would take years to carry through the reforms. After all, it took Alderson nine years as a chief constable to get the Devon and Cornwall force to where it was when he announced his retirement. It took David Webb four years to make whatever progress he did in Handsworth. The Met alone is a force ten times bigger than Devon and Cornwall. This is not to say that it couldn't be done, still less that it shouldn't; it is to say that it is a huge task and that the police may simply be too far down a completely different road for the changes to be practicable as things stand.

The riots, however, pointed the urgency of change, although the debate about policing methods took place among those who never rioted. Nobody went on to the streets demanding reform of accountability, the police complaints system or even policing methods. In so far as these issues have subsequently been debated on the streets, community policing is widely seen as a cosmetic. This undeniable fact stimulated and reflected a tendency which is implicit in the work of those who have pointed to the repressive nature of much modern policing – that the police are not only unreformed but unreformable, and that policing as such is repressive, no matter how it is organized or what its ideals.

Yet the riots made this view appear unsatisfactory. The riots and the Scarman process raised policing issues more widely than ever before. They didn't raise them in the abstract. They raised them because policing had gone wrong and it now became possible to question the direction of policing without meeting an undivided response. It was reflected in a more critical attitude to policing in the media and among political representatives. Labour's official position at national level has undergone a massive shift since the party lost office in 1979, for example, which cannot simply be explained away in terms of the change in the internal balance of power within the party. For many years, Labour's approach to policing had been marked by acquiescence. At national level, the Home Office was seen at best as marginal to the priority economic and spending departments, at worst as a ministry doing a necessary 'apolitical' job and doing it well. At local level, Labour members have sat for years on police authorities without doing much more than collect their attendance allowances. There has now been a shift, to which the riots gave great impetus. As one writer has accurately put it: 'A political space has been opened up which was previously closed because of the apparently impenetrable and widespread belief in the inestimable British bobby.'[20]

It is a space which many of the critics have been strangely reluctant and ill-equipped to fill. In 1978, E. P. Thompson warned of the dangers. He wrote:

There has been around, for a decade or more, on the unofficial left a general rhetoric which passes itself off as a 'Marxism' ... Common elements in this rhetoric are some of the following: first, there is a platonic notion of the true, the ideal capitalist state ... This state is inherently profoundly authoritarian, as a direct organ of capitalist exploitation and control, and any inhibitions upon its powers are seen as 'masks' or disguises, or as tricks to provide it with ideological legitimation and to enforce its hegemony ... This may easily consort with a profoundly pessimistic determinism in which that kind of authoritarian state can be seen as the necessary concomitant 'structure' of the 'capitalist formation'. And this may, and often does, consort with a loose rhetoric in which civil rights and democratic practices are discounted as camouflage or as the relics of 'bourgeois liberalism'. And, to cut short the list, this very often goes along with a wholesale dismissal of *all* law and *all* police, and sometimes with a soppy notion that *all* crime is some kind of displaced revolutionary activity.[21]

The riots faced the left with a choice. Some chose to see the policing of the riots merely as further proof of what Thompson called a pessimistic determinism. Tony Bunyan, for example, the author of the most important left-wing critique of repressive policing, saw them as an attack by the state on the people, the passing of a liberal-democratic phase in policing in favour of an authoritarian democratic framework. Bunyan regards community policing simply as part of an alternative control mechanism, engineering consent for the police and spying more effectively on communities.[22] He is part of a tradition which still prefers to see Alderson, for example, as a wolf in sheep's clothing rather than to welcome his significance and the opportunities which he has helped to open up. There is a tendency on the left to judge Alderson on a 'worst case' extrapolation from his sometimes muddled writings, rather than on the practical achievements – however limited – of the Devon and Cornwall experiments. Other writers have urged a different analysis. Ian Taylor, for instance, wrote that the left was wrong to abstain on the argument between reactive and community policing. To conflate them was both too absolutist (ignoring real differences of practice) and too conspiratorial (ignoring the complex demands placed on the police, notably the wish of working-class communities for police protection). Taylor argued that the left must participate in the debate to urge new forms of policing.

There is now some evidence of an attack on left abstentionism on law and order and policing. But there is precious little evidence of it at the grass roots. Those who are participating in the debate do so either in the bureaucracy of the police authority or the élite forum of the universities or the academic journals. Moreover, the critics of abstentionism have confined their remarks within a socialist tradition, criticizing the left. They have not extended their views to the more sensitive areas of black attitudes to the police.

At the beginning of 1982, the evidence suggests that the debate about policing has not directly involved black people's and young people's views to any greater degree than it did in the past. On the contrary, it has moved ahead without them. For them, issues like accountability, complaints and above all methods of policing remain firmly based in their own perceived experience. Despite some of the changes which have taken place, they see the same officers in their streets as they did before, the same supervising officers in the stations as they did before, the same police commanders in the police headquarters as they did before and the same politicians in charge of law and order as they did before. There have been no apologies, only a series of internally determined compromises and fudgings on the proposals put forward by a judge in whom they had little confidence. The opportunities for change seem to have beckoned briefly and now to be more distant. If things weren't changed by what happened in 1981, how on earth are they ever going to be any different?

Does this then mean that there is no future in police reform? The answer depends upon police and public alike. 1981 showed that the power and practice of the police are neither inviolable nor unchallengeable. The danger of locking oneself within theories of a drift into a law and order democracy is that they rule out the possibility of change. Drifts can be fast, drifts can be slow and drifts can be uneven. Drifts can also be stopped.

9 In conclusion: A riotous future?

At the heart of any serious explanation of the British riots of 1981 must be the catastrophically bad relationships between the police and young black people. Theirs is an antagonistic relationship. They expect, on the basis of long mutual experience in particular areas, that each is up to no good. Each regards the other as suspicious, likely to be violent and likely to lie about whatever they are doing. Young blacks and the police are in a somewhat similar position. Both generally consider – for quite different reasons – that they are misrepresented and unappreciated by large sections of the public. Both groups have a powerful and self-reliant culture which is highly protective of its members and within which news travels fast. That of young blacks has been created by the common disadvantage and discrimination to which they have been subjected as a racial group. That of the police has been created by the job that they do, by the way they are trained into it and the way that, over the past fifteen years in particular, they actually do it.

This does not mean that they are equally 'to blame' for the riots. They are not equal. They are not like two groups of football supporters spoiling for a fight in the high street. The one has power while the other is powerless. The way in which that relationship has evolved and hardened has been documented in this book and in others on which our account has drawn. It has hardened in different ways. Among West Indians in London it has come from the experience of sus, street searches and arrests on a large scale and from the harassment of social gatherings. Among Asians in Southall it has come from the handling of racist violence and racist organizations bent on attacking their community's right to exist. In Liverpool 8, the use of police powers against the young of all races in an exceptionally deprived area was especially acute. None of these local aspects and none of the particular problems experienced by different ethnic groups was self-contained. All the areas where the riots occurred had experienced each type of conflict in some measure. The recent history of police–black relations – or, to put it more broadly, perhaps of state–non-white relations – had created a common consciousness of mistreatment or oppression, call it what you will. Moreover, it was fed by experience of other areas of the criminal justice system, not just of the police. Cases such as the death in Ashford remand centre in March 1980 of Richard 'Cartoon' Campbell, the inquest into the Deptford fire of January 1981 and the death of Winston Rose on his way to mental hospital in July 1981 helped to feed an acute sense of racial injustice in black communities generally. It is neatly summed up in the phrase frequently heard in black political literature and the press: 'we are a community under attack'.

Look from the local community's viewpoint at the events which sparked four of the most important riots. In Bristol in April 1980, it was a raid on the only black café in St Paul's at a time when other black cafés had been closed down for breaking health regulations and licensing laws. In Brixton a year later, young blacks saw one of their number bleeding and being chased by police and later saw him stopped in a car, still bleeding, and two officers bending over him. In Southall in July, Asians saw white skinheads advancing down their streets smashing windows. In Toxteth, local people saw the son of a well-known local Jamaican who was at that time trying to sue Kenneth Oxford for alleged police harassment being arrested on the assumption that his motorcycle was stolen. In each case, a community with its own local experience of police injustice, and with some sense that theirs was an experience shared by blacks throughout the country, saw what seemed to them to be incidents of serious injustice.

In Moss Side the initial disturbance was caused by the taunting of young blacks by whites outside a local club. In Leeds there was a police raid on a private drinking club. In other areas rumour took over. But to call the rioting which followed 'mindless' or 'pure hooliganism' is inaccurate and insulting. It is only mindless if you accept that one may not think about the police, if you think that the police can only be supported. And what of 'copycat' riots? Accusations that some riots were imitative are obviously intended to disparage the reasons why they occurred. Yet why did some groups and communities copy and not others? The conspiracy explanation that the riots were organized by outsiders can be dismissed in almost every single case. This leaves the simple answer that other riots took place because people with a sense of grievance felt encouraged to commit acts of defiance and destruction which require a level of bravery and example. Attempts to explain the riots by reference to mindlessness, criminality and imitation are all attempts to deny to the rioters the right to have their actions recognized as chosen behaviour for which they have some level of responsibility.

The same criticism applies to those who insist that the riots are caused by a set of general social or economic conditions. The problem with attempts to link the riots directly to joblessness, poor housing or other indices of deprivation is that they are imprecise and mechanistic. As we have tried to show, the incidence of such conditions bears no obvious direct relation to the incidence of riots. Indeed such a link is contradicted by many important cases where riots did occur and where they did not. But the objection to the economic explanation of the riots is also that it allows no nuances of analysis. The rhetoric of law and order is unsatisfactory for a number of reasons but at least it recognizes the fatuousness of the notion that unemployment causes riots. Norman Tebbit was right, in one sense, to point out that his father did not riot when he was unemployed. Nor have millions of other people, black and white alike.

The pundits, the politicians, the leader writers and the analysts came up with many different theories about the riots. But they seemed to owe a lot to their own existing assumptions and rather little to actual study of the riots. It is really very striking that these theories took so little account of the rioters themselves – who they were (and who they were not), what they thought (and what they didn't think) and what they did (as well as what they didn't do). Striking, but perhaps not unexpected.

We have already pointed out that what started many of the riots was not the closure of a local factory, the failure to introduce a multi-racial curriculum or even the breakdown of liaison between local leaders, councillors and police chiefs. Instead, the major riots – certainly in Brixton and Toxteth – were started because people witnessed specific acts of street injustice which no longer seemed tolerable. Equally significant was the way that some of the riots then developed. There was obviously much indiscriminate destruction, but the rioters also showed some discrimination in their choice of targets. These choices were disciplined not by some string-pulling general but by the rioters' own shared assumptions. Why not allow these acts to speak for themselves?

In Bristol the attack was on police vehicles and a bank, rather than on people's homes. In Brixton, an anarchist bookshop was left untouched but a pub with a reputation of refusing to serve blacks was burned to the ground; the stores that were looted were big chains – Curry's, John Collier, Burton – not the shops of black people. In Toxteth, too, the Asian shops were still standing after the riots and so was a Chinese chippy. Gone were the Toxteth racquets club, an establishment watering hole, and the Rialto, which was barred to blacks when it was a dance hall. In Chapeltown in Leeds, the first building to go up was the district's only sex shop, against which a local campaign had been mounted. As one black Toxteth woman put it in July: 'We weren't frightened, because we knew just what people were going for.'

Looting, too, needs to be seen as something more than mere wickedness. 'Last night saw a greater redistribution of wealth than any government will ever allow,' a Brixtonian told the *Daily Star* on 13 April. Perhaps. But what is also true is that the looting had a kind of modesty about it. Most of the evidence on looting shows us people helping themselves to very ordinary things: shoes, suits, bottles of beer, television sets, washing machines. There is always a danger of romanticizing such activity but it is surely at least relevant that the looted goods were the very things that advertising and marketing relentlessly tell the public that they should desire and possess. Such observations don't necessarily 'justify' the riots. But both sets of cases bring the actions of the rioters or the looters, who in Brixton at any rate were different people from the rioters, into the sphere of chosen and explicable conduct. This is something which the theories of mindlessness or deprivation both deny to the rioters.

It is no easier to explain the riots than it was to predict them. An explanation must show why the events that did happen took place where, when and how they did. As Margaret Thatcher has recently observed, many of one's worst fears do not ever come to pass. But in 1981 the frequently voiced fears that young people – above all, young black people – would rise up against the police and lay claim to a respect which had been denied them became a dramatic reality. The subsequent response of British society has not eradicated the likelihood that it will happen again.

References

Introduction: A riotous history

1 *Brownlie's Law of Public Order and National Security* (2nd edn, Butterworth 1981), pp. 131–9.
2 *Race and Class*, vol. XXXIII, nos 2/3 (autumn 1981/winter 1982).
3 George Rudé: *Paris and London in the Eighteenth Century* (Fontana 1970), pp. 268–92.
4 A. J. Peacock: 'Village Radicalism in East Anglia' in J. P. D. Dunbabin: *Rural Discontent in Nineteenth Century Britain* (Faber 1974), pp. 39, 60.
5 E. P. Thompson: *The Making of the English Working Class* (Gollancz 1963), p. 592.
6 Charles Lock Mowat: *Britain between the Wars* (Methuen 1955), p. 317.
7 Richard Clutterbuck: *Britain in Agony* (Penguin 1980), p. 19.
8 Rudé: op cit., pp. 17–34.
9 E. P. Thompson: 'The Moral Economy of the English Crowd in the Eighteenth Century', *Past and Present* (February 1971).
10 Tony Hayter: *The Army and the Crowd in mid-Georgian England* (Macmillan 1978), p. 36.
11 Richard Cobb: *The Police and the People* (OUP 1970), p. 20.
12 Rudé: op. cit., p. 280.
13 E. J. Hobsbawm and George Rudé: *Captain Swing* (Penguin 1973), p. 202.
14 Christopher Hill: *The World Turned Upside Down* (Penguin 1975), pp. 16–17.
15 Cobb: op. cit., p. 20.

1 The forerunner: Bristol 1980

1 Home Affairs Committee 1980–81;
  Racial Disadvantage, HC 424-II, p. 6.
2 Ken Pryce: *Endless Pressure* (Penguin 1979),
  p. 26.
3 Home Affairs Committee: op. cit., pp. 132–3.
4 Ibid., p. 42.
5 Pryce: op. cit., p. 131.
6 Cited in the *Sunday Times*, 6 April 1980.
7 Prosecution evidence to crown court at Bristol riot
  trial.
8 Memorandum placed in library of the House of
  Commons by the Home Secretary after report to him
  from Chief Constable of Avon and Somerset.
9 Memorandum by the Home Office: *Review of
  Arrangements for Handling Spontaneous Disorder*.
10 Bristol TUC: *Slumbering Volcano?*
11 Bristol Teachers Association (NUT) equal
  opportunities subcommittee: *After the Fire*, a report
  on education in St Paul's Bristol and multi-ethnic
  education in Avon.
12 *Race and Class* (autumn 1981–winter 1982),
  p. 223.

2 Immigration and racism: Blacks in Britain

1 Nigel File and Chris Power: *Black Settlers in Britain
  1555–1958* (Heinemann Educational Books 1981), p.
  6.
2 Ibid., p. 1.
3 Ibid., p. 43.
4 The Times News Team: *Black Man in Search of Power*
  (Nelson 1968), p. 128.
5 Dilip Hiro: *Black British White British* (Pelican 1973), p.
  23.
6 *The Times*, 2 January 1982.
7 Robert Moore: *Racism and Black Resistance in Britain*
  (Pluto Press 1975), p. 16.
8 Dilip Hiro: op. cit., p. 22.

9 David Smith: *Racial Disadvantage in Britain, the PEP report* (Pelican 1977), p. 288.

10 A. Sivanandan: 'From Resistance to Rebellion: Asian and Afro-Caribbean struggles in Britain', *Race and Class* (autumn 1981/winter 1982), p. 119.

11 Ann Dummett: *A Portrait of English Racism* (Pelican 1973), p. 189.

12 Richard Crossman: *The Diaries of a Cabinet Minister*, vol. I (Hamish Hamilton and Jonathan Cape 1975), pp. 149–50.

13 Ibid., p. 299.

14 Derek Humphry: *Police Power and Black People* (Panther 1972), pp. 68–77.

15 Martin Walker: *The National Front* (Fontana 1977), p. 224.

16 *New Society*, 9 August 1979, 13 March 1980.

3 People don't like being lined up against a wall: Black people and the police

1 *Daily Mail*, 30 October 1981.

2 Michael Ignatieff: 'Police and People: The Birth of Mr Peel's Blue Locusts', *New Society*, 30 August 1979.

3 *City Limits*, 23–9 October 1981.

4 *Observer*, 14 June 1981.

5 *Searchlight*, September–December 1981.

6 *The Times*, 18 November 1981.

7 Information from Newham Rights Centre.

8 *Southall 23 April 1979; the Report of the Unofficial Committee of Inquiry* (the Dummett inquiry), pp. 11–12.

9 *Guardian*, 4 September 1976.

10 *Report of the Commissioner of Police for the Metropolis for the year 1978* (Cmnd 7580), p. 8.

11 Robert Moore: op. cit., p. 63.

12 *Observer*, 10 January 1982.

13 Paul Gordon: *Passport Raids and Checks* (Runnymede Trust 1981), p. 37.

14 North Islington Law Centre: *Passports to Health?*; Vijay Sharma: *Race and Social Security* (CPAG).

15 Robert Reiner: 'Black and Blue: Race and the Police', *New Society*, 17 September 1981.
16 *Police Studies*, September 1978.
17 *The Times*, 24 September 1981.
18 Philip Stevens and Carole F. Willis: *Race, Crime and Arrests* (Home Office Research Study no. 58).
19 Mary Tuck and Peter Southgate: *Ethnic Minorities, Crime and Policing* (Home Office Research Study no. 70).
20 Michael Pratt: *Mugging as a Social Problem* (Routledge 1980).
21 Home Affairs Committee 1979–80; *Race Relations and the 'Sus' Law*.
22 *The Times*, 21 January 1981.
23 Ann Brogden: '"Sus" is Dead: But What about "Sas"?', *New Community* (spring–summer 1981).
24 Joanna Rollo: 'The Special Patrol Group' in Peter Hain (ed.): *Policing the Police*, vol. 2 (John Calder 1980).
25 Ben Whitaker: *The Police in Society*, (Methuen 1979), p. 68.
26 Robert Mark: *In the Office of Constable* (Collins 1978), p. 303.
27 *The Times*, 27 September 1980.

4 The explosion: The Brixton riots of April 1981

1 Cited in the *Guardian*, 13 April 1981.
2 Lord Scarman: *The Brixton Disorders 10–12 April 1981* (Cmnd 8427 HMSO), p. 10.
3 Ibid., p. 11.
4 Capital Radio survey in *The Times*, 14 May 1981.
5 Caroline Tisdall, freelance journalist, in evidence to Lord Scarman.
6 John Clare, education and community relations correspondent of the BBC, in evidence to Lord Scarman.

5 Deprived and disadvantaged?

1 Nicholas Deakin: 'Why Nothing Seems to Work in the Inner Cities', *Guardian*, 7 September 1981.
2 Gordon Cherry: 'New Towns and Inner City Blight', *New Society*, 8 February 1979.
3 S. G. Checkland: *The Upas Tree: Glasgow 1875–1975* (2nd edn, Univ. Glasgow Press 1976), p. 97.
4 Peter Hall: 'Spending Priorities in the Inner City', *New Society*, 21–28 December 1978.
5 Stan Taylor: 'The Politics of Enterprise Zones', *Public Administration* (winter 1981), p. 436.
6 Lee Bridges: 'Keeping the Lid On: British Urban Social Policy 1975–81', *Race and Class* (autumn/winter 1981).
7 *The Times*, 26 August 1981.
8 Chaim Bermant: 'No Mean City Without a Riot', *Observer*, 6 September 1981.
9 Home Affairs Committee 1980–81; *Racial Disadvantage*, HC 424-I, p. viii.
10 *Report of the Moss Side Enquiry Panel* (Hytner Report), p. 17.
11 HC 424-I, p. lxxii.
12 Alan Simpson: *Stacking the Decks: a study of race, inequality and council housing in Nottingham* (NCRC 1981), pp. 32–4.
13 HC 424-I, p. liv.
14 HC 424-I, p. lviii.
15 George Gaskell and Patten Smith: 'Are Young Blacks Really Alienated?', *New Society*, 14 May 1981.

6 The uprising: the riots of July 1981

1 Cited in *The Times*, 6 July 1981.
2 Ibid.
3 *Guardian* 9 December 1981.
4 *Sunday Times* magazine, 1 November 1981.

5 *New Statesman*, 7 August 1981.
6 *The Times*, 24 July 1981.
7 *LAG Bulletin*, October 1981.

7 'There must be causes for them': Explanations of the riots

1 *New Society*, 3 December 1981.
2 *The Times*, 10 July 1981.
3 *Hansard*, 16 July 1981.
4 Most of the MPs' comments quoted in this chapter are from the debate 'Civil Disturbances', reported in *Hansard*, 16 July 1981. Unless otherwise indicated the MPs' quotes are from this debate or *Hansard* for 6, 7, 9, 14 and 15 July 1981.
5 *Daily Telegraph*, 6 July 1981.
6 *Police Review*, 15 May, 2 October, 13 November 1981.
7 *Police*, May 1981.
8 *Police Review*, 29 May, 24 July, 14 August 1981.
9 P. Lupsha: 'On Theories of Urban Violence' in Murray Stewart (ed.): *The City: Problems of Planning* (Penguin 1972), p. 460.
10 *Police Review*, 17 April 1981.
11 *The Times*, 9 July 1981.
12 *The Times*, 11 July 1981.
13 *The Times*, 10 August 1981.
14 *The Times*, 6 January 1982.
15 *Sunday Telegraph*, 29 November 1981.
16 *Police*, May 1981.
17 *The Times*, 2 July 1981.
18 *The Times*, 7 July 1981; *Guardian*, 14 July 1981.
19 *Guardian*, 7 September 1981.
20 *Police Review*, 17 July 1981.
21 The polls are in: *New Standard*, 11 May 1981; *The Times*, 14 May 1981; *The Times*, 8 October 1981; *Guardian*, 30 November 1981.
22 *The Times*, 13 November 1981.

23 *Police Review*, 6 November 1981.
24 *Observer, Sunday Telegraph*, 12 April 1981;
    Guardian, 13 April 1981.
25 *The Times*, 23 November 1981.
26 Hytner Report, pp. 52–4.
27 Mary Tuck and Peter Southgate: *Ethnic Minorities,
    Crime and Policing* (Home Office Research Study no.
    70), p. 44.
28 *The Brixton Disorders 10–12 April 1981; report of an
    inquiry by the Rt Hon The Lord Scarman OBE* (Cmnd
    8427, November 1981).
29 Scarman Report, pp. 15–16.
30 Scarman Report, p. 45.

8 Beginning of the end or end of the beginning? The riots and policing

 1 *New Society*, 12 June 1980.
 2 *Observer*, 15 November 1981.
 3 'The Police and the Public', James Smart Lecture, 17
    September 1980.
 4 *Observer*, 27 September 1981.
 5 *Police*, October 1981.
 6 *Guardian*, 17 December 1981.
 7 *New Statesman*, 7 August 1981.
 8 Scarman Report, p. 95.
 9 Robert Mark: op. cit., p. 102.
10 Derek Humphry: op. cit., p. 170.
11 Scarman Report, p. 118.
12 Scarman Report, p. 88.
13 Norman Fowler: *After the Riots* (Davis-Poynter 1979),
    p. 176.
14 *Report of the Commission of Inquiry relating to Police
    Complaints, Internal Discipline and Grievance Procedure
    with the Royal Canadian Mounted Police*, p. 84.
15 The main books are: Tony Bunyan: *The History and
    Practice of the Political Police in Britain* (Quartet 1977);
    Carol Ackroyd, Karen Margolis, Jonathan
    Rosenhead, Tim Shallice: *The Technology of Political*

Control (2nd edn, Pluto Press 1980); Peter Hain (ed.),
Martin Kettle, Duncan Campbell, Joanna Rollo:
Policing the Police, vol. 2 (John Calder 1980); Crispin
Aubrey: *Who's Watching You?* (1981).

Important pamphlets include: State Research:
Policing the Eighties, The Iron Fist (1980); Duncan
Campbell: *Phonetappers and the Security State* (New
Statesman Pamphlets 1981); *State Research*
(bimonthly) is an indispensable regular monitor of
these developments.

16 *Police Review*, 6 April 1979.
17 *The Times*, 9 January 1982.
18 John Alderson: *Policing Freedom* (Macdonald & Evans
    1979), p. 162.
19 Colin Moore and John Brown: *Community versus
    Crime* (Bedford Square Press 1981), p. 120.
20 Ian Taylor: 'Policing the Police', *New Socialist*,
    November/December 1981.
21 E. P. Thompson: *Writing by Candlelight* (Merlin Press
    1980), pp. 166–7.
22 Tony Bunyan: 'The Police Against the People', *Race
    and Class* autumn 1981/winter 1982).

Bibliography

Official publications

The Brixton Disorders 10–12 April 1981; Report of an Inquiry by the Rt Hon The Lord Scarman OBE (Cmnd 8427, 1981).

West Indian Children in our Schools: Interim Report of the Committee of Inquiry into the Education of Children from Ethnic Minority Groups (Chairman Anthony Rampton OBE) (Cmnd 8273, 1981).

Home Affairs Committee: *Race Relations and the 'Sus' Law* (1979–80 HC 559)

Home Affairs Committee: *Deaths in Police Custody* (1979–80 HC 631)

Home Affairs Committee: *Racial Disadvantage* (1980–81 HC 424)

Home Affairs Committee: *Commission for Racial Equality* (1981–82 HC 46)

Home Office Research Study no. 58; Philip Stevens and Carole F. Willis: *Race, Crime and Arrests* (1979)

Home Office Research Study no. 68; Simon Field, George Mair, Tom Rees and Philip Stevens; *Ethnic Minorities in Britain* (1981)

Home Office Research Study no. 70; Mary Tuck and Peter Southgate: *Ethnic Minorities, Crime and Policing* (1981)

Police Complaints Board: *Triennial Review Report 1980* (Cmnd 7966)

The establishment of an independent element in the investigation of complaints against the police (Cmnd 8193, 1981)

Report of the Commissioner of Police for the Metropolis (published annually)
Report of Her Majesty's Chief Inspector of Constabulary (published annually)
Criminal Statistics (published annually)
Parliamentary Debates (Hansard)

Books and pamphlets

J. Alderson: *Policing Freedom* (Macdonald & Evans 1979)
All Faiths For One Race: *Talking Blues (Centerprise 1976)*
All Lambeth Anti-Racist Movement: A Cause for Alarm (1979)
Bethnal Green and Stepney Trades Council: *Blood On The Streets* (1978)
A. Blaber: *The Exeter Community Policing Group* (NACRO 1979)
N. Blake: *The Police, the Law and the People* (Haldane Society 1981)
C. Bolt: *Victorian Attitudes to Race* (Routledge 1971)
Bristol Teachers' Association: *After The Fire* (1980)
J. Brown: *Shades of Grey* (Cranfield Police Studies 1977)
Brownlie's Law of Public Order and National Security (Butterworth 1981)
E. Canetti: *Crowds and Power* (Penguin 1981)
E. Cashmore: *Rastaman* (Allen & Unwin 1979)
R. Clarke and J. M. Hough: *The Effectiveness of Policing* (Gower 1980)
R. Clutterbuck: *Britain in Agony* (Penguin 1980)
R. Cobb: *The Police and the People* (OUP 1970)
Commission for Racial Equality: *The Fire Next Time* (1980)
Communist Party: *Black and Blue: Racism and the Police* (1981)
B. Cox: *Civil Liberties in Britain* (Penguin 1975)
T. A. Critchley: *A History of Police in England and Wales* (Constable 1978)
W. W. Daniel: *Racial Discrimination in England* (Penguin 1968)
A. Dummett: *A Portrait of English Racism* (Penguin 1973)

A. Dummett: *A New Immigration Policy* (Runnymede Trust 1978)

N. File and C. Power: *Black Settlers in Britain 1555–1958* (Heinemann Educational 1981)

N. Fowler: *After the Riots* (Davis-Poynter 1979)

P. Gordon: *Passport Raids and Checks* (Runnymede Trust 1981)

P. Hain (ed.), D. Humphry, B. Rose-Smith: *Policing the Police*, Vol. 1 (John Calder 1979)

P. Hain (ed.), M. Kettle, D. Campbell, J. Rollo: *Policing the Police*, Vol. 2 (Calder 1980)

P. Hall (ed.), *The Inner City in Context* (Heinemann Educational 1981)

S. Hall, C. Critcher, T. Jefferson, J. Clarke, B. Roberts: *Policing the Crisis* (Macmillan Press 1978)

S. Hall: *Drifting into a Law and Order Society* (Macmillan 1980)

W. Hannington: *Unemployed Struggles* (1936, EP Publishing 1973)

T. Hayter: *The Army and the Crowd in Mid-Georgian England* (Macmillan 1979)

D. Hiro: *Black British, White British* (Penguin 1973)

E. J. Hobsbawm: *Primitive Rebels* (Manchester UP 1972)

E. J. Hobsbawm and G. Rudé: *Captain Swing* (Penguin 1973)

D. Humphry: *Police Power and Black People* (Panther 1972)

D. Humphry and G. John: *Because They're Black* (Penguin 1971)

D. Humphry and M. Ward: *Passports and Politics* (1974)

D. Humphry and D. Tindall: *False Messiah, The Story of Michael X* (Hart-Davis 1977)

Institute of Race Relations: *Police Against Black People* (1979)

G. John: *In the Service of Black Youth* (Nat. Assn of youth Clubs 1981)

R. Kapo: *A Savage Culture* (Quartet 1981)

V. G. Kiernan: *The Lords of Human Kind* (Penguin 1972)

A. Lester and G. Bindman: *Race and Law* (Pelican 1972)

R. Littlewood and M. Lipsedge: *Aliens and Alienists* (Penguin 1982)

London Borough of Lambeth: *Report of the Working Party on Community/Police Relations in Lambeth* (1981)

J. McClure: *Spike Island* (Pan 1981)

R. Mark: *In the Office of Constable* (Collins 1978)

R. I. Mawby and I. D. Batta: *Asians and Crime: The Bradford Experience* (Nat. Assn for Asian Youth 1980)

R. Miles and A. Phizacklea: *Racism and Political Action in Britain* (Routledge 1979)

C. Moore and J. Brown: *Community versus Crime* (Bedford Square Press 1981)

R. Moore: *Racism and Black Resistance in Britain* (Pluto Press 1975)

H. Ouseley: *The System* (Runnymede Trust 1981)

C. Peach, V. Robinson and S. Smith (eds.): *Ethnic Segregation in Cities* (Croom Helm 1981)

M. Pratt: *Mugging as a Social Problem* (Routledge 1980)

K. Pryce: *Endless Pressure* (Penguin 1979)

M. Punch: *Policing the Inner City* (Macmillan Press 1979)

P. Ratcliffe: *Racism and Reaction* (Routledge 1981)

Report of the Moss Side Enquiry to the Leader of the Greater Manchester Council (1981)

Report of the National Advisory Commission on Civil Disorders (Bantam 1968)

Review of the Race Relations Act 1976 (Runnymede Trust 1979)

J. Rex and S. Tomlinson: *Colonial Immigrants in a British City* (Routledge 1979)

G. Rudé: *Paris and London in the 18th Century* (Fontana 1970)

Runnymede Trust and Radical Statistics Group: *Britain's Black Population* (1980)

E. B. Schaffer: *Community Policing* (Croom Helm 1980)

A. Simpson: *Stacking the Decks* (1981)

A. Sivanandan: *Race and Resistance: The IRR Story* (Inst. of Race Relations 1974)

D. J. Smith: *Racial Disadvantage in Britain* (Penguin 1977)

D. J. Smith: *Unemployment and Racial Minorities* (Policy Studies Institute 1981)

Southall: 23 April 1979; the report of the unofficial committee of enquiry (NCCL 1980)

G. Stedman Jones: *Outcast London* (Oxford 1971)

M. Stewart (ed.): *The City: Problems of Planning* (Penguin 1972)

I. Taylor: *Law and Order: Arguments for Socialism* (Macmillan 1981)

E. P. Thompson: *The Making of the English Working Class* (Gollancz 1963)

E. P. Thompson: *Writing by Candlelight* (Merlin Press 1980)

The Times News Team: *The Black Man in Search of Power* (Nelson 1968)

M. Walker: *The National Front* (Fontana 1977)

B. Whitaker: *The Police in Society* (Methuen 1979)

K. Young and N. Connelly: *Policy and Practice in the Multi-Racial City* (1981)

Articles

Lee Bridges: 'Keeping the Lid On: British Urban Social Policy 1975–81', *Race and Class* (autumn 1981–winter 1982)

Tony Bunyan: 'The Police Against the People', *Race and Class* (autumn 1981–winter 1982)

Courtney Griffiths: 'Black People, the Police and the State', *Haldane Society Bulletin* (winter 1981)

Stuart Hall: 'Summer in the City', *New Socialist* (September/October 1981)

Dacus Howe: 'From Bobby to Babylon' part 2, *Race Today* (November 1980)

Michael Ignatieff: 'It's a Riot', *London Review of Books*, 20 August 1981

Chris Harman: 'The Summer of 1981; a post-riot Analysis', *International Socialism* (autumn 1981)

C. L. R. James: 'An Accumulation of Blunders', *New*

Society, 3 December 1981

Martin Kettle: 'The March of Black Outcast London', *New Society*, 12 March 1981

Robert Reiner: 'Black and Blue: Race and the Police', *New Society*, 17 September 1981

Rob Rohrer: 'A Law unto Themselves', *New Statesman*, 7 August 1981

A. Sivanandan: 'From Resistance to Rebellion: Asian and Afro-Caribbean Struggles in Britain', *Race and Class* (autumn 1981–winter 1982)

Ian Taylor: 'Policing the Police', *New Socialist*, November/December 1981

Stan Taylor: 'The Politics of Enterprise Zones', *Public Administration* (winter 1981)

Ian Walker: 'The Voices of the Kids of Toxteth', *New Society*, 26 November 1981

Michael Williams: 'The Tents at the Gates of the City', *New Society*, 16 July 1981

Periodicals and newspapers

Caribbean Times
City Limits
Daily Express
Daily Mail
Daily Mirror
Daily Star
Daily Telegraph
Economist
Evening Standard (later *New Standard* and *The Standard*)
Guardian
Legal Action Group Bulletin
Leveller
New Society
New Statesman
News of the World
Observer
Police
Police Journal
Police Review
Police Studies
Rights
Race and Class
Race Today
Runnymede Trust Bulletin
Searchlight
State Research Bulletin
Sun
Sunday People
Sunday Telegraph
Sunday Times
The Times

Index